DATE DUE

HOW CHILDREN LEARN TO BUY

PEOPLE AND COMMUNICATION

Series Editors: F. GERALD KLINE   *Department of Journalism*
PETER CLARKE   *University of Michigan*

This study of children and advertising launches a new series of books entitled PEOPLE AND COMMUNICATION. Volumes published in this series report original research by scholars and professionals in many diverse fields which bear upon the general focus of the series. Each book in the series develops an individual theme and conveys the results from a coordinated program of studies.

Contributions are selected for the urgency of their findings to policy makers in communications fields and for their appeal to other readers concerned with media in contemporary society.

F.G.K.
P.C.

Volumes in this series:

Volume 1: How Children Learn to Buy: The Development of Consumer Information-Processing Skills
SCOTT WARD, DANIEL B. WACKMAN, ELLEN WARTELLA

Volume 2: Big Media, Little Media: Tools and Technologies for Instruction
WILBUR SCHRAMM

The Development of
Consumer Information-Processing Skills.

SCOTT WARD, *Harvard University*

DANIEL B. WACKMAN, *University of Minnesota*

ELLEN WARTELLA, *Ohio State University*

 SAGE PUBLICATIONS   Beverly Hills   London

For information address:

SAGE PUBLICATIONS, INC.
275 South Beverly Drive
Beverly Hills, California 90212

SAGE PUBLICATIONS LTD
St George's House / 44 Hatton Garden
London EC1N 8ER

Printed in the United States of America

Library of Congress Cataloging in Publication Data

Ward, Scott, 1942-
    How children learn to buy.

    (People and communication   ; v. 1)
    Bibliography: p. 193
    Includes index.
    1. Youth as consumers. 2. Television and children.
3. Television advertising. I. Wackman, Daniel B., joint
author. II. Wartella, Ellen, joint author. III. Title.
HC79.C6W37   658.8'34   74-77291
ISBN 0-8039-0424-X
ISBN 0-8039-0744-3 pbk.

FIRST PRINTING

CONTENTS

Introduction 7
  GERALD A. LESSER

Preface 11

PART I. INTRODUCTION

1. Overview: The Development of Consumer Behavior Skills 17

2. Research Methodology 31

PART II. COGNITIVE DEVELOPMENT AND CONSUMER SOCIALIZATION

3. Cognitive Aspects of Children's Consumer Behavior 43

4. Children's Consumer Information Processing 51

5. Children's Consumer Behavior: Money Use and Purchase Requests 81

PART III. THE FAMILY'S ROLE IN CONSUMER SOCIALIZATION

6. A Developmental View of Family Influences in Socialization 95

7. The Family Context for Children's Consumer Learning 113

8. Influences on Children's Consumer Learning 145

PART IV. IMPLICATIONS OF THE RESEARCH

9. Public-Policy Issues 165

10. Summary and Implications 175

CONTENTS *(continued)*

Bibliography   193

Appendix A: The Interview Schedules and Questionnaire   199

Appendix B: Excerpts from Code: Child's Interview   229

Appendix C: Regression Analyses: Separately by Grade Level   239

Indexes   261

About the Authors   269

INTRODUCTION

This work looks superficially like a lot of other social-science efforts to grapple with questions of public intent. In this case we explore issues about how children learn, or fail to learn, to become intelligent consumers. We have grown accustomed to seeing such social-science efforts miss their mark. This book does not miss. Ward, Wackman, and Wartella actually deliver on their promise to connect research to public policy. They describe their studies and then tell us what they have learned about the influences that help or harm children who are trying to understand how our consumer society operates.

This book is not just another social-science exercise, trying but failing to touch reality. Neither is it just another "view-with-alarm" over the great menace of television. Almost everything else we read about television catalogues and deplores its abuses: its teaching of violence and passivity, its disruption of family life, its dehumanization, its diverting of children from more useful or healthier activities, its bombardment of commercials that fill our children with avarice and cynicism. Suddenly, we have a book about television that goes beyond hand-wringing or self-flagellation. Ward, Wackman, and Wartella neither apologize for nor attack televised advertising directed to children. They try to understand both its benefits and abuses by studying the children and their parents. The authors set out to discover the effects of televised advertising in a systematic, careful manner that takes the question beyond opinion and advocacy and into the realm of evidence and information.

How do they achieve this? As a conceptual base, they stress the information-processing capabilities of children and try to identify the conditions that foster or interfere with the development of these skills and attitudes, emphasizing the family context. They argue that consumer behavior is simply one instance of a larger class of information-processing behaviors, which does seem a useful way to put the learning of consumer skills and attitudes into a greater perspective. They also assume that looking at children of different ages (or at different levels of cognitive development) will help them to understand the nature of consumer strategies.

With these ideas as general guides, they proceed to interview 615 kindergarten, third-grade, and sixth-grade children and their mothers from blue-collar and middle-class neighborhoods in Boston and Minneapolis-St. Paul, using carefully constructed sets of interview questions with both children and mothers. Children are asked about such matters as recall of information from television advertising, awareness of brand names, comprehension of the selling purpose of commercials, judgment of the truth of television advertising, purchase requests, and use of money for saving or spending. Mothers are asked about their own goals for their children as consumers, their methods for teaching these goals and the opportunities they provide their children to decide about purchases, as well as about the mothers' own consumer strategies and purchasing decisions for themselves and their families. Often interview questions for the children and their mothers are identical, such as the question of frequency of purchase requests by children and other aspects of children's consumer behavior.

What did the authors find out? Not unexpectedly, there are clear and consistent differences among kindergartners, third-graders, and sixth-graders in their attention to televised commercials, the influence the commercials have on them, the information they use in making brand or product requests, their understanding of persuasive intent, and their skepticism about the commercials' truthfulness. Neither sex differences nor social-class differences are nearly as prominent as age differences in their influence on consumer behavior. As children get older, they are more flexible in their use of the information-processing strategy that Ward, Wackman, and Wartella consider fundamental to consumer behavior.

Less predictable are Ward, Wackman, and Wartella's findings about the influence of the family on the ways in which children learn to become intelligent consumers. By the time their children reach kindergarten, mothers have pretty well decided what they want to teach them about how to use money wisely and how to purchase quality products. These goals and the ways in which mothers go about teaching them do not change much as their children get older. At no age is this teaching very planned or deliberate; rather it seems to occur mainly in informal ways, usually through providing examples rather than through exhortation, though most mothers apparently do not like the televised commercials directed toward children and often discuss their negative reactions with their children.

Since it may take some time for the children to benefit from observing their mothers' examples, younger children do not show this effect as strongly as older children. Providing children with their own buying opportunities also has different effects on children at different ages. Surprisingly, Ward, Wackman, and Wartella do not find that increased opportunities for older children to play the consumer role result in increased consumer skills. Kindergartners learn through their buying opportunities, but this effect seems to drop away for the older children. Apparently, providing older children with consumption opportunities results in hit-or-miss learning. Less complex is the finding that mothers can teach kindergarten children that commercials have a persuasive intent. It is perhaps for this reason that Ward, Wackman, and Wartella also report that more exposure to commercials does not result in increased spending or purchase requests by children.

I shall let the readers discover for themselves the authors' conclusions from these and other data, conclusions that are significant for several audiences, including government regulators, educators, consumer advocates, corporate managers, and parents. Though this is a book full of careful exposition and technical analysis, it gives all these readers some new, meaningful, and important conclusions about how children succeed or fail in becoming intelligent consumers.

Gerald A. Lesser
Bigelow Professor of Education
in Development Psychology
Harvard University

PREFACE

It is probably safe to conclude that the only organized group of individuals which has historically been much interested in the question of how children learn to buy has been the small band of teachers who have produced secondary textbooks and curricula in "consumer education." Major national advertisers marketing to children (primarily for food and toy products) have naturally enough been interested more in the immediate effects of advertising on children's buying behavior than in underlying causes of this behavior. Widespread concern about the effects of television advertising on children has changed this situation. This major "consumerism" issue has, in turn, focused attention on the broader picture of how children acquire knowledge, attitudes, and skills relevant to their effective functioning in the marketplace—in short, on how "consumer socialization" proceeds. The controversies surrounding television advertising directed to children have also resulted in a call for research-based approaches to consumer education, in contrast to previous efforts based on individual teachers' assessments of what children of different ages need to know.

Research on consumer socialization processes can help to identify children's abilities to process information about the marketplace, as well as identify gaps in children's knowledge and skills which might be addressed in the classroom. Thus, this research should be valuable for consumer-education programs, which may ultimately be the most effective antidote for many of the alleged abuses of marketing stimuli on children. The research reported here should also be relevant to planners in corporations, self-regulatory groups, and government agencies who are concerned with both short-term and long-term policy decisions regarding the use of advertising directed to children. Finally, this research should be of use to those designing communication programs for young people. Of particular relevance are findings on children's cognitive abilities, which mediate messages, and the family context which forms the communication environment.

This book represents a continuation of the two senior authors' long-standing interest in the effects of mass media on socialization. This interest began when, as doctoral students at the University of Wisconsin, both were deeply involved in research in the area of political socialization and interpersonal persuasion among adolescents. This interest continued with some of the early research examining effects of television advertising on preadolescents. This published research was particularly useful in defining the scope and conceptual approach adopted in the present research. The results of that early research suggest the utility of looking at children's responses to advertising in terms of an information-processing approach, rather than in terms of the traditional "effects" model of mass communication. Consequently, Piagetian notions from cognitive development theory form the major conceptual underpinning to the research reported here.

This approach has benefited from the research interests of the third author, Ms. Wartella. As a doctoral candidate in the Communication Research Division, School of Journalism and Mass Communication at the University of Minnesota, Ms. Wartella has been concerned with applications of cognitive development theory to problems of children's responses to television programming, as well as applications of theory to the process of consumer socialization.

Aside from the normal conflicts one can expect from three co-authors, this book contains a deeper conflict. On the one hand, our objective is to provide relevant information for corporate and government policy makers, and for educators. On the other hand, we are quite aware that the issues are complex and that it is quite likely that no data can ever really resolve them. Thus, we are faced with an opposing tendency to follow the traditional route—simply present the findings and let others worry about applying them to policy issues in the "real world."

Despite this conflict we elect to present the data and to suggest conclusions and areas of potential application of the results. We proceed on the basis of three premises, all of which have been strengthened by the research reported in this volume:

1. Consumption for children is as legitimate an activity as it is unavoidable. Efforts would seem to be better spent on preparing children for efficacious interaction with the marketplace than on protecting them from the multiple influences on product preferences and purchasing which are indigenous to childhood.

2. The inevitability of consumption among children should not be taken as an excuse for advertising excesses. Children are clearly a special audience, and there is an important need to understand their abilities to process information contained in the most prevalent marketer-controlled stimuli affecting children: mass media advertising. We do not subscribe to the "hot stove" theory—i.e., the position that advertising to children need not be carefully scrutinized because children become skeptical of advertising claims as they grow older. We feel this position can be misused by diverting attention from legitimate problems in children's comprehension of marketing stimuli. Moreover, we feel that children, like adults, have a right to be able to fairly evaluate messages designed to appeal to them.

3. There is a need for policy and research to work together toward policy decisions assuring fairness in advertising communication designed to appeal to children, and toward educational programs to improve children's consumer training.

In recent years, there has been a trend toward litigation as a basis for policy decisions in the area of promotions and children. Behavioral science has not presented a viable alternative to litigation, perhaps because research too often proceeds without some attention to policy issues and the setting for policy formulation and applications. Even so, we have not approached our research from the perspective of what would be useful in litigative and judicial proceedings. While proper uses of behavioral research in such proceedings are gradually being perfected (Gerlach, 1972), we feel that the issues concerning promotion and children are not delineated clearly enough to permit such an approach. In any case, we feel that ample opportunities exist for creative and positive approaches to the issues outside of the judicial and quasi-judicial arenas, and that such approaches are preferable to policy making via litigation and government regulation. Consumer education to prepare children for sound marketplace interaction is one such approach. Another possibility for policy action is through industry self-regulation based on research to ascertain children's comprehension of commercials.

We hope our research addresses the question of whether various policy options are desirable and feasible. To do so demands that we move beyond findings of "it depends" toward findings which specify what "it depends upon," as Raymond Bauer (1967) reminds us. We hope our research takes that step.

Data collected in this study were made possible by a grant from the Office of Child Development (OCD-CD-380). Many individuals and organizations have made important contributions to this book, and we gratefully acknowledge their assistance. Professor Stephen A. Greyser, Executive Director of the Marketing Science Institute, provided support, assistance, and invaluable suggestions throughout this volume, as did Seymour Banks, Ph.D., of the Leo Burnett Company. Financial support for these analyses was provided by the Marketing Science Institute and the Educational Foundation of the American Association of Advertising Agencies. The excellent cooperation of the Mounds View school district in Minnesota and the Somerville school district in Massachusetts enabled us to locate children for our study.

Our colleagues and friends at the School of Journalism and Mass Communication at the University of Minnesota helped us in coordinating the Minnesota data collection. Various graduate students in the Communication Research Division helped in computer work and data analyses; particularly, we wish to thank Leo Jeffres and Joseph Wong. Professor W. Andrew Collins at the University of Minnesota's Institute of Child Development provided assistance and clarification of our notions of developmental psychology and Professor James Terwilliger of the School of Education consulted with us about statistical questions we had. Professor F. Stewart DeBruicker, Harvard University, and Professor William Wilkie, University of Florida, also made many helpful suggestions regarding this manuscript.

At the Marketing Science Institute, computer assistance was provided by Wing-Hing Tsang and Jane Ross; we are also grateful for editorial assistance provided by Katherine Bock at MSI. Excellent typing services were provided by Carol Jorgensen at Minnesota, Louise Ringle at Harvard, and Vicki Schwartz, Willow Twyford, and Elaine Snow at MSI. Ronald Faber made valuable contributions to all phases of this research. His graduate training was in Education, and he will pursue doctoral studies in Communication Research; hopefully his future studies will enable him to solve some of the issues raised in this research.

S.W.
D.B.W.
E.W.

PART I

INTRODUCTION

Chapter 1

OVERVIEW: THE DEVELOPMENT OF
CONSUMER BEHAVIOR SKILLS

Perhaps as an outgrowth of the emergence of "consumerism," much concern has been evidenced in recent years in the consumer behavior of preteenage children. Consumer groups and government regulators have been especially concerned with determining the nature and extent of influences on children's consumer behavior—most notably, television advertising. Marketers of products and services to children have long been concerned with understanding children's consumer behavior in order to design appealing products and promotion programs.[1] More recently, marketers and their industry associations have been increasingly interested in understanding children's consumer behavior and influences on its development, as a basis for setting advertising guidelines which may preempt possible government regulatory intervention. At the same time, industry spokesmen have urged going beyond the questions of advertising's short-range effects on children, and taking a broader view of how children become acculturated into the consumer marketplace. Through all of this, parents and educators wonder what effects commercials have on children. At the same time, they gradually evolve rules of thumb for helping children to develop some set of consumer skills.

It is hoped that this book can offer some help to these diverse groups and their particular concerns with children's consumer behavior. We report results of a large-scale survey of parents and children which was conducted in an attempt to describe and understand the process children go through in developing consumer attitudes, knowledge, and skills—a process we call "consumer socialization." The term refers to the gradual development of a broad range of attitudes, knowledge, and skills which are related to consumption, e.g., attitudes toward television commercials, knowledge of the purpose of commercials, knowledge of brands and products, and skills, such as how to most effectively allocate discretionary monies.

In this chapter, we provide an overview of the major concepts which underlie the research reported here. We begin by defining the "information-processing" framework which underlies the research. We next describe cognitive development theory, which provides a basis for explaining differences in how children of different ages select, evaluate, and use information as part of the consumer socialization process. Finally, we argue that research in this area best proceeds from understanding how children respond to a range of consumption situations, rather than simply attempting to predict children's behavior from a set of variables describing their family environment, media behavior, or some other singular aspect of the child's world. We do stress that consumer socialization is best understood if one takes into account the interaction of the child's cognitive abilities and his environment—such as family and media influences. In later chapters, we describe in more detail cognitive development theory, and theories pertaining to family influences on children. Our purpose in this chapter is simply to give readers a feeling for the various concepts and theories which underlie our approach to research on consumer socialization.

THE INFORMATION PROCESSING FRAMEWORK

Our first task was to decide upon a conceptual viewpoint which would help us to structure research in consumer socialization. There were several alternatives. We could have looked carefully at the *inputs* to consumer socialization. For example, some have examined the amount and kind of television commercials children see (Barcus, 1971).

On the other hand, we could have focused on the *outputs,* i.e., catalogued the kinds of things children buy at different ages (McNeal, 1964), or assessed the variety of responses children have to television commercials (Wells, 1965). But the process of consumer socialization means that the inputs and the outputs are connected—we should be able to specify the relationship between influences, such as television advertising, family activities, etc. and outputs, such as children's skills at using money, their responses toward commercials, and so forth.

One alternative would be to view the process in learning theory terms. This point of view would lead one to explain consumer socialization as follows: Children are exposed to various stimuli, such as commercials, products in stores, etc., and they obtain these products, either by buying them directly or by urging their parents to buy them. To the extent that children obtain these products and enjoy them, the consumer behavior patterns are rewarded and, eventually, established. Another explanation would be that children strive to imitate activities and role models they see, such as their friends using a new toy, or an activity portrayed in television commercials. These learning and imitation processes probably account for some of children's consumer socialization, but more complete explanations are possible. For example, no matter how rewarding some consumption experiences have been for children, they do not buy, or request that their parents buy, every product they see, no matter how rewarding the child may believe it would be. Clearly, some screening or selection of information occurs. Children desire some products and haven't the slightest interest in others; they believe some advertising claims and reject others.

Our view is that consumer socialization is best understood in terms of children's developing abilities to select, evaluate, and use information relevant to purchasing. We call these abilities "information processing." This framework indicates that we believe children are active participants in communication processes—attending to some messages and ignoring others, selecting some information in one commercial to compare with product information gained through experience, and so on. This framework suggests that children vary in the quantity of information they process, and in the quality of information processing. Finally, as we will explain, a child's environment can influence how he processes information—for example, some families may mediate the impact of television advertising on children more than other families.

This "information processing" view is expressed graphically in the pictorial model of a specific purchasing situation in Figure 1-1. The

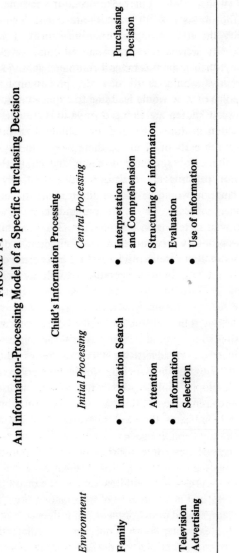

FIGURE 1-1

An Information-Processing Model of a Specific Purchasing Decision

Child's Information Processing

Environment	Initial Processing	Central Processing	
Family	• Information Search	• Interpretation and Comprehension	Purchasing Decision
	• Attention	• Structuring of information	
Television Advertising	• Information Selection	• Evaluation	
		• Use of information	

model depicts two influences on children's consumer behavior—the family and television advertising. Obviously, there are other influences, such as peers, in-store displays, and so forth, but these two are considered to be of major importance. We divide the process into "initial" and "central" processing, to describe the different cognitive activities children go through in acquiring information (searching for it, in some cases, attending to it, and selecting what information to use), and in structuring, interpreting, and using information—what we call "central processing." "Purchase decision" refers to the outcome of the child's decision as to whether he wants a particular good or not. If he decides he wants it, strategy for obtaining it follows—e.g., deciding how to approach his parents.

To illustrate the model further, consider the example of how a boy might decide what new toy he wants—say a new truck. He may have a pretty clear idea of the specific truck he wants, but he may also want to explore the range of trucks available to him. In the course of this information search, he may consider other factors as well, such as where toy trucks can be purchased. The nature of the child's information search activities is influenced by several different factors. First, there may be variations from child to child in awareness of different sources of information about the product (should he examine a store catalogue? watch TV commercials? ask a friend or parent?); there may be differences in the availability of information sources to the child; and finally, children may vary in the allotted time they are willing to give to the search.

As the child gathers information about the kinds of trucks available, he needs to select those "bits" of information he will consider in his decision. The child's attention to advertising messages and interpersonal communication is selective. The kinds of product attributes selected from the various sources of information may be age-related or may be determined by the particular product (a toy truck) under consideration.

Once product information is selected for further processing, subsequent cognitive activity involves interpretation, e.g., Am I likely to get this truck given its price? Does the truck have all the gadgets I want it to have? Interpreting the information requires that the child evaluate new information against past experience, stored knowledge, and goals for product use. For example, the child who wants to purchase a toy truck may be faced with two or more similar brands. He will then have to compare and evaluate the brands; such comparison may involve information which has previously been selected and stored.

Once the child has interpreted, evaluated, and structured the information about the toy truck, he will decide which one to buy, or ask his parents to buy it for him. The child may then use the experience in future product-purchase situations.

Several comments are in order about this model of information-processing. First, children do not go through the process just described for every purchase decision. In some cases, for example, a child may want a toy on the basis of one and only one attribute—its size, for example. In many cases, there is no real information "search"—children may simply see a desirable toy while walking through a store. Second, when the events depicted in the model do occur, they may take place over a few seconds or over a considerably longer period of time, as a child deliberates a "Christmas list," for example. In short, the model is useful as a basis for generating questions for research: it does not require that we view all children as attending to the same message in the same manner, nor does it assume that all children select the same kinds of product information or use the information in the same way. Yet, as a starting point for the research reported in this volume, the model is useful for three primary reasons.

First, the model depicts an essentially "rational" decision-making process. Precisely because it is so rational, it clearly does not *always* apply to children's purchase decisions, as any parent will attest! But this process—or something like it—is what we would often *like* children to go through in making a purchase decision. Parents, for example, often admonish their children to think about what they want before making a decision; regulators of advertising would clearly prefer that children weigh *all* the attributes before making a decision.

A second reason for the model's utility is that it relates to broader streams of research in psychology, consumer behavior, and communication research. In consumer behavior, for example, research on multi-attribute models focuses on the central-processing aspects of the information-processing model presented here. These models essentially refer to how people implicitly weigh the importance of various product attributes in making purchase decisions. Other consumer researchers have traced the sequence of consumer decision-making (Bettman, 1971), examined the quality of consumer decisions as a function of amount and kind of information (Jacoby, 1975), and assessed the thoughts consumers have while attending to marketing communications (Wright, 1974; Ward and Ray, 1974).[2]

A final reason for using the information processing model is that it orients research toward actionable results. Our findings should be useful to those responsible for making decisions about communication practices affecting children, and to parents and educators who may wish to help children develop sound consumer skills. Results might suggest, for example, various kinds of training which could help children in learning to evaluate various purchase alternatives.

THE CONCEPT OF COGNITIVE DEVELOPMENT

To this point, we have introduced the information-processing perspective underlying the research reported here, and suggested some of the outputs of information-processing which comprise the process of consumer socialization. We will elaborate on these outputs—particular kinds of attitudes, knowledge, and skills which make up consumer socialization—in Part II. It is necessary to describe one other conceptual viewpoint in order for us to fully describe our point of view in this research. This is the concept of "cognitive development," which is briefly described below.

In our discussion of the information-processing model (Figure 1-1), we suggest that not all children select, evaluate, and use information in the same way. Obviously, for example, younger children can be expected to process information differently than older children. The latter have more consistent attention spans and greater memory capacities and, as we will see, process information in qualitatively different ways than younger children.

These age-related differences are explained by cognitive development theories. These theories stem from the seminal work of Jean Piaget (1928; 1952; 1954), a Swiss psychologist primarily interested in trying to understand how we come to "know" about the world as adults, i.e., what knowledge is, and how it is acquired. To answer these questions, Piaget decided to study mental growth processes in children. He began his work in the 1920s and is continuing it to this day.

As with all cognitive theories, Piaget's theory posits a cognitive representational or coding process intervening between a stimulus and a child's response. These cognitive representations are organized patterns of thought and behavior which change with age. Piaget's work is the most completely articulated theory in terms of specifying the cognitive structures which constitute the various "stages of development" characterizing age-related differences in children's thinking processes. Furthermore, his theory attempts to explain *how* cognitive development occurs, i.e., the process of development. Although not all cognitive development theorists agree exactly with Piaget's description of the process, most agree with the general notions of cognitive structure, stages of development, and developmental growth.

A cognitive structure is a theoretical construct referring to the child's cognitive representations of the world and to organized patterns of actions. The underlying structure of a set of actions are those features common to all members of the set. For example, an infant may bring a spoon of food to his mouth in slightly different ways at different times, but the structure underlying the action remains the same. With an increase in the age of the child, interest shifts from behavioral structures to cognitive structures, such as classifying objects, connecting events in time or space, or thinking abstractly.

The behavioral structures of the infant are obviously different from the cognitive structures of the adolescent. The qualitative changes in thought which occur as children grow older are conceptualized by Piaget and other developmental theorists as proceeding in "stages." That is, since these cognitive structures are assumed to be rather tightly organized or integrated, cognitive development can be described as proceeding through a sequence of stages.

Piaget has theorized that there are four main stages of cognitive growth which roughly correlate with chronological age: *sensorimotor* (birth to two years), *preoperational* (two to seven years), *concrete operational* (seven to eleven years), and *formal operational* (eleven through adulthood). These age ranges are approximate, but the qualitative differences in cognitive capabilities available to children at different ages have been well articulated by Piaget and his colleagues (Flavell, 1963). The stages of concern in the present study are the middle two—preoperational and concrete operational.

The use of cognitive development theory in this research gives us a basis for "translating" children's cognitive development to help us identify and predict qualitative changes in children's consumer-information processing. As an example, cognitive development theory provides some notions of how children's perceptual and conceptual abilities change over time. These notions are useful to us as a basis for predicting age-related changes in consumer socialization, such as changes in how children perceive, select, and evaluate information relating to their consumer behavior (as depicted in Figure 1-1).

Our purpose at this point is simply to give the reader an introduction to the theory, and to explain its role in the information-processing model which is the basis for the research. We will discuss in detail the cognitive development approach and our specific hypotheses in Chapter 3.

THE RESEARCH APPROACH

In the last section we described how cognitive development theory gives us a basis for explaining how and why children at different ages process information differently. Referring back to the information-processing model (Figure 1-1), we also said that the *same* children may process information differently, depending on the situation. For example, when children are deciding what candy bar to buy for themselves, their decision process may be quite different than when they are garnering arguments to use in trying to get their parents to buy them a new bicycle.

We determined, then, that our approach to this research would best proceed by using the information-processing model to examine the nature of children's information processing across a variety of situations. Rather than attempting to formally test the model posited in Figure 1-1, we decided that the most fruitful course of action would be to elaborate the model and assess its viability across a range of consumer situations encountered by children.

Our decision to apply the information-processing model to a range of consumption-related activities was based largely on what we considered to be a deficiency in current research on children's consumer socialization research, including our own. Much of this research has focused on children's processing of consumer information, but it has proceeded largely in a piecemeal fashion, examining various elements of the process, but not all aspects. For instance, Caron and Ward (1975), Robertson and Rossiter (1974), and Reilly (1973a) have investigated children's information search. Other research has focused on children's attention behavior when exposed to commercials; some age-related differences have been found in children's attention to television commercials relative to programming (Ward and Wackman, 1973) and depending upon the degree of audio and visual complexity (Wartella and Ettema, 1974). Research on children's reactions to premium advertising has focused on children's selection of information (primarily premium attribute information) from commercial messages (Rubin, 1972). Atkin (1974) has examined children's use of premium information in requesting cereal purchases.

Little research has been devoted to central information processing, although Shimp et al. (1975) recently examined children's reactions to commercials varying in the proportion of time devoted to premium offers and product attributes.

These studies of specific aspects of children's cognitive processing are useful, but we approached our research with a view toward elaborating and testing a broader conceptual scheme. To do this, we have examined initial and central processing across different products and different consumption situations for different-aged children. Further, sampling various consumer-related situations has allowed us to examine the impact of different family consumption patterns on children's own use of consumer information. Finally, this research approach lends itself to further theoretical development of information-processing concepts, since it provides a fruitful research strategy for examining developmental changes in the scope of information-processing capabilities of children.

Environmental Influences on Consumer Socialization

In describing our research approach to this point, we have stressed intra-individual notions—that is, cognitive processing of information, going on "inside the heads" of children. The information-processing perspective by definition focuses on intra-individual processes, and cognitive development theoretical notions provide some basis for helping us to explain how children's capabilities are translated into information-processing strategies. Cognitive developmental theorists are often criticized for failing to take into account the interaction of the environment with the intra-individual processes posited by the theory. In this research, we have chosen *not* to ignore the environment—indeed, common sense tells us that a complete picture of consumer socialization demands that we at least take into account family and media influences on the child. The pictorial model (Figure 1-1) shows these two important aspects of that environment which bear on consumer socialization—television advertising and the family. As noted earlier, there are other environmental influences—peers, in-store displays, school courses, etc. But socialization research in other contexts (e.g., political socialization) leads us to suggest that family and media influences are of relatively major importance. Since television is the primary medium by which children are exposed to advertising, we focus on that medium as opposed to other mass media.

Our assumption is that television advertising provides children with some knowledge of the range of goods and services available, and it provides children with attributes and criteria which they could employ in evaluating various purchase alternatives. On the other hand, socialization research leads us to believe that the family is a more important influence on consumer socialization than television advertising. In many cases, family members—especially parents—may mediate the impact of commercials, as when parents refuse to purchase a product a child saw in a television commercial. Further, they may have major impacts on the development of broader consumer skills.

Researchers interested in determining the family's impact on children have usually identified and measured general child-rearing variables and correlated them with children's behavior or personality traits (Hoffman and Lippitt, 1960). Both Freudian and learning theories have provided the conceptual basis for many of the variables employed in such research. However, past research on family influences indicates that this approach has not been very successful in explaining children's behavior at a particular age. Moreover, it has been even less successful in explaining *changes* in children's behavior over time. Perhaps the history of this research led Kohlberg (1969) to his conclusion about family socialization research:

> An appropriate naturalistic study of social learning would not relate individual differences in parental practices of a global nature to individual differences in later global personality traits. Instead, it would relate trial-by-trial changes in children's situational behavior to the trial-by-trial training inputs of parents. (p. 365)

Our research on the family's role in consumer socialization has attempted to follow Kohlberg's advice by adopting a "situational" view of children's consumer learning. That is, we have conceptualized the family context as a series of specific learning situations in which the child may be exposed to various consumption behaviors by his mother, or situations in which the child may engage in various kinds of consumption-related interaction with his mother. Thus, the family pattern the child experiences is a set of situationally based response tendencies. This approach is a substantial departure from most family socialization research which conceptualizes (or at least measures) family patterns in terms of general, nonsituational response tendencies.

We will present a detailed discussion of our conceptualization of the family context and its role in consumer socialization in Part III. Here we simply want to note that we take the family and media influences into account in this research, and that the theoretical literature and some empirical data suggest that environmental influences may operate quite differently for children at different age levels (Baldwin, 1969; Crandall et al., 1958; Kagan and Moss, 1962). Thus, we expect some differences in the impact of the various aspects of the family context on different-aged children's consumer behaviors.

The Research Model

Figure 1-2 portrays an expansion of the information processing model of consumer socialization pictured in Figure 1-1. This expanded model shows the key independent (or causal) variables: family influences and television advertising, and child's stage in cognitive development. Aspects of the family context measured in this study include parent's own consumer behavior, which may indirectly influence children, more direct parent influences, such as parent-child interaction about consumption, and parent's making independent consumption opportunities available to the child.

These independent variables should affect information processing—both initial processing and central processing—as portrayed in the model. But consumer socialization is more than children's cognitions and their structuring of these cognitions: ultimately we expect the model to be successful in predicting some patterns of children's consumer behaviors. Compared to adults, of course, children engage in fewer and simpler consumer tasks. Nonetheless, we would hope to explain some patterns of children's money use, spending and saving behavior, and purchase requests. These are elementary forms of consumer behavior measured in this research, which may underlie the development of more complex patterns of adult consumer behavior.

Finally, we stress that our intention is not to test this model, in the formal sense, but to elaborate it. Therefore, parts of our analysis examine children's consumer information processing and consumer behavior across a variety of consumer situations.

ORGANIZATION OF CHAPTERS

This chapter has attempted to introduce the central concepts underlying the research reported here; the next chapter describes the research design. Subsequent chapters in the book are organized into sections

FIGURE 1-2

Research Model: Children's Consumer Socialization

Independent Variables	Child's Information Processing		Behaviors
	Initial Processing	*Central Processing*	
Cognitive Development			
Family context	Information search	Interpretation and comprehension	Money use
	Attention		Spending
• Parent's own consumer behavior	Information selection	Structuring of information evaluation	Saving
• Parent-Child Interaction		Use of information	Purchase requests
• Children's independent consumer opportunities			
Television Advertising			

permitting more extended discussion of the central concepts than would have been possible in this introductory chapter.

The second part presents results pertaining to effects of stage in cognitive development: Chapter 3 discusses the theory in depth and Chapter 4 presents results pertaining to effects of cognitive development on information processing. Chapter 5 presents results relating cognitive development to actual behaviors—money use and purchase requests.

Part III examines environmental influences on consumer socialization. Chapter 6 discusses various views of the family and what impact it may have on consumer socialization processes; Chapter 7 discusses various patterns of family behavior which may influence children's consumer learning; and Chapter 8 presents results relating the family variables to children's information processing and behavior.

The final part presents analyses which are pertinent to public policy issues (Chapter 9) and, in Chapter 10, a discussion of the implications of the present research for cognitive development theory and for public policy, education, and marketing decisions.

NOTES

1. Children can directly purchase products for their use (e.g., candy), influence others to buy products and brands for them (e.g., breakfast cereal), and may influence consumption of others, as well as themselves, as in the case of children choosing which fast-food outlet to patronize. The scope and complexity of children's consumer behavior make reliable estimates of expenditures hard to come by. One source estimated that children spend—or influence the spending of—about $20 billion per year (McNeal, 1964).

2. Extended discussion of these recent and provocative streams of research in consumer behavior is not possible here. However, the reader may wish to review various directions in information-processing research in consumer behavior by referring to recent edited works, e.g., Hughes and Ray (1974) and Ray and Ward (1975).

Chapter 2

RESEARCH METHODOLOGY

▓▓▓

Data for this study were gathered in a survey of 615 mother-child pairs. The sample was drawn entirely from families in blue-collar and upper-middle-class neighborhoods. A major interest in this research was the role parents play in the socialization of young children. We could reasonably expect that family environments differing in social status would involve different patterns of parent-child interaction related to consumer information processing and behavior.

Since time and budget constraints made a longitudinal study impractical, we wanted to maximize cognitive development differences among the children we interviewed by drawing a sample of children at age levels which reflect particular stages of cognitive growth. Thus, we chose to sample children from kindergarten, third grade, and sixth grade, with the assumption that children in these grades would span the Piagetian stages of preoperational and concrete-operational thought.

Strategies for training interviewers, constructing interview schedules, and coding and analyzing data all had to reflect cognitive developmental differences in the children as well as provide indicators of information use. Each of these matters is considered below.

SAMPLING

Samples were drawn in Boston and Minneapolis-St. Paul from designated school district populations of kindergarten, third-grade, and sixth-grade students. Mothers and fathers of these children were then asked to participate in the study. In Boston, interviewing was conducted in Somerville, a predominantly working-class community; in Minneapolis-St. Paul, it was carried out in the Mounds View district, an area comprising several middle-class suburbs north of St. Paul.

The student samples from both communities were drawn from class lists of students in area schools. For the Boston sample, we used classroom lists from nine schools in the Somerville school district. These schools did not supply telephone numbers, so we had considerable difficulty contacting prospective respondents and scheduling appointments. Consequently, a random sample of 550 names was drawn in an attempt to obtain at least 300 child interviews in Boston. A response rate of 55 percent for this sample resulted in 301 child participants.

For Minneapolis-St. Paul, lists of students in kindergarten, third grade, and sixth grade in four schools in the Mounds View school district were used as the basis for the sample. Through a simple random-sampling procedure, 120 students per grade were chosen, yielding a sample of 360 students. The school district provided telephone numbers, making scheduling of interviews fairly easy. An 87 percent response rate yielded 314 student responses in Minneapolis-St. Paul.

The Sample

The total sample consisted of 615 child-mother pairs who participated in personal interviews. Only 55 percent of the fathers participated in the study by returning self-administered questionnaires through the mail, even after being contacted twice.

The Boston sample is similar to the Somerville population in terms of income level, proportion of female heads of households, and mother's and father's education levels. On the other hand, the Minneapolis-St. Paul sample is slightly skewed upward compared to the Mounds View population in terms of income and both parents' education levels.

The Boston sample generally falls at the lower end of the socio-economic scale; 70 percent of the respondents fall in the lowest half of the Census Bureau's Occupational Classification System. The Minneapolis-St. Paul sample is generally middle class, with only 31 percent of the respondents in the lowest half of the occupational scale.

The total sample of children is divided almost equally among grades and, in each grade, between Boston and Minneapolis-St. Paul. Also, there are approximately equal numbers of boys and girls and nearly equal numbers of children from the various socio-economic status levels at each grade level.

INTERVIEW PROCEDURES

In both cities the interviewers were women. For the Boston sample, interviewers were primarily students in child development at Harvard University. In Minneapolis-St. Paul, interviewers were middle-aged women with experience as professional interviewers in local polling agencies. Interviewer selection was based on observations of candidates' performance in child interviews with pretest instruments by one of the three authors. Independent assessment was also made by a child psychologist with extensive experience in individual interviews with children. The criteria included interviewer's abilities to elicit information from children, verbal probing abilities, and consistency of ability to establish good rapport with child subjects.

Interviewer training in both cities focused heavily on specific techniques for interviewing young children. The main thrust of the training procedures was to prepare the interviewers to follow and record the logic of the child's thought, to keep the child interested in the questionnaire, and to maintain as much standardization as possible in probing for complete responses. In both cities, interview schedules were pretested with children and their mothers from the same school district as in the final sample, although children interviewed in the pretest came from different schools in the district.

The survey was conducted in March and April, 1973. Identical field procedures were used in both Boston and Minneapolis-St. Paul. Initial contact with the families was made through an introductory letter, which outlined the purpose of the project, the amount of time the family would be expected to spend in the interview, and the name of the interviewer who would be calling for an appointment within the week. In the next step, interviewers telephoned the mother to schedule an appointment.

As soon as the interviewer arrived in the home for an appointment with either the mother or the child (whenever possible the appointments were scheduled consecutively), she gave the mother a consent form to read and sign before the interview. This form acknowledged the mother's consent to her child's participation in the interview and informed her of her right to read over the child's questionnaire to delete any questions she deemed inappropriate. No mothers deleted any questions.

Mothers' and children's interviews lasted an average of one hour each. At the completion of the mother's interview, she was given a self-administered questionnaire to fill out. This questionnaire took about twenty minutes to complete and was collected by the interviewer before leaving the home. Finally, a second self-administered questionnaire, to be filled out by the father, was left in the home. These questionnaires were returned by mail. Follow-up letters were sent to fathers who had not returned their questionnaires within a month of the interview with the mother. Since only about half of the fathers returned questionnaires, we have not included these data in any following analyses.

Thus, data were gathered from four sources: personal interviews with children and with their mothers, and self-administered questionnaires for mothers and fathers.

The Child's Interview Schedule

Items in the children's interview were developed to gauge children's skills in initial and central processing of consumer information relative to television advertising and consumer decision making. Measures of children's money use behaviors and purchase requests were also developed. Specific variables included in these various categories are listed in Table 2-1.

About 90 percent of the items consisted of open-ended questions. Interviewers were taught nondirect techniques to elicit answers to these items. For example, a common probe to many of the open-ended items was "anything else?" or "can you think of anything else?"

Furthermore, items on the children's schedule were pretested to insure that they could be understood by the youngest children in the sample. When kindergartners seemed not to understand certain concepts, probes were used to make the questions more concrete and

TABLE 2-1

Table of Variables for Child's Interview Schedule

Information Processing Variables: Initial Processing
1. Recall of information from TV advertising
2. Awareness of sources of information about new products
3. Awareness of brand names of products
4. Information selection about a TV set in a hypothetical purchase situation.

Information Processing Variables: Central Processing
1. Comprehension of the purpose of commercials
2. Evaluation of truth of TV advertising
3. Attitudes toward TV advertising
4. Brand comparison: attributes used in comparing brands of a product
5. Strength of brand preference

Consumer Behavior Variables: Money Use and Purchase Requests
1. Money use norms:
     Prescriptive—what   to do with money
     Proscriptive—what not to do with money
2. Money use behavior: frequency of saving and spending behavior
3. Purchase requests

understandable. For example, in a question asking children to identify different brands from a list of products, interviewers were instructed to rephrase the question for children who did not understand the concept of brand (i.e., children who gave nonsense or nonbrand name responses to the item). The reworded question then became: "Can you tell me the name of different kinds of toothpaste?" Interviewers probed at least three times in relevant, open-ended questions. In this way, we hoped to elicit the maximum level of response each child could provide.

Coding of the open-ended items proceeded after thorough content analyses of responses. Coding categories were developed to capture theoretical categories of interest (such as those which reflect dimensions of cognitive growth) and to represent the range of different responses. A child's first five responses to each open-ended question were coded. Intercoder reliability on the open-ended questions was 90 percent agreement.

An important issue in survey research with children is whether age-related increases in performance of various skills are simply a function of the greater verbal abilities of older children, or whether these differences are a function of developmental growth in cognitive capabilities, as cognitive development theory might suggest. The issue is

TABLE 2-2

Correlations Between Grade Level and Open-Ended Children's Consumer Behavior Variables*

	r
Higher-Level Information Processing Skills	
1. Awareness of the purpose of TV commercials	.66
2. Asking about performance attributes in TV purchase	.50
3. Comparing brands on the basis of performance and ingredient characteristics	.54
4. Awareness of multiple sources for information about new products	.58
5. Awareness of brand names	.73
Lower-Level Information Processing Skills	
1. Asking about perceptual attributes in TV purchase	.09
2. Comparing brands on the basis of perceptual characteristics	.04
3. Awareness of in-store shopping for information about new products	.16
Money Use Skills	
1. Perscriptive norms–savings	.23
2. Proscriptive norms–don't waste money	.21
3. Proscriptive norms–don't buy specific products	.23
4. Number of perscriptive money norms	.15
5. Number of proscriptive money norms	.34
6. Money behavior–savings	.14
7. Number of money behaviors	.25
Nonskill Behaviors	
1. Prescriptive norms–spending	−.13
2. Money behavior–spending	.25

*See Chapter 3 for a fuller description of the conceptualization of children's consumer behavior.

particularly significant in the present research, since almost all of our questions were open-ended, with extensive probing, by adults not previously known by children.

The correlation between grade level and the children's variables derived from open-ended questions are shown in Table 2-2. These data clearly indicate that the relationships between grade level and children's behavior are not simply a function of increased verbal abilities. Only five of the seventeen measures of children's skills and behaviors are substantially correlated with grade level (.35 or higher).

The average correlation between grade level and higher-level information-processing skills is .60 (see Chapter 3). For the three other classes of variables, average correlations with grade level are as follows:

.10 for lower-level information-processing skills, .22 for money use skills, and .06 for nonskill purchase behaviors. This pattern of correlations indicates that the open-ended measures were not severely biased in favor of children with presumably greater verbal ability (such as the older children).

The Mother's Interview Schedule and Questionnaire

The mother's interview schedule and questionnaire provide the basic data for a description of the family context for children's consumer socialization. For example, each mother was asked several questions

TABLE 2-3

Table of Variables for Mothers' Interview Schedules and Self-Administered Questionnaire

Consumer-Education Goals and Attitudes Variable
1. Consumer-education goals and teaching mode for child
2. Attitude toward commercials designed for children

Modeling Variables: Mother's Own Consumer Behavior
1. Use of different sources for information about products
2. Use of information (effectiveness and efficiency) about products in a decision-making situation
3. Frequency of shopping at more than one store

Parent-Child Interaction Variables
1. Talking to child about product decision making
2. Talking to child about commercials
3. Purchase requests and parental yielding to children's purchase requests
4. Parent's responses to child's request for product in different situations

Child Opportunity Variables
1. Frequency of taking child shopping
2. Child's purchasing power
3. Money provided child:
   - allowance
   - money just given to child
   - money earned
   - bank account
4. Child's TV use

Demographics
1. Age of mother and father
2. Income
3. Number of children
4. Occupation of mother and father
5. Ages of children

about her goals for her child as a consumer and her methods for teaching these goals. We expected that children may model certain parental consumer behaviors, so a number of questions concerned the mother's consumption patterns and purchase decision making. Other items probed the mother's interaction with her child about consumption and the kinds of opportunities she gives her child for consumption. These variables are listed in Table 2-3.

Mothers were also given some items identical to those asked in the children's interviews, such as frequency of purchase request and several items regarding the child's consumer behavior. In subsequent analyses several of these items are used as measures of the child's behavior.

ANALYSES

The principal explanatory variables in the present study are the child's cognitive capabilities, which cognitive development theory typically groups together in the concept of "stage." This concept is best thought of as a summary term, encompassing the major cognitive capabilities of children within a particular age range. It is possible to measure the various cognitive abilities directly, but such a procedure is very time consuming and, as a consequence, was not feasible in the present study. In child-development research, age or grade level is often used as a surrogate measure of the child's stage or level of development.

In the present study, we attempted to sample age groups for which the majority of members would clearly fall in a particular stage of development. Thus, we selected kindergartners to represent the "preoperational" stage, sixth graders to represent the "concrete-operational" stage, and third graders to represent a transitional stage between preoperational and concrete operational.

To test the validity of our use of grade level as a cognitive stage surrogate, we devised a measure of cognitive development. A central concept of the process of cognitive development is "perceptual boundedness," which refers to relative differences in children's abilities to comprehend and evaluate stimuli in terms of perceptual cues or in terms of more abstract dimensions. The concept is basic to children's progress from perception to inference—the major theme of cognitive growth. We therefore included questions designed to measure perceptual boundedness, i.e., to identify children who discriminate objects largely on the basis of perceptual attributes (preoperational children) and those who use more abstract conceptual and functional attributes (concrete-operational children).

In three open-ended items, children were asked to describe differences between pairs of objects: (1) school versus house, (2) car versus truck, and (3) father versus mother. The many actual differences between these objects allow children a great deal of latitude in responding. For each item, the children's heavily probed responses were coded on a four-point scale:

1. Coincidental reasoning—lack of ability to focus on dimensions differentiating objects;

2. Perceptual—focus on physical aspects of object, e.g., house is smaller than school;

3. Transitional—differentiation on basis of activities objects perform, e.g., fathers work at an office, mothers work at home;

4. Conceptual—focus on functional difference, e.g., school is where you get an education, home is where you live.

Based on the distribution of responses to these three items, we divided the sample into five levels of cognitive capabilities, from low (predominant use of perceptual distinctions among objects) to high (predominant use of functional distinctions among objects). The relationship between these levels of cognitive capabilities and grade level is

TABLE 2-4

Relationship Between Grade Level and Perceptual Boundedness

			K %	3 %	6 %	Total %
Low	1		42	13	4	20
Low-Transitional	2		23	20	3	15
Medium-Transitional	3		18	26	22	22
High-Transitional	4		10	25	30	22
High	5		7	15	41	21
		Total	100	100	100	100
		N =	(204)	(202)	(207)	(613)

$x^2 = 194.81$ (8 d.f.) $p < .001$

shown in Table 2-4. The cognitive ability groupings are strongly related to grade level, indicating that grade level is a good surrogate measure of cognitive stage.

Within each grade level, we compared children of different sexes and differing socio-economic status levels on the measure of cognitive capabilities. There are no sex differences, but there is a slight positive relationship between socio-economic status and the level of cognitive capabilities at each grade level. This is to be expected, since the presumably enriched home environment of middle-class and upper-middle-class children should contribute to the somewhat more rapid development of their cognitive capabilities.

In the next three chapters, which examine children's information-processing and consumer behavior, we focus entirely on age-related differences, using grade level as the independent variable. In conducting analyses for these chapters, we also examined sex and socio-economic status differences within grade level. Few differences by sex or by socio-economic status were observed; in fact, they occurred only at about chance frequency.

When the family context variables are analyzed (Chapter 7), both grade level of the child and family socio-economic level appear as independent variables. We shall show that the family context for children's consumer socialization differs in important ways in terms of both variables.

Data analysis in Chapter 8 employs multiple regression techniques to examine the relationship between the family context variables and the children's consumer skills and behaviors. The major analysis presented there focuses on patterns of relationships within each of the grade levels.

Final data analyses in Chapter 9 report data relevant to various policy issues of current concern.

PART II

COGNITIVE DEVELOPMENT AND CONSUMER SOCIALIZATION

COGNITIVE ASPECTS OF CHILDREN'S CONSUMER BEHAVIOR

▓▓▓

In Chapter 1 we introduced Piaget's theory of cognitive development. This theory is useful because it provides a basis for explaining age-related differences in children's patterns of information processing, which we see as the primary process of consumer socialization. In this chapter, we explain cognitive development theory in more detail, paying particular attention to aspects of the theory which are pertinent to information processing over the course of children's consumer socialization. We advance some hypotheses based on this discussion and test them in Chapters 4 and 5.

COGNITIVE DEVELOPMENT THEORY

While there are several distinct theories of cognitive development, most are anchored in concepts advanced by Piaget; therefore we simply refer to "cognitive development" theory, recognizing that there are differences among various theories.

Developmental theory posits that children undergo qualitative changes in the way they organize and use information to direct their behavior. For Piaget, this process constitutes intellectual development; tightly organized and integrated "structures" of cognition characterize the thought processes of the child at distinct, age-related "stages" of intellectual development.

The concept of cognitive states has several implications for how children perceive and think (Kohlberg, 1969). First, stages imply distinct, qualitative differences in children's modes of thinking or problem solving at different stages. Second, stages of thought form an invariant sequence in individual development, so although environmental factors may alter the rate of growth, they do not change the sequence. Third, stages of thought form structured wholes, so that a child will show thinking typical of his stage in numerous situations that may differ widely. Fourth, cognitive stages are hierarchial and integrative: higher stages become increasingly differentiated and at the same time integrate lower stages at a new level of organization; in short, one stage "melds" into another.

A brief description of the four stages of development Piaget identifies is a useful way of elaborating the qualitative differences in children's thinking. In the *sensorimotor* stage, the infant's behavior is not at all mediated by thought as we know it, but rather by set behavior patterns that Piaget calls "schema." For example, the infant may see an object, then reach for and grasp it, but he does not think about what he is doing.

In the *preoperational* stage, the child is developing symbolic abilities (such as language and mental imagery), but his behavior is still very closely linked to perception. Piaget characterizes the mental processes of this stage as a "mental experiment" in which the child's thought is a replication in mental imagery of various stimuli which often bear no logical relation to each other.

By the *concrete-operational* stage the child has developed conceptual skills which enable him to effectively mediate perceptual activity, but only when dealing with concrete objects. For example, the child can sort objects into subordinate and superordinate classes and answer questions about the inclusion of one class in another, but only if the objects are visually present.

Finally, in the *formal-operational* stage, he develops adult-like thought patterns, including abstract thought. The formal-operational child can perform many complex cognitive operations and, unlike his younger concrete-operational counterpart, can do so hypothetically and abstractly.

We chose to view the cognitive abilities characterizing children at different stages as rules of information processing which characterize the child's thought. Indeed, Kohlberg (1969) refers to stage-related cognitive structures as "rules for processing information and connecting experienced events." Underlying cognitive stages are several dimensions which explain the changes in perceptual and conceptual abilities differentiating younger, preoperational and older, concrete-operational children. Since these are the particular age-related groupings of children in this study, we will elaborate each of these particular dimensions of cognitive growth in turn.

A basic dimension underlying changes in cognitive stages in the course of development is the movement from perception to inference (Wohlwill, 1962). Wohlwill argues that the most important aspect of cognitive growth is the child's increasing ability to organize his conceptual skills to mediate incoming stimuli, rather than to simply respond to what he perceives. We use the term perceptual-boundedness—the tendency to focus on and respond primarily to perceptual aspects of the environment—to refer to this dimension of growth. Younger, preoperational children tend to be perceptually bounded in their interactions with the environment. However, older, concrete-operational children do not simply accept what is perceived as reality, but can mentally manipulate perceived elements. In short, younger children cannot engage in abstract thought, to the extent that older children can.

The concept of perceptual boundedness suggests a number of specific research questions: do younger children attend primarily to visual attributes to the exclusion of other attributes when they watch television commercials? Are younger children more likely to evaluate products on the basis of perceptual characteristics with little regard to their functional attributes? Do older children employ more varied repertoire of attributes to use in distinguishing among and evaluating products? These are questions we will examine in Chapter 4.

A second dimension characterizing changes in cognitive abilities between six and twelve years of age is the growing ability of children to "decenter" their attention. Piaget describes the thought of younger preoperational children as being characterized by *centration*—the tendency to focus on a limited amount of available information. In contrast to the young child who largely operates on one dimension, the older, concrete-operational child can focus on several dimensions of a situation and relate these dimensions. This movement toward decentration of thought suggests that older children may perceive and select more information from advertising messages than younger children. It also suggests that younger children may use fewer attributes than older children in evaluating a product or comparing two products.

Several other dimensions of cognitive development which may have an impact on consumer information processing are (1) the gradual development of *causal reasoning processes* such that older children are better able to relate events in a causal sequence; (2) the development in middle childhood (about ten or eleven years of age) of the *ability to infer motives* in evaluating actions, such as identifying the motives of advertisers in commercials; and (3) the general growth in more flexible *information-gathering strategies* as children proceed from the preoperational to the concrete-operational stage.

What propels these changes in cognitive abilities—how does the child learn new ways of processing information? Ginsburg and Opper (1969) identify two basic processes in Piaget's theory: development and learning.

For Piaget, development is the result of four factors: (1) maturation of the physical abilities of the child; (2) the child's own experience with objects in the world; (3) social transmission, such as parents talking with the child, knowledge gained in classroom education; and (4) equilibration, the child's self-regulatory processes. Equilibration is particularly significant since it is *the* factor which integrates all aspects of development, i.e., equilibration refers to how the child adapts to his environment.

Piaget maintains that development occurs as the child attempts to cope with his environment, as he is constantly accommodating to new events and assimilating these new events into his present cognitive abilities. When there is cognitive conflict, or "disequilibrium" between the child's cognitive functioning and his ability to understand a new event, the child is propelled to readjust his cognitive structures—to adapt them in order to assimilate the experience. The child is in a state of "dynamic equilibrium," constantly trying to accommodate and assimilate new events. How well he accommodates and assimilates new events is a function of the "fit" between the new experience and the child's level of cognitive ability. For example, we might expect a child to readily classify dogs and cats into a structure concerning animals; however, the intense emotions of young children experiencing novel zoo animals for the first time provides testimony to the difficulty young children have in assimilating radically new experiences into existing cognitive structures. With age, this process is easier, and new structures are formed which subsume the earlier ones.

Piaget's theory of development is not solely a maturational theory—indeed the richness of the child's environment is thought to propel some changes in development more quickly than other changes. Recent research by Pascual-Leone and Smith (1969) and Case (1974) has examined the impact of the environment on cognitive development. Their research shows that one can teach a child a particular item of knowledge or cognitive ability far earlier that Piaget suggests the child should be able to acquire that ability. Case suggests that "the acquisition of any particular item of knowledge depends upon the match between the pragmatic structure of the situation in which the child first has a chance to construct that particular item of knowledge, and the functional limitations of his thought process at the stage in his life when he first encounters such a situation" (Case, 1974, p. 572). Case demonstrated that, through a highly structured training technique, bright seven- and eight-year-old children could be taught to perform and understand a "control of variables" logical problem, although Inhelder and Piaget (1958) hold that such problems cannot be solved until the stage of formal operations. Case's results, in particular, show that the child's environment affects cognitive development. In Part III we will have more to say about how family and media influences, as part of the child's environment, affect children's information-processing and consumer behavior.

The second process propelling changes in cognitive abilities is learning. For Piaget, learning, in a very narrow sense, refers to the acquisition of new behavioral responses over time to a specific situation.

This form of learning considers the use of reinforcements and repeated experiences with a particular situation such that the child "learns" a response to that situation—but only that one. For instance, we may be able to teach a five-year-old child to ask whether a toy train comes with a battery, but the child's understanding of this action (i.e., his assimilation of it into his general cognitive functioning) may not have developed at the same time; the child may still be in a state of "disequilibrium." If he has not assimilated the action, he is unlikely to ask about batteries in other product-choice situations in which the question would be relevant (e.g., in considering a flashlight, toy truck, etc.). If the child has assimilated this question into his repertoire of attributes to examine across a variety of products then he had "developed" a new cognitive ability.

Unfortunately, at times Piaget uses the two terms of "learning" and "development" interchangeably—that is, he may refer to the definitive changes in cognitive growth as the "learning" of a new cognitive structure rather than the "development" of a new cognitive structure. Therefore, some confusion in distinguishing these two terms, learning and development, may arise when reading Piaget.

In order to avoid this confusion, we have restricted the use of the term "learning" to mean the very narrow sense of acquisition of a behavioral response to a specific situation. Thus, a child may "learn" to ask about such a nonperceptual attribute of toothpaste as "does it have fluoride?" However, if the child has generalized across many products and can ask about nonperceptual attributes of different products, such as TV sets, snack foods, etc., then the child is said to have "developed" a new cognitive skill.

These cognitive developmental notions should be relevant to differences between preoperational and concrete-operational children in their patterns of consumer-related information-processing and consumer behaviors. In the following sections we advance hypotheses for consumer socialization which are based on this discussion of cognitive development theory.

CHILDREN'S CONSUMER SKILLS

Piaget is mainly concerned with intellectual development—behaviors which require logical thinking abilities. But not all consumer behavior is a function of cognitive growth, nor is all consumer behavior cognitively based. We have distinguished between two types of consumer activities: (1) consumer skills, or consumer activities which have a cognitive basis in that they involve information-processing activities or other "thinking" capabilities which might follow the course of general cognitive growth; and (2) "nonskill" consumer activities which are not thought to have a cognitive basis or follow the course of general cognitive development. We will discuss both "consumer skills" and "nonskill purchasing behaviors" below.

We define consumer information-processing skills as either "high"- or "low"-level skills. *Lower-level information-processing skills* refer to the use of relatively concrete perceptual attributes in consumer information processing, i.e., in asking about products, comparing brands, or processing television advertising. *Higher-level information-processing skills* refer to the use of more abstract conceptual and functional types of information in consumer information processing.

Our general hypotheses for these consumer skills are as follows: (1) *the use of higher-level skills will increase* substantially with age, because the cognitive capabilities necessary for utilizing these skills in consumer information processing undergo major development from ages five to twelve. (2) *The use of lower-level skills will not change with age,* because the cognitive capabilities necessary for utilizing these skills are possessed by even the youngest children in our study. Since cognitive abilities which develop early are not replaced by later cognitive structures, but rather are elaborated upon and used more efficiently, the older children in our study can and will perform with lower-level skills depending on the situation.

In addition to cognitive information-processing skills, we examine two aspects of children's consumer behavior—their use of money and their requests to parents for products, perhaps the method by which children acquire most goods. *Money use skills* refer to the child's awareness of norms regarding savings and the wise use of money, as well as his own savings behavior. *Purchase behaviors* refer to the frequency of the child's use of money for spending and the frequency of his purchase requests.

Our general hypotheses about changes in money use skills and purchase behaviors are as follows: first, *we expect money use skills to increase as children grow older.* This prediction is only partly based on cognitive development theory. Even though developmental changes in children's comprehension of marketplace economic transactions have been found to follow general cognitive growth (Scheussler and Strauss, 1950), the relationships between money use skills and cognitive development are not well specified. However, since norms of saving and actual saving behavior involve somewhat abstract notions, we would expect some increase in money use skills as a consequence of cognitive changes. A second major basis for this prediction is the increased experience of older children in dealing with money.

Regarding other consumer behavior, *we expect little or no increase with age in the frequency of nonskill purchase behaviors.* Children learn early to ask their parents for products they want. They also learn to allocate available monies for products they want. We have little reason to expect any change in the frequency of children's desire for products as they grow older. Consequently, we see little reason to expect changes in the frequency of the behaviors children use for obtaining products. A possible exception may be some decrease in asking for products among older children as their incomes increase and they are better able to purchase products themselves.

In the next chapters we will discuss, first, children's consumer information-processing skills and, second, children's money use skills and nonskill purchasing behaviors. As we indicated in Chapter 2, our major independent variable in both these chapters is child's grade in school. Thus, our analysis will focus on age-related changes in children's skill and nonskill consumer activities. Use of grade level as a surrogate measure of the child's general level of cognitive ability is a common practice in developmental research. In this way, we can maximize the differences among the three age groups in our sample since we assume that children at one grade level should be more similar in cognitive ability than children from different grade levels.

Furthermore, preliminary analyses conducted on all of the children's consumer activities data indicate that both sex and SES differences within age groups were minimal. In fact, we found such differences at only about the chance level across the fifty-six child-consumer behavior variables we examined. Therefore, we will only discuss sex and SES differences in children's behaviors where they seem particularly appropriate.

Chapter 4 ░░

CHILDREN'S CONSUMER INFORMATION PROCESSING

░░

Children can and do use various sources of information in making consumer decisions to buy or not buy a particular item, or, as often happens, to ask their parents to buy for them. Television, parents, siblings, friends, in-store displays, and catalogues are kinds of information sources available to children. Children's frequent exposure to television programs, and thus commercials, makes television advertising a primary information source. Recent estimates suggest that elementary school children watch about thirty hours of television per week (Lyle, 1972). Analyzing several sources of audience information, Faber (1975) concludes that five- to twelve-year-olds are exposed to an average of nearly 400 commercials per week. While one can debate the meaning or implications of such "average" figures, there can be little doubt that television advertising provides children with early and frequent exposure to the marketplace and products. Furthermore, research shows that children frequently name television as a primary source of ideas for Christmas gifts (Caron and Ward, 1975).

For these reasons one major topic we examine in this chapter is children's consumer information processing of television commercials. The ability of children to comprehend commercial messages on television adequately and therefore avoid being "misled" or deceived is an issue of considerable current interest, particularly in light of this high exposure children—even very young ones—have to commercials. Previous studies conducted by us and by other researchers (Ward and Wackman, 1973; Robertson and Rossiter, 1974) have shown a clear relation between stage of development and children's ability to understand the purpose of commercials. Typically, these studies have involved rather small samples. In the present research, we decided to test this proposition again with a considerably larger sample, as well as to broaden our measurement of children's processing of television advertising.

Secondly, we focus on children's awareness, selection, and use of several types of product attributes which may be utilized in comparing consumption alternatives: brand information, "premium" information, and other physical and functional characteristics of products. Obviously, how children use product information when making purchases or when requesting products from parents is at the crux of children's consumer learning. Our goal here is to sample various purchasing situations and various types of products in order to examine the kinds of product information which may be salient to children at particular ages, or for particular products.

The specific aspects of children's information processing of television advertising and product information selected for analysis were:

TELEVISION ADVERTISING

Initial Processing:
1. Attention to TV advertising
2. Selection of information about products from specific commercials
3. Recall of information across a variety of commercials
4. Awareness of TV advertising as a source of new product information

Central Processing:
1. Comprehension of the purpose of TV advertising
2. Evaluation of TV advertising

PRODUCT INFORMATION

Initial Processing:	1. Brand knowledge
	2. Selection of information about products in considering product purchases
Central Processing:	1. Brand comparison
	2. Brand preference
	3. Use of information in product purchase requests

INFORMATION PROCESSING OF TELEVISION ADVERTISING

Initial Processing Related to Television Advertising

The first step in information processing involves perceptual processes: (1) children's actual looking behavior or attention to television commercials; (2) children's selection of information from the commercials for further processing; and (3) children's use of advertising in gathering information about new products. Our basic predictor in these and succeeding analyses is grade in school.

Attention behavior. Attention to the advertising stimulus is a necessary condition for subsequent processes of information selection, comprehension, and evaluation. Attention is the process which "filters information" and determines what part of the environment will occupy thought; that is, it determines what will be processed (Simon, 1972).

Two of our studies have examined the nature of children's attention to TV commercials, although in different contexts. Wartella and Ettema (1974) studied young children's attention to specific commercials in an experimental setting; Ward and Wackman (1973) examined attention behavior across a variety of commercials in an in-home viewing situation. In both studies, cognitive developmental differences in children's information-processing capabilities were used to predict the children's attention behavior. The basic proposition tested in these studies was that the more perceptually bound the child (i.e., the younger the child), the greater the influence of perceptual characteristics of commercials on his attention; the less perceptually bound the child (i.e., the older the child), the greater the influence of content or conceptual aspects of commercials on his attention. Data from both studies support this proposition.

Wartella and Ettema (1974) examined the sequential nature of children's attention to television advertising. In a school setting, they observed 120 three- to eight-year-olds' attention to twelve commercials that were manipulated for differences in visual and auditory complexity. Content was controlled by using commercials which advertised similar products. The commercials were presented in three two-minute time blocks during the course of a one-half hour program. Attention behavior was recorded by observers before the commercial, at the onset of the commercial, and at ten-second intervals during the commercial. At each observation, attention was coded into one of three categories: full attention (child in viewing position and eyes on the screen); partial attention (eyes not consistently on the screen and/or child not in viewing position); and no attention (eyes not on the screen and child not in viewing position).

Wartella and Ettema found some evidence that attention behavior of young children varies according to the perceptual characteristics of the commercials. For instance, the difference in attention to high- versus low-complexity commercials was greatest for nursery schoolers although the difference was small. Furthermore, they found evidence of movement toward full attention during the transition from program to commercial. The authors interpret these findings as indicating that even children as young as three are aware of the visual and auditory cues signifying the interruption of the program by a commercial. Apparently, young children can discriminate between commercials and programs *perceptually* (as indexed by their attention behavior), even though they have difficulty conceptualizing differences, as data reported below indicate.

Evidence of the relative unimportance of content or conceptual aspects of commercials in directing young children's attention behavior is provided by Ward and Wackman's (1973) observation study. In this study, mothers of ninety five- to twelve-year-olds observed their children watching television in the home. The same threefold coding scheme discussed above was employed here.

When data on attention to a variety of different types of commercials were compared, the younger, perceptually bound children showed *less* differentiation in their attention behavior, i.e., the younger children are less sensitive to the content differences across television programming. However, when content is controlled, as in the Wartella and Ettema study, young children do show more differentiation in attention to stimuli varying in terms of perceptual aspects. In short, research evidence on children's attention to television advertising indicates that age-related changes in children's attention behavior are consistent with the overall development of consolidating conceptual skills. The movement from heavy reliance on perceptual aspects of stimuli to increasingly more reliance on conceptual aspects appears to be at least one important factor influencing children's attention behavior.

Information selection. When children attend to a commercial, they select different kinds of information from it. Questions of interest here include: What attributes of the advertised product do children select for further processing? Is there a developmental trend in the kind of information selected from commercials? These questions have been addressed in research on the information-selection strategies of children, as indexed by recall measures, in two contexts: (1) information selection from a specific commercial and (2) information selection after exposure to a variety of commercials.

In an experimental study of information selection from a specific commercial, Rubin (1972) exposed seventy-two first-grade, third-grade, and sixth-grade children to a thirty-second cereal commercial, either with or without a premium offer. Here the stimulus commercial was manipulated to examine differences in the content of children's information selection. Immediately after exposure, children were asked the question, "Tell me, what happens in the movie you just saw? . . . Anything else?" The specific elements recalled were coded into three major categories: brand name, product symbol, and premium.

Rubin found a clear developmental trend in recall of only one type of information—brand name. Very few first-graders recalled the brand name in either experimental condition (two out of twelve children), while sixth-graders had a reasonably high recall of brand name in both conditions (seven out of twelve in the premium, and nine out of twelve in the nonpremium condition). Recall for third-graders fell in between these two groups. Both the product symbol and the specific premium (in the premium condition) were accurately recalled by a relatively high percentage of all children.

In contrast to Rubin's study, we examined the kinds of advertising information children focus on across a variety of television commercials. Our measure of information selection is children's recall of what happens in their "favorite" commercial. We expected from developmental theory and previous research on children's recall of television programs (Leifer et al., 1971) that as children grow older, recall of advertising becomes increasingly complex, multi-dimensional, and complete. The survey results support this hypothesis (Table 4-1). The youngest children are most likely to describe just a single element in a commercial (e.g., "there was a man on a horse") or to recall several images, but in random fashion. With increased age, children recall more features and relate these features in the proper sequence to represent the story told in the commercial. Some of the children gave responses which not only told the story but also contained references indicating knowledge of the persuasive intent of the "favorite" commercial.

Thus there appears to be a major developmental change in children's information selection from television advertising. Rubin's data suggest that a clear representation of an information item, such as the highly specific visual representations of the product symbol and premium, facilitates younger children's recall, since these children tend to remember only a few dominant perceptual images from the commercial. As age increases, recall embraces more and more different kinds of information, including brand name and other, more abstract information about the product and the commercial.

Sources of new product information. A basic component of children's learning about the marketplace is knowledge of sources of information about products. Here we will examine children's awareness of advertising and other sources of new-product information. In particular, we will discuss the relative usefulness of these sources in providing information about different types of products.

Children were asked open-ended questions about where they would

TABLE 4-1
Recall of Favorite Commercial by Grade Level

	K %	3 %	6 %	Total %
Recall Unidimensional	31	12	9	17
Recall Multidimension and Random	50	36	27	37
Recall Multidimension and Coherent	17	48	52	40
Recall Multidimensional, Coherent and with Selling Message	2	4	12	6
	100	100	100	100
N =	(166)	(187)	(193)	(546)

$x^2 = 93.40$ (6 d.f.) $p < .001$

"find out about" three kinds of new products: toys, snack foods, and clothing. Across the three product groups, the average number of information sources mentioned increases with age: from 3.66 for kindergartners to 5.90 for third-graders and 6.68 for sixth-graders.

Children's awareness of advertising as a source of information about new products increases substantially with age and also becomes more varied and selective (Table 4-2). Kindergartners rely on personal in-store experiences as their principal information source; only a third of the

TABLE 4-2
Knowledge of Sources of Information About New Products at Each Grade Level*

Source	Toys %	Clothes %	Snacks %
Kindergartners			
Mass Media	40	23	32
TV commercials	31	16	28
Newspaper print	5	2	4
Catalogues	6	7	–
Store	77	77	68
Interpersonal	13	20	18
N =	(190)	(179)	(184)
Third Grade			
Mass Media	79	67	65
TV commercials	56	35	55
Newspaper print	19	30	8
Catalogues	20	23	2
Store	82	71	78
Interpersonal	23	29	24
N =	(200)	(200)	(200)
Sixth Grade			
Mass Media	82	78	71
TV commercials	57	31	60
Newspaper print	29	36	17
Catalogues	25	35	1
Store	41	78	76
Interpersonal	33	31	25
N =	(207)	(207)	(208)

*Because of multiple responses columns total to more than 100 percent within each grade level. Similarly, subcategories of mass media total to more than the overall category because some respondents cited several media sources.

kindergartners also utilize TV commercials and just one-fifth mention other people as a second source. Kindergartners demonstrate little differentiation across products in the sources they use, although they appear to have some recognition that TV commercials are more likely to be a useful information source for toys and snack foods than for clothes.

Older children do not abandon personal in-store experiences as a source of new-product information, but they are much more aware of advertising. Two-thirds or more of the third-graders and the sixth-graders name media sources for each product, compared to a maximum of 40 percent of the kindergartners who mention media sources for toys. Furthermore, unlike kindergartners, substantial numbers of both groups mention print media and catalogues as well as TV commercials.

Both groups of older children appear to recognize variations in the media used to advertise different products. For example, 20 percent fewer third-graders mention TV commercials as a source for clothes compared to snacks or toys; at the same time, 21 percent more third-graders mention print media as a source for clothes compared to snacks. The percentage of third-graders mentioning catalogues as a source for snacks declines to near zero. Results are similar for sixth-graders. Thus, both groups of older children appear to be aware of more sources of advertising and to view the various media as functional alternatives.

These data may just reflect the fact that older children, who can read, learn that newspapers, magazines, and advertising catalogues contain product information, whereas kindergartners, who typically cannot read, simply don't know the kinds of information these media contain. However, the developmental pattern indicated here also resembles a general dimension of cognitive growth mentioned by developmental theorists such as Baldwin (1969): with increased age, children become more flexible in the use of information-gathering strategies. Baldwin suggests that information-gathering strategies of children are circumscribed by their ability to comprehend and intelligently make use of the information. As children acquire more efficient and elaborate processing capabilities, they are able to use more of the kinds of information they may gather about a product. If this is the case, then the younger children's lesser reliance on mass-media sources of product information, particulary television advertising, may reflect low comprehension of the functions of advertising. Thus, our subsequent analyses focus on children's comprehension and evaluation of television advertising. These are *central* information-processing activities in our research model.

Central Processing Related to Television Advertising

In earlier research with small samples of children, we explored the nature of children's reactions to television advertising (Ward and Wackman, 1973; Ward, 1972). The general findings have been highly consistent with predictions from cognitive development theory. Relative to younger children, third-grade through sixth-grade children exhibit more elaborate and multi-dimensional recall of commercials (data presented earlier) and more accurate understanding of the purposes of commercials. They are also more likely to base attitudes toward specific commercials on message characteristics than on attitudes toward the product itself, and are less likely to feel that commercials always tell the truth. Since children's processing of information in television advertising is fundamental to consumer socialization processes, we were eager to test our earlier results against data from the larger sample in the present study.

Data were obtained by asking a series of open- and closed-ended questions concerning:

1. children's understanding of the nature and intent of commercials;

2. children's belief in advertising messages;

3. various attitudes of the children toward commercials.

Understanding of commercials. To measure their understanding of the nature and intent of commercials, children were asked:

"When you watch TV you must see a lot of commercials. What is a TV commercial?"

"Why are commercials shown on television?"

"What do commercials try to do?"

Coding categories for the first question were derived from developmental theory. "Low degree of awareness" responses are simple perceptual descriptions of commercials (e.g., "they show kids playing with dune buggies") or affective responses ("they're funny"). "Medium-awareness" responses reflect some knowledge of the concept of advertising but no understanding of advertising's persuasive intent. "High-awareness" responses show understanding of the intent of advertising, and some notions of sponsorship and/or technique.

Results show a strong linear relationship between awareness and age (Table 4-3). Similar results were found regarding children's understanding of "why commercials are on TV" and "what commercials try to do" (Tables 4-4 and 4-5). Responses to these two questions were grouped into three scaled categories, each defined in terms of information-processing differences between the younger and older children (see Appendix B for detailed code). These data strongly support the developmental hypothesis and our prior findings.

Evaluation of commercials. An important mediator in the processing of advertising information is the extent and the nature of truthfulness one attributes to advertising messages. The concept of "truth in advertising" is a difficult one. Adults can normally deal with puffery and

TABLE 4-3
Awareness of "What a Commercial Is" by Grade Level

	K %	3 %	6 %	Total %
Low Awareness	68	18	2	27
Medium Awareness	26	57	57	48
High Awareness	6	25	41	25
	100	100	100	100
N =	(167)	(199)	(207)	(573)

$x^2 = 114.63$ (4 d.f.) p < .001

TABLE 4-4
Awareness of "Why Commercials Are on TV" by Grade Level

	K %	3 %	6 %	Total %
Low Awareness	56	12	3	23
Medium Awareness	40	73	59	58
High Awareness	4	15	38	19
	100	100	100	100
N =	(193)	(200)	(208)	(601)

$x^2 = 215.23$ (4 d.f.) p < .001

TABLE 4-5

Understanding of Purpose of Television Commercials by Grade Level[*]

	K %	3 %	6 %	Total %
Low Understanding	50	7	1	16
Medium Understanding	46	67	58	58
High Understanding	4	26	41	26
	100	100	100	100
N =	(140)	(200)	(207)	(547)

$$x^2 = 214.11 \text{ (4 d.f.) } p < .001$$

[*] Sixty-five kindergartners did not attempt to answer this question and therefore do not appear in this table. Consequently, this table probably underestimates the percentage of kindergartners with low understanding of the purpose of commercials.

other distortions of literal truthfulness in selecting information from television commercials, but children may not be able to do so. Indeed, our earlier research indicated that even sixth-grade children do not always make subtle distinctions in evaluating advertising truthfulness. Consequently, we asked the children whether commercials *always* tell the truth, knowing that inclusion of the word "always" poses a particularly difficult test for advertising truthfulness. In subsequent questions, we examined evaluation of commercial truthfulness further, recognizing that children may have particular difficulty in verbalizing their full understanding of this subject.

Kindergartners are nearly evenly split in response to the question about television advertising always being truthful; however, the proportions of older children saying "sometimes" or "no" increase markedly to 88 percent of third-graders and 97 percent of sixth-graders.

We asked these skeptical children "how often" commercials don't tell the truth, how they know when commercials "lie," and why they don't tell the truth. Children do make some discriminations regarding the frequency of truthfulness, although one-fifth of the sixth-graders feel commercials lie "most of the time" compared to only 7 percent of the kindergartners. Further, three-fifths of the children in the younger two age groups report that commercials lie only "once in a while," but only one-third of the sixth-graders report this low frequency of untruthful commercials.

When asked how they know when commercials "lie," many sixth-graders gave answers to this open-ended question that suggest they respond to television advertising as they may respond to some other authority figures and institutions—with a generalized skepticism or distrust (Table 4-6). Both third- and sixth-graders are more likely than kindergartners to cite a specific negative experience with an advertised product as a basis for determining when advertising "lies."

Children who thought TV commercials don't always tell the truth were asked why commercials don't tell the truth (Table 4-7). The youngest children typically can give no reason or respond in egocentric terms, e.g., "they just want to fool you," "they just lie." On the other hand, older children give responses which reflect their developing abilities to infer and attribute motives, a more complex information-processing skill, e.g., "they want to sell products to make money, so they have to make the product look better than it is."

We also asked children who had agreed with the statement that "TV commercials always tell the truth" why they feel this way. Unfortunately, data are not sufficient to permit detailed age-related analyses (N=132). However, it appears that the youngest children often refer to authority concepts ("they'd get in trouble if they lied"), while older children frequently base their attitude on positive experiences with advertised products ("products are like they are in commercials"). Though the data are tentative on this point, it appears that the reason at least some of the older children feel commercials tell the truth is their positive experiences with advertised products.

On the other hand, negative experiences with advertised products were the primary reason why children were skeptical of advertising. To probe this matter further, we asked children directly about experiences with products they had seen advertised:

> Did you ever see something on TV that you got and then when you got it, it wasn't as good as you thought it would be? (If yes.) Tell me what happened?

Two-thirds of third-grade children and three-quarters of sixth-grade children answered "yes" to this question compared to 38 percent of kindergartners. Responses regarding specific experiences with the product indicate that about one-third of older children experienced functional problems (e.g., "it didn't work right") or quality problems (e.g., "it fell apart") or said the product was inadequate (e.g., "smaller than it showed" or "not as much in the box").

TABLE 4-6
How Children Judge TV Commercial's Truthfulness by Grade Level*

	K %	3 %	6 %	Total %
Confused	49	13	3	15
Authority-based	3	3	2	3
Concrete-specific Experience	36	70	58	58
Understanding Advertising Technique	0	1	8	4
Generalized Distrust	12	13	29	20
	100	100	100	100
N =	(89)	(171)	(200)	(460)

$x^2 = 133.69$ (10 d.f.) $p < .001$

TABLE 4-7
Children's Explanations of Why TV Commercials Are Untruthful*

	K %	3 %	6 %	Total %
No Reason or Egocentric Concept	68	13	3	19
Idea of Desire to Motivate	28	53	71	56
Understand Advertising Profit Motive	4	34	26	25
	100	100	100	100
N =	(83)	(166)	(199)	(448)

$x^2 = 178.03$ (4 d.f.) $p < .001$

*Respondents in these two tables are children who believe commercials do not always tell the truth.

Even though many children indicate having negative experiences with advertised products, we must keep in mind that at least some children, especially older ones, cite positive experiences with products as a basis for judging advertising truthfulness. Unfortunately, we cannot precisely determine to what extent positive or negative experiences with some products generalize to attitudes about the credibility of other advertising.

Children's general attitudes toward commercials were addressed in a series of closed-ended questions. Two-thirds of the kindergartners said they would like to have most things they see on TV commercials, but such generalized "wanting" decreases with age (Table 4-8). Nevertheless, half of both the third-graders and sixth-graders also indicate they would like most things shown in TV commercials. Further, two-thirds of the kindergartners and more than five-sixths of both the third-graders and the sixth-graders agree with the statement that "commercials on TV make you want to have things." Although this statement merely indicates a child's attitude and is not a valid indicator of commercials' actual effects, it is interesting to note the older children's high agreement.

On the other hand, when children were asked if the "things shown on TV commercials are the *best* you can buy," half of the kindergarten children agreed with this statement, compared to only 17 percent of the third-graders and 8 percent of the sixth-graders. And in responding to a related question concerning whether they can "tell how good something is from the TV commercial," only one-fifth of the third-graders and sixth-graders said yes. On the other hand, kindergartners are about evenly split on this item.

It appears that children's attitudes toward commercials are complex indeed. Their attitudes are consistent in that they report disappointment with advertised products, skepticism toward commercials, and general rejection of the proposition that commercials indicate product quality. However, in spite of these attitudes, which may cognitively "filter" commercial messages, about half of the children still report wanting much of what they see in commercials. No doubt this finding reflects the fact that commercials to which children are exposed are frequently for products they regularly desire and consume, e.g., toys and foods.

To summarize the findings regarding children's comprehension and evaluation of television advertising, the data are highly consistent with our earlier, smaller-scale research and with findings reported by other

TABLE 4-8

Children's Verbal Attitudes Toward Commercials and Their Effects by Grade Level*

	K %	3 %	6 %
Question: *"Would you like to have most things they show on TV commercials?"*			
Yes	66		
No	34		
Yes, really think so		21	14
Yes, sort of think so		30	35
No, sort of think not		24	24
No, really think not		25	27
Question: *"Do you think commercials on TV make you want to have things?"*			
Yes	67		
No	33		
Yes, really think so		40	35
Yes, sort of think so		47	50
No, sort of think not		8	11
No, really think not		5	4
Question: *"Do you think the things they show in TV commercials are the best you can buy?"*			
Yes	55		
No	45		
Yes, really think so		4	1
Yes, sort of think so		13	7
No, sort of think not		48	52
No, really think not		35	40
Question: *"Can you tell how good something is from the TV commercial?"*			
Yes	44		
No	56		
Yes, really think so		4	3
Yes, sort of think so		17	18
No, sort of think not		38	37
No, really think not		41	42

*Kindergartners were provided with only two response alternatives—yes or no. Third and sixth graders were given the four alternatives shown.

investigators (Robertson and Rossiter, 1974; Atkin, 1975a, b). The general picture of children becoming more "sophisticated" with increasing age is certainly not surprising. Moreover, the consistency with which the results correspond to cognitive development notions about children's ability to process information increases confidence in the results. This consistency is also helpful in suggesting broad strategies to ensure that children can comprehend advertising messages. For example, the findings regarding young children's difficulty in understanding commercials would suggest the advisability of clearly separating programming and advertising content. We will have more to say about this later.

INFORMATION PROCESSING OF PRODUCT INFORMATION

In the next sections, we will consider how children select and use information about products in making purchase decisions. The question of how consumers use information in forming attitudes and shaping behavior has commanded a great deal of attention in consumer research. The principal research thrust has attempted to apply multi-attribute attitude models to the consumer context. Some of these models are outgrowths of expectancy-value theories in psychology (e.g., Rosenberg, 1956); Fishbein's model (1967), on the other hand, is based on behavior theory principles of mediated generalization. The latter model has been usefully modified in consumer research, in that attitudes are conceptualized as a function of the importance of various product attributes to the consumer and of the consumer's belief that the object (product) possesses each attribute.

The importance of these multi-attribute models for the present research is that they suggest kinds of variables to examine in looking at how children perceive, select, evaluate, and use information in product decisions. The first two operations—perceptions and selection of information—refer to "initial processing" of product information; the latter two—evaluation and use of information—refer to "central processing" in our research model.

Children's information processing of product information can be viewed in terms of the following object/attribute model, which is a simplified version of the multiattribute models:

	Alternative		
	Object A	*Object B*	*Object n*
Attribute 1	A_1	B_1	n_1
Attribute 2	A_2	B_2	n_2
Attribute 3	A_3	B_3	n_3
Attribute n	A_n	B_n	n_n

The "perfectly rational" consumer implicitly (or explicitly) fills in the cells, with appropriate attribute weighting, combines the attributes, and makes the appropriate choice. The utility of this matrix for the present purposes is not, however, to test the "rationality" of child consumers. Rather, it serves to focus our attention on the various kinds of product information (attributes) children may select and use in making a product or brand choice. For example, we would expect brand name to be a salient attribute across a range of child-relevant products, since establishing brand recognition is a major objective of much advertising children see. However, as children grow older, their increased interaction with the marketplace and their greater cognitive abilities should lead them to use a greater number and wider variety of product attributes in product and brand evaluation and selection.

Initial Processing of Product Information

Selection of product information is the initial step in consumer information processing in purchase decision situations. Before further processing of the information can take place and a purchase decision be reached, children select various product attributes by which to compare consumption alternatives. We examined two aspects of information selection: (1) children's awareness of brand as a relevant product attribute and (2) children's selection of different kinds of product attributes in specific purchase situations, such as perceptual, price, and functional product attributes.

Brand awareness. We consider children's awareness of brands of consumer goods to be an indicator of their ability to select this kind of information as a product attribute. Children were asked to name as many brands as they could in four product categories. The four products vary both in terms of their relevance to the child (chewing gum and soft drinks versus gasoline and cameras) and in terms of the relative amount of advertising children may see for each product (gasoline and soft drinks are more heavily advertised than cameras and gum).

Because children may recognize many brand names, but not the concept of "brand," we developed a series of questions to circumvent possible difficulties with children's verbal abilities. First, children were asked "What are some different brands of toothpaste?" If they could not identify a brand, they were asked, "What are some different kinds of toothpaste?" and "What are some different toothpastes?" If a child then gave one or more brand names, we told him he was correct: "That's right, that's what a brand is. It's the name of a certain kind of product." Following this series of questions, virtually all children could name some brands of toothpaste. Next we asked them to identify brands of chewing gum, gasoline, soft drinks, and cameras.

Table 4-9 presents the average number of brands children mention for each of the four products. While brand knowledge for each product increases with age, product relevance and amount of advertising differentially affect the brand knowledge of the younger and older children. For kindergartners, product relevance and amount of advertising appear to have independent impacts on brand knowledge, producing what seems to be an additive effect. The greatest number of brands kindergartners mention is for soft drinks, a heavily advertised, highly child-relevant product. On the other hand, for third-graders and sixth-graders, either high advertising or high product relevance increases brand know-

TABLE 4-9

Mean Number of Brands Identified for Different Types of Products at Each Grade Level

		Child Relevance		
		Low		High
Amount of Advertising	Low High	Camera Gasoline		Gum Soft Drinks
	Camera (Lo Ad Lo Rel)	Gum (Lo Ad Hi Rel)	Gasoline (Hi Ad Lo Rel)	Soft Drinks (Hi Ad Hi Rel)
K (N = 205)	.1	.6	.6	1.2
3 (N = 202)	.8	2.3	2.6	2.4
6 (N = 208)	1.4	3.2	3.3	3.3

ledge substantially, but the combination of the two factors does not result in any additional increment to brand knowledge.

Selection of product information. In addition to our measure of children's brand knowledge, we obtained a measure of children's product-information selection in a specific decision-making situation. Children were asked to consider a hypothetical product purchase situation: "Suppose you wanted to buy a new television set. What would you want to know about it?" From the first three responses coded for analysis, scales were constructed of the number of mentions of physical attributes (e.g., color versus black and white), performance attributes (e.g., easy to operate), price attributes, and functional attributes (e.g., good quality).

Table 4-10 presents the percentage of children at each grade level mentioning the various product attributes at least once. A large majority of all children mention physical attributes, making this the most frequently requested type of information. However, fewer sixth-graders than younger children mention physical attributes. Performance characteristics of the television set are the second most likely type of information children request, with nearly half of all children mentioning such product information. Price and functional attributes are mentioned by less than one-third of the children. Requests for all types of information other than physical attributes increase with age, particularly for price and functional attributes.

These data suggest that as children grow older they are more likely to request nonperceptual types of product information when considering a product purchase. The specific product, a TV set, did elicit

TABLE 4-10

Children's Information Selection About a Television Set by Grade Level[*]

	K %	3 %	6 %	Total %	x^2
Physical Attributes	84	87	71	80	19.48 (2 d.f.) p<.001
Performance Attributes	36	49	57	48	16.84 (2 d.f.) p<.001
Price Attributes	15	31	41	30	27.99 (2 d.d.) p<.001
Functional Attributes	13	26	43	28	38.21 (2 d.f.) p<.001
N =	(157)	(199)	(202)	(558)	

[*] Because of multiple responses, columns total more than 100 percent.

frequent mention of performance information (such as "how does the TV set work" and "is it long-lasting"), probably reflecting even the kindergartners' substantial experience with this product. As expected, both third-graders and sixth-graders are more likely to mention performance attributes than are kindergartners.

In sum, data from children's brand knowledge and product-information selection indicate developmental differences in the kinds of information children focus upon when considering products. Young children focus primarily on physical, perceptual kinds of information, while older children include additional, nonperceptual types of information, such as brand and functional product attributes, in their product decision making.

Central Processing of Product Information

Age-related changes in children's cognitive capabilities and in their experience with product decision making should lead to developmental differences in children's central processing of product information. Specifically, we expect older children to use *more* information and more *kinds* of information in comparing consumption alternatives and reaching purchase decisions.

A basic cognitive task in consumer activity is that of comparing consumption alternatives. To assess children's development of this skill, we asked a series of questions concerning choice between two brand alternatives, strength of preference, and attributes used to differentiate the two brands. To ensure that all children responded to the same brand alternatives, interviewers showed children actual packages of two major brands in each of three product categories: toothpaste, peanut butter, and milk additives. Package sizes were the same in each case.

Strength of brand preference. For each product pair, children could choose the brand they would rather have, or express indifference. For toothpaste, Brand A was chosen by nearly two-thirds of the children; it was favored slightly more by third-graders than by the other two groups. For peanut butter, Brand A was chosen by most of the children, with the choice becoming more pronounced among older children. However, for milk additives, kindergartners expressed nearly equal preference for both brands, but older children clearly favored Brand B.

Regarding degree of preference for the chosen brands, data indicate that nearly half of the kindergartners say their choice is "a lot better," compared to less than one-third of the older children. This result holds

TABLE 4-11
Strength of Brand Preference by Grade Level

	K %	3 %	6 %	Total %
Low	16	32	34	27
Medium	34	38	41	38
High	50	30	25	35
	100	100	100	100
N =	(205)	(202)	(208)	(615)

$x^2 = 35.93$ (4 d.f.) $p < .001$

for all product categories regardless of the particular brand chosen. Third- and sixth-graders were quite similar in their strength of preference. About two-fifths of the older children rated the two brands "about the same" in each product group compared to 30 percent of the kindergartners.

A brand-strength scale was developed by summing up the children's degrees of preference across all three products. The scale ranges from those saying all brands are "about the same" (low brand preference) to those indicating one brand is "a lot better" in each of the three product categories (high brand preference). By this measure, strength of brand preference decreases with age, especially between kindergarten and third grade.

A possible explanation for these results can be derived from developmental theory. The older children (third-graders and sixth-graders) should be able to evaluate brands on more dimensions than the kindergartners. If older children feel one brand is better on some dimensions but the other brand is better on other dimensions, then they are likely to perceive the chosen brand as just slightly better overall.

Information used in comparing brands. The explanation for older children's lesser brand preference implies that the older children fill in more of the attribute-object matrix discussed earlier, and it also assumes an additive model of brand selection. If the explanation is valid, there should be a relationship between age of the child and the number of dimensions children use to distinguish between brands. Indeed, we do find that across all three product pairs, the average number of attributes used to compare the brand pairs increases from 4.50 (kinder-gartners) to 5.55 (third-graders) to 5.94 (sixth-graders).

These differences in the total number of attributes used to differen-tiate between brands may simply reflect greater verbalization among older children. However, across product groups, the kinds of attributes used to compare brands also vary by age. The attributes children used to compare the product pairs were grouped into three categories: perceptual, ingredient, and functional. Table 4-12 presents the mean number of each type given per product. All three age groups are similar in mentioning perceptual attributes of the products, but older children are more likely to mention ingredients and functional attributes, which are more conceptual in nature (e.g., "the way the milk additive mixes with water" or "the toothpaste keeps you from getting cavities").

Thus, while the kindergartners express stronger brand preferences for the products examined here, their choices appear to be made on a relatively narrow basis of brand comparison. Kindergartners use fewer dimensions to compare brands and these are primarily perceptual at-tributes; older children use perceptual and functional attributes about equally.

Information used in product requests. In addition to examining children's brand knowledge and their use of information in making brand comparisons, we also queried the children about their use of brand information in requesting products from their parents. Since children have relatively little disposable income (or, at least, few means of independently purchasing consumer products), an early kind of consumer behavior involves the decision to attempt to influence paren-tal purchases.

Children were asked about their brand requests for four food pro-ducts (soups, soft drinks, candy, and cereal). The question was, "Do you ask for certain kinds or brands of (soups)?" If the answer was yes,

TABLE 4-12

Mean Number of Different Types of Attributes per Product Used to Compare Brands at Each Grade Level

	Perceptual Attributes	Ingredients	Functional Attributes	Total Information
K	.88	.17	.45	1.50
3	.93	.26	.66	1.85
6	.93	.35	.70	1.98

they were asked, "Which ones?" The probe, "Any other?" was used once.

As can be seen in Table 4-13, among children who ask for the specified products, brand is a significant attribute in the child's decision. For three of the four food products (the exception being soup), a substantial majority ask for an item by brand name. For each food class except cereals, large numbers of children ask for items in terms of generic attributes too, most often flavors. However, for cereals, brand is a much more dominant attribute, probably because brand is perceived as nearly synonymous with flavor.

The data also indicate a developmental pattern *toward* increased brand asking and away from generic asking with increased age. Indeed, sixth-graders are more likely to ask by brand than by generic attributes in all four food classes. These data suggest that brand name is a highly salient attribute in children's purchase requests across a variety of food classes that they often use and enjoy. This is the case even for kindergartners, who typically cannot read.

We see then that brand asking increases as children grow older, but that brand preference decreases with increased age (data reported earlier). This apparent contradiction can be explained by the finding that older children are more likely to ask for several different brands of

TABLE 4-13

Asking for Item in Terms of Brand Name or Generic Attribute
by Grade Level[*]

		K %	3 %	6 %	Total %
Soft Drinks	brand	60	70	84	71
	generic	59	57	35	50
Soup	brand	40	47	66	51
	generic	60	57	43	50
Candy	brand	50	78	83	71
	generic	66	41	23	43
Cereal	brand	93	97	97	96
	generic	15	12	12	13
	N =	(205)	(202)	(208)	(615)

[*] Because of multiple responses, columns total to more than 100 percent for each product.

an item. For instance, only 17 percent of the kindergartners report asking for two or more brands of soft drinks, as compared to 34 percent of the third-graders and the 43 percent of sixth-graders. Thus, the third-grade and sixth-grade children's lessened preference for any one brand appears to reflect their greater use of several different brands of a product.

While we have focused primarily on brand attributes of products in purchase decision making, other researchers (Atkin, 1974; The Gene Reilly Group, 1973b) have queried children about their use of other product attributes. For example, Atkin has conducted research on children's use of "premium" attributes in cereal purchase requests. In a supermarket observation study including approximately one hundred observations, he found that 48 percent of all in-store child requests for cereals involved explicit mention of the premium obtained with the product. On the other hand, only a few children expressed a desire to buy a cereal for nutritional reasons. These findings were supported in a subsequent survey of grade-school children's mothers: 47 percent reported their child mentions premiums as a reason for requesting a particular type of cereal. Other frequently mentioned reasons included "he just wants it" (24 percent) and ad-related comments (18 percent). Nutrition reasons were mentioned by only 3 percent. In direct follow-up questions, an additional 36 percent of the mothers said their child had asked for a cereal to receive a premium, but only an additional 16 percent reported their child had ever mentioned the nutritional value of a specific cereal.

Thus, Atkin's data suggest that "premium" is a highly salient attribute for at least one class of food products: cereals. Neither Atkin's research nor our own study, however, has examined the *relative* importance of various product attributes in children's purchase requests. That is, neither study has examined such questions as whether brand name is more or less important than premiums for children's requests.

Research conducted by The Gene Reilly Group (1973b) did include children's evaluation of the relative importance of several different types of information about advertised products. In this research, a national sample of six- to twelve-year-old children was asked a series of paired comparison questions involving product attributes: "Would you like a TV commercial product more if it was nutritious or tasted good? If it tasted sweet or was nutritious? If it had a prize inside or was nutritious?" Since not all possible comparisons of product attributes were made, a complete ranking of attributes is not possible. Nevertheless, the available data do provide some indication of the relative importance of nutritional, premium, and taste attributes of food products for children.

As Table 4-14 indicates, good taste is the most highly valued attribute for all children. The relative importance of the remaining attributes varies by age level. For six- and seven-year-olds, receiving a prize is second in importance to good taste; sweetness and "an offer to send for" are rated similarly and are more important than nutrition, the younger children's least-favored product attribute. For eight- to ten-

TABLE 4-14

**Relative Importance of Product Attributes
in Evaluation of Product by Age Level***

Attribute Pairs	6-7 %	8-10 %	11-12 %
Nutritious	22	28	23
Tasted Good	72	68	70
No Difference	6	4	7
	100	100	100
N =	(152)	(289)	(239)
Tasted Sweet	51	50	51
Nutritious	43	45	41
No Difference	6	5	8
	100	100	100
N =	(148)	(290)	(239)
An Offer to Send For	52	40	34
Nutritious	43	54	58
No Difference	5	6	8
	100	100	100
N =	(145)	(285)	(240)
Prize in Box	57	51	38
Nutritious	35	42	51
No Difference	8	7	11
	100	100	100
N =	(152)	(288)	(234)

*Data presented here were taken from The Gene Reilly Group, Inc. (1973b).

year-olds, the attributes of sweetness and prizes in the box appear to be equally important, followed by nutrition and an offer to send for. Lastly, for eleven- and twelve-year-olds, sweetness is the second most important attribute, followed by nutrition. Both in-box and send-for premiums appear to be relatively unimportant for this age group.

The decrease in the relative importance of premiums with increased age may simply reflect the lesser attractiveness of the typical plastic toy premium to older children. The data pitting good taste against nutrition show no change with age, indicating no greater emphasis on the nutritional value of food products among the older children.

In summary, age-related changes in children's central processing of product information do conform to our expectations: children use more information and different kinds of information in purchase decision making as they grow older. Moreover, information processing is more elaborate among older children—at least in the specific aspects of initial and central processing indexed in this research. Specifically, the data indicate that with increased age there are: (1) increases in the number of attributes employed in comparing products; (2) increases in the use of functional and other more abstract attributes, such as brand; (3) decreases in strength of brand preference, perhaps as a consequence of the use of more attributes in product comparisons; and (4) decreases in the importance of premium as a product attribute.

HIGHER AND LOWER INFORMATION PROCESSING SKILLS

Data in this chapter suggest that children's information processing in relation to product-purchase situations becomes more elaborate and "sophisticated" with age. However, not all of the children's consumer information processing can be classified as skilled behavior. Clearly, information-processing skills vary in terms of their usefulness to the child in helping him to function effectively within the marketplace. We distinguish two levels of information-processing skills.

"Lower-level skills" are characterized by use of perceptual attributes in consumer information processing, i.e., in asking about products, comparing brands, or processing television advertising. Our measures of lower-level skills include (1) children's selection of perceptual attributes in considering a television purchase, (2) comparison of brands on the basis of perceptual characteristics, and (3) awareness of in-store shopping for information about new purchases. Such consumer behaviors reflect a less developed level of cognitive capabilities and are most characteristics of younger children.

In contrast, "higher-level" information-processing skills involve the use of more conceptual and functional types of information. In the present study, these skills include (1) selection of performance attributes in considering a television purchase, (2) comparing brands on the basis of functional characteristics, (3) awareness of a variety of sources of information about new products, (4) awareness of brands, and (5) level of understanding of television advertising.

Thus, we have divided information-processing skills into two groups, lower- and higher-level skills, which describe a major age-related change in children's cognitive development. It is this developmental continuum from selection and use of limited, perceptual kinds of information to selection and use of more abstract and conceptual kinds of information that underlies the age-related differences in information-processing skills we have examined in this chapter. We have earlier referred to this general cognitive capability dimension as the movement from perception to inference.

The pattern of our findings indicates rather clearly the developmental nature of the higher-level information-processing skills we have measured in this research. A consistent pattern of age-related development emerges in children's selection and use of more conceptual and functional kinds of information in their processing of both advertising and product information. For instance, the data indicate that with increased age children become more aware of the function of commercials. Similarly, with increased age children are more likely to select functional and performance attributes of products when considering product purchases. Further, just as brand awareness, indexed by children's ability to name different brands of products, increases with age, children's recall of brand name from a television commercial is found to increase as children grow older (Rubin's research). These higher-level information-processing skills appear to tap the upper end of the developmental continuum.

In contrast, the lower-level skills we have measured tap the lower, perceptual end of the continuum and, therefore, should be available to even the young children. Since early cognitive capabilities are not replaced by new abilities as children grow older, but rather are elaborated upon and used more efficiently, we should not expect a developmental trend toward decreased use of lower-level skills among older children. Instead, as we have seen, younger and older children use these lower-level skills to about the same extent. This clearly indicates that the increasing cognitive capabilities of the older children do not displace the lower-skill capabilities; rather, they add on to these skills.

In examining intercorrelations among the information-processing skills, we would expect rather low correlations among lower-level skills. All of the children can utilize these skills, but whether they do so in a particular situation depends largely on the specific information-processing task at hand, the product involved, and so forth. Furthermore, we should expect these skills to be relatively less integrated in their application to consumer tasks than higher-level skills. On the other hand, we would expect relatively high correlations among our measures of higher-level skills, since they are available to only a limited number of children, typically older children. For example, we would expect that children who cannot recognize conceptual distinctions or functional attributes in one situation generally cannot do so in another. On the other hand, children with these processing capabilities are likely to use these skills in a variety of situations.

Correlations among the higher-level processing skills are substantially greater than those among lower-level skills—an average of .43 compared to an average of only .07. As suggested above, this pattern of relationships probably reflects the underlying developmental continuum of cognitive capabilities from perception to inference. The higher-level skills are more consistently related to each other, since they clearly tap the upper end of the developmental continuum, which involves the ability to describe and make conceptual distinctions among objects such as products and television commercials.

The measures we have used in indexing children's consumer information processing have focused primarily on one aspect of information processing—the *kinds* of information children of different ages use in thinking about TV commercials, brands, and products. Our research has ignored other important aspects of children's consumer information processing, such as how children structure information, how they connect previously stored information with new incoming information, how past behavior may feed back to alter information processing, and how children use various strategies when employing information in consumer decision making. Knowledge of these activities is important for understanding how children learn to become consumers, but since they are dependent upon the kinds of information children select for further processing, we addressed what appeared to be the most fundamental aspect. Subsequent research should examine these other aspects of children's consumer information processing.

In conclusion, the data we have presented indicate that across various consumer behavior situations involving information processing of television advertising and product information in purchase decision making, there are consistent age-related changes in the kinds of information children attend to, select, and use to describe and conceptualize the consumer environment. This change appears to reflect basic developmental growth in children's cognitive capabilities toward increased awareness and use of more abstract, functional kinds of information in consumer information processing.

In the next chapter, we consider two other aspects of children's consumer behavior: their money use and purchase requests.

Chapter 5

CHILDREN'S CONSUMER BEHAVIOR:
MONEY USE AND PURCHASE REQUESTS

This chapter examines some outcomes of children's consumer information processing. One obvious outcome is spending behavior. Since other authors have examined the specific products children buy (McNeal, 1964), we chose to focus instead on more general patterns of spending and saving. We also examine the genesis of norms for spending and savings, which may develop as children have increasing amounts of money to spend and as they gain experience in marketplace transactions. Finally, we examine a ubiquitous form of children's consumer behavior: asking parents to buy.

We reasoned that some kinds of children's consumption behaviors are quite elementary and do not become elaborated upon or improved over time. We labeled these "nonskilled" behaviors; examples are the frequency of children's use of money for spending and the frequency of purchase requests to parents.[1]

On the other hand, other money-related behaviors involve more abstract notions and develop with experience. We call these "skilled" behaviors, and they include children's holding of savings and money use norms, as well as actual savings behavior. These skilled behaviors rest on somewhat abstract concepts, which older children should grasp more readily than younger children because of their cognitive capabilities (Schuessler and Strauss, 1950), and their greater experience in the marketplace. Consequently, grade level is the major independent variable for the analyses in this chapter too since it is an index of both cognitive development and marketplace experience. It also seems reasonable to expect that children from more affluent family backgrounds may achieve more elaborate consumer norms and skills than children from lower-income family environments. Early research suggests this is the case, perhaps due to differences in the amounts of money children have to spend as well as differences in opportunities for consumption and for modeling parents' consumer behavior (Marshall and Magruder, 1960). Therefore, social status will also be used as an independent variable in the chapter.

We will first examine the norms children hold for using money and their own money use. Next their requests for products from their parents will be discussed. Finally, selected interrelationships among these behaviors will be examined.

CHILDREN'S MONEY USE

Money Use Norms

By "money use norms" we refer to children's ideas about what should and should not be done with money. Since saving necessitates denying immediate gratification as well as understanding the notion of accumulating money as a goal, this activity would seem to represent an important dimension in children's early consumer learning. Furthermore, understanding the concept of saving requires the ability to project future states of affairs from present behavior. This would appear to be a difficult task for younger children since development theorists have demonstrated age-related changes in children's comprehension of such concepts, e.g., time (Piaget, 1950). Thus, we expect the percentage of children having savings norms to increase as children grow older, while norms regarding spending money should show no such age-related changes.

We assessed children's money use norms by the following questions: "Pretend you are a mother/father and you gave your child $25. Now you're going to have to tell him/her what he/she should do with the

$25. What would you tell him/her? What would you tell him/her *not* to do with the money?" The first question attempted to measure the kinds of *prescriptive* norms the child has for how money should be used. The second question is an index of *proscriptive* norms the child has for how money should not be used.

Data presented in Table 5-1 indicate spending norms are mentioned by more kindergarten than third-grade or sixth-grade children. Very few children (only one-tenth of the total sample) mentioned short-term saving as a norm, and more third-graders do so than younger or older children. In contrast, mention of long-term savings as a norm increases linearly with age. Further, 70 percent of the high-SES third-graders mentioned long-term savings norms, compared to about half of middle- and lower-SES third-graders.

Thus, it appears that the norm of saving is acquired by some very young children and that this norm becomes more entrenched as children grow older. Moreover, older children are more likely to mention both spending norms and savings norms. One-quarter of the older children mention both types of norms compared to 12 percent of the kindergartners. This suggests that older children are more flexible in their money use, i.e., they perceive saving as an alternative to spending rather than as a replacement. In contrast, kindergartners appear to perceive money behavior as primarily spending.

The kinds of proscriptive money norms children hold are presented in Table 5-2. The themes of "don't waste" and "don't buy specific things" are mentioned by a majority of third-graders and sixth-graders, but admonitions to be careful with money appear to be an equally

TABLE 5-1
Children Mentioning Different Types of Prescriptive Money Norms by Grade Level[*]

	K %	3 %	6 %	Total %	x^2
Spend	71	56	56	61	12.67 (2 d.f.) p<.01
Short-term Save	6	16	8	10	11.07 (2 d.f.) p<.01
Long-term Save	35	57	69	54	44.73 (2 d.f.) p<.001
N =	(188)	(195)	(190)	(593)	

[*]Cell entries add up to more than 100 percent in each column because respondents often gave multiple responses to this question.

TABLE 5-2

Children Mentioning Different Types of Proscriptive
Money Norms by Grade Level*

	K %	3 %	6 %	Total %	x^2
Don't Waste	35	54	62	52	26.88 (2 d.f.) p<.001
Be Careful	34	25	22	26	6.77 (2 d.f.) p<.05
Don't Buy a Specific Product	44	62	60	56	13.02 (2 d.f.) p<.01
N =	(154)	(189)	(202)	(545)	

*Cell entires add up to more than 100 percent in each column because respondents often gave multiple responses to this question.

salient norm for kindergartners. Perhaps the relatively greater emphasis of kindergartners on "being careful" with money is a reflection of parents' warnings that they shouldn't lose their money. On the other hand, it is likely that parents of third-grade and sixth-grade children are less concerned that these older children will lose their money and more concerned that they will not spend it wisely.

As with prescriptive norms, only 10 percent of the kindergartners mentioned more than one type of proscriptive money norm, and one-quarter did not answer the question at all. In contrast, about 40 percent of the older children mentioned two proscriptive norms.

It is clear that both third-grade and sixth-grade children have better-developed ideas about what should and what should not be done with money. This may reflect the greater time period parents have had to counsel the older children about money use, but it may also reflect their greater ability to understand the relatively abstract notions of savings and savings behaviors. Furthermore, older children have had more experience with money—both with spending and with saving—and may have developed their own norms. In the next section we will examine this possibility when we consider children's own money use behavior.

Money Use Behavior

Before considering data on how children use their own money, we should discuss the amount of money available to them. Our data show that the majority of children at each grade level do have available money. However, as would be expected, the amount of weekly allowance and number of sources of income (e.g., a job outside the home, money simply given to the child, etc.) increase with age. Kindergartners' total weekly income averages about 50 cents compared to $1.00 for third-graders and $2.00 for sixth-graders. Oddly enough, lower-income children report receiving *more* money than do middle-class or upper-class children, except among sixth-graders. In Chapter 7 we will discuss in more detail the various sources of children's money.

Our interest in the present chapter is in examining how children use their money. Since older children both receive more money than do younger ones, and hold long-term savings norms more often, we expect older children to engage in long-term savings more frequently than kindergartners. Data presented in Table 5-3 indicate that indeed half of the third-graders and sixth-graders do report saving for long periods of time (a month or more), compared to slightly less than two-fifths of kindergartners. Third-graders are the age group most likely to save for short-term items, such as snack foods and soft drinks. At each grade level, smaller percentages of children say they save for short-term items than for long-term items. The vast majority of children at all age levels report spending some of their income.

The only social-class differences in children's use of money are found for long-term savings behavior among sixth-graders. For these older children, long-term savings behavior increases with social class. This could be related to increased parental training regarding savings (a more frequent activity among higher-social-class parents—see Chapter 7).

Older children are also more flexible in using their money. About

TABLE 5-3
How Child Uses Own Money by Grade Level[*]

	K %	3 %	6 %	Total %	x^2
Spend	69	68	81	73	5.68 (2 d.f.) n.s.
Short-term Save	14	25	17	19	7.86 (2 d.f.) n.s.
Long-term Save	38	47	50	45	8.56 (2 d.f.) p $<$.05
N =	(185)	(197)	(204)	(586)	

[*]Cell entries add up to more than 100 percent in each column because respondents often gave multiple responses to this question.

two-fifths use their money in at least two ways—usually both saving and spending—compared to only one-fifth of the kindergartners. It would seem the increased income available to older children does enable them to use their money for multiple purposes.

To summarize briefly, increased savings behavior and greater flexibility in use of money among older children appears to be a function of several factors: the amount of money available to the children, older children's greater awareness of savings norms, and perhaps parental training regarding savings.

A second measure of children's money use was the regularity with which children spend or save their money. This was obtained by asking mothers how often their children spend their weekly income for candy,

TABLE 5-4

Regularity of Spending Money for Specific Products by Grade Level

	K %	3 %	6 %	Total %
High Regularity	17	44	47	36
Medium Regularity	57	43	40	47
Low Regularity	26	13	13	17
	100	100	100	100
N =	(205)	(202)	(208)	(615)

$x^2 = 51.28$ (4 d.f.) $p < .001$

TABLE 5-5

Regularity of Saving Money by Grade Level

	K %	3 %	6 %	Total %
High Regularity	20	28	29	26
Medium Regularity	43	51	53	49
Low Regularity	36	21	18	25
	100	100	100	100
N =	(205)	(202)	(208)	(615)

$x^2 = 20.82$ (4 d.f.) $p < .001$

snacks, or other products. They were then asked how frequently their child saves money for specific items. Mothers responded on a four-point scale: usually, sometimes, not too often, and never. Measures were then constructed of the regularity of children's spending and specific savings behaviors.

Data in Table 5-4 clearly indicate that third-grade and sixth-grade children spend their money more regularly than do kindergartners—no doubt partly because they have more money to spend. However, these older children also engage in savings behaviors more regularly than do the younger children (see Table 5-5).

Among third-grade children, both regularity of spending and of saving vary according to social class. While about half of low- and high-SES third-graders report high regularity of spending, less than one-third of medium-SES children do so. Similarly, medium-SES third-graders save money less regularly than do children of lower and higher social classes at this grade level.

The data regarding children's money use suggest the higher incomes of the third-graders and sixth-graders largely account for greater frequency of both spending and saving. Thus, data taken from two measures of children's money use—mother's and child's reports— indicate that by the time children reach the third grade they regularly spend their money for products; however, even among sixth-grade children fewer than one-third save money regularly.

Lastly, we examined the relationship between the prescriptive norms children have regarding how money should be used and how children actually use money. There is little consistency between children's norms and their own behavior; all correlations are less than .23. However, consistency does appear to increase slightly with age. Only among sixth-graders is there a statistically significant relationship between norms and behavior of all three types—spending, short-term saving, and long-term saving—but even among children at this grade level correlations are quite low (.15 for spending money and .20 for long-term savings).

To summarize money use behavior, older children have more norms regarding saving money and engage in more saving behavior, as predicted. However, children at all grade levels are more likely to report spending their money than saving for either short-term or long-term periods. Furthermore, with increased age children become more flexible in their money use. The older children's money use flexibility cannot be accounted for by their higher awareness of saving as a norm, since we find little consistency between children's behavior and the norms they hold for using money, at least as these norms were measured in this research. Rather, the greater money use flexibility is probably a consequence of the larger income available to third- and sixth-grade children. These findings are consistent with earlier research by Scheussler and Strauss (1950) and Marshall and Magruder (1960) indicating greater comprehension of money concepts and increased money experience (including savings behavior) as children grow older.

CHILDREN'S PURCHASE REQUESTS

Since children have relatively little disposable income (or at least few opportunities for independently purchasing many consumer products they might want) an early kind of consumer behavior involves the attempt to influence parental purchases, usually for products which will ultimately be consumed by the child himself. Our interest here is in examining the frequency with which children of different ages request products from parents. Though our earlier research did indicate a small decrease in purchase requests as children grow older (Ward and Wackman, 1972), these differences were so small as to suggest no important differences among five- to twelve-year-olds. Therefore, we decided to examine this relationship with our larger sample of children.

The frequency of children's purchase requests was measured by giving children a list of products and asking how often they asked their parents to buy each item. Children could choose one of four responses: often—once a week or more; sometimes—once a month or more; not too often—less than once a month; or never. The products children were queried about were (1) food products, e.g., cereal, snack foods, candy, soft drinks, and soup; (2) nonfood grocery-store products, e.g., shampoo, toothpaste, aspirin, and household cleaners; (3) child products, e.g., a game or toy, clothing, and record albums. As can be seen, products were chosen which have a high likelihood of being desired and requested by children of various ages.

Table 5-6 presents the frequency of children's purchase requests for food products. Virtually no differences are found among children at the three grade levels or at the three social-class levels. Furthermore, requests for food products are uniformly high, with over 90 percent of all children reporting medium or high frequency of requests for these products.

TABLE 5-6

Frequency of Children's Purchase Requests by Grade Level

		K %	3 %	6 %	Total %
Food Products					
High		42	46	40	42
Medium		50	48	49	49
Low		8	6	11	9
		100	100	100	100
	N =	(204)	(202)	(208)	(614)
		$x^2 = 4.00$ (4 d.f.) n.s.			
Other Grocery Products					
High		2	2	1	2
Medium		15	7	12	11
Low		47	46	52	49
Very Low		36	45	35	38
		100	100	100	100
	N =	(203)	(202)	(208)	(613)
		$x^2 = 9.40$ (4 d.f.) $.05 < p < .10$			
Child-Relevant Products					
High		14	22	21	19
Medium		47	55	47	50
Low		39	23	32	31
		100	100	100	100
	N =	(203)	(202)	(208)	(613)
		$x^2 = 14.20$ (4 d.f.) $p < .01$			

In contrast, the frequency of children's requests for nonfood grocery-related products is relatively low; more than four-fifths of the children in each grade report low or very low frequency in requesting these products. Data on social-class differences in purchase requests for these products indicate that the frequency of such requests is negatively related to social class among kindergartners, but not among older children.

The only major age-related difference in purchase requests is found for child-relevant products (Table 5-6). About one-fifth of the third-grade and sixth-grade children report high frequency of requests compared to only 14 percent of kindergartners. These findings are not too surprising, since it seems likely that requests for clothing and record albums should increase as children progress toward teenage years. The frequency of requesting child products is related to SES only among third-grade children; one-fourth of low- and medium-SES third-graders report high request frequency for these products compared to less than one-tenth of the upper-class children.

We examined these data for the consistency of children's purchase requests across product types by correlating the different types of purchase requests at each grade level (Table 5-7). All of the relationships are statistically significant. Correlations between food product and child-relevant product requests are uniformly high for all children. For kindergartners and third-graders, a relatively modest relationship is found between food and nonfood grocery-product requests; however, this relationship increases among sixth-graders.

All of the product-request questions were asked in a similar manner. Therefore, the high correlations may be a function of yea-saying on the part of children. However, the relatively low correlation between food

TABLE 5-7

Correlations Among Frequency Purchase Request for Food, Other Grocery and Child-Relevant Products Within Grade Level[*]

	Other Grocery	Child Relevant
Kindergarten		
Food products	.19*	.43*
Other grocery products		.38*
N = (203)		
Third Grade		
Food products	.12*	.35*
Other grocery products		.25*
N = (202)		
Sixth Grade		
Food products	.29*	.44*
Other grocery products		.26*
N = (208)		

[*]Pearson product-moment correlations were run between different types of product-purchase requests. Coefficients marked with an asterisk are statistically significant.

products and nonfood grocery products at each grade level suggests that children probably were making discriminations among these products. The large differences in the average frequency of requests for product categories also suggests substantial discrimination by product.

The data show a fairly consistent pattern of purchase requests in general. Children in all three grades ask for food products more frequently than they ask for other types of products. Moreover, within each grade children who frequently ask for one type of product are also likely to ask for other types of products. Only for child-relevant products, such as clothing, movies, and record albums, do purchase requests differ by grade level, increasing as children grow older.

SUMMARY

In this chapter we have examined two aspects of children's consumer behavior that fall outside our model of consumer information processing: children's money use and purchase requests. Our measures of the frequency of these behaviors are only indirectly related to cognitive processing skills. However, several of the measures regarding wise use of money and actual savings behavior may depend partly on increases in cognitive capabilities, since comprehension of the notion of savings involves the cognitive capability to project events in time. We have conceptualized these behaviors as money use skills.

In contrast, the remaining measures of frequency of spending, holding spending norms, and frequency of purchase requests constitute nonskilled money use behaviors. They are not indicative of either effective consumer activity or of processing capabilities, and they do not develop with age and experience.

As expected, children's money use skills increase as children grow older. However, the average correlation among these measures is a rather low .11. This is not too surprising, since we earlier found low consistency between money use norms and money use behavior, two major components of money use skills. The low consistency among money use skills suggests that comprehension and advocacy of norms regarding sound money use are not enough to insure actual practice of these activities. Further, we might suggest that, considering the age range of children surveyed in this research, it is quite understandable that they do not engage in much actual savings behavior. For one thing, these children receive relatively little money each week—even for the sixth-graders, as has already been noted, average weekly earnings are only about $2.00. Second, parents generally take care of the needs of grade-school children, whereas teenagers have additional wants and desires that parents often will not fulfill. Perhaps what we have uncovered here is the beginning step in the process of learning how to save money: children initially learn savings norms in the later elementary grades; then, when greater income is available and the cost of products requires saving, adolescents engage in more regular and substantial savings behavior.

We did not expect age-related changes in children's nonskilled money use behaviors, and we did not find them. We find that the average correlation among these measures is only .06, indicating no consistency in the frequency with which children hold spending norms, spend their money, or request products. Clearly, children's performance in requesting products and using money is a reflection of factors other than cognitive growth or simply growing older. Environmental factors, such as parental modeling behaviors, yielding patterns, or discussions with the children, may have a greater impact on these consumer activities. Therefore, we now turn our attention to these kinds of influences, and consider the family context within which children learn to be consumers.

NOTE

1. In earlier research (Ward and Wackman, 1972) we found a small negative correlation between age and frequency of purchase requests ($r = -.13$). That is, older children make purchase requests to their parents less frequently than younger children. While some differences in purchase-request frequency might occur with age, as parents come to know their children's product preferences (perhaps making requests less necessary), there is little reason to expect purchase-request frequency to be related to cognitive abilities.

PART III

THE FAMILY'S ROLE IN CONSUMER SOCIALIZATION

Chapter 6 ▨▨▨▨▨▨▨▨▨▨▨▨▨▨▨▨▨▨▨▨▨▨▨▨▨▨▨▨▨▨▨▨▨

A DEVELOPMENTAL VIEW OF FAMILY
INFLUENCES IN SOCIALIZATION

▨▨▨▨▨▨▨▨▨▨▨▨▨▨▨▨▨▨▨▨▨▨▨▨▨▨▨▨▨▨▨▨▨▨

Cognitive development theory provides a basis for understanding and predicting age-related changes in children's consumer information-processing skills. The strong empirical support for our hypotheses in the preceding two chapters clearly indicates the utility of the theory for understanding aspects of consumer socialization. However, as we suggested in Chapter 1, consumer socialization depends on more than the child's general information-processing abilities implied by his level of cognitive development. There are many external influences on children which can also influence consumer socialization. Chief among the "external factors" on children, of course, is the impact of the family group.

Developmental theorists, including Piaget himself, stress the importance of "the environment," or "external influences" on children. However, there is very little research which examines *how* external influences interact with cognitive development stage in determining behavioral outcomes.

Our purpose in this chapter is to explore this relatively ignored area: how does the family[1] influence children? How does this impact vary depending on the child's stage in cognitive development? By what processes do families affect children's consumer learning? Because we are integrating family influences and cognitive development notions in a socialization perspective, and because there is little prior research and theory to guide us, the discussion in this chapter is necessarily complex.

In order to most clearly state our position, we begin with an overview of the family's impact on children's consumer socialization at different developmental stages. Then we trace the development of this position, beginning with a review of previous research on family impacts on children, and discuss new directions in cognitive development theory which help in integrating the literature of family impacts and developmental notions. Finally, we detail our view of the family context for children's consumer socialization and specify hypotheses, which are tested in Chapters 7 and 8.

OVERVIEW

Our viewpoint is strongly influenced by two premises. First, we believe that children learn in series of *situations,* i.e., configurations of people, places, and circumstances in which actions occur providing opportunity for learning.[2] Second, we believe that *what* and *how* children learn—the quality of learning—is determined by how a child interprets given situations.

We do not believe, as a strict reinforcement-learning model would have it, that children's learning is simply a function of reinforcement histories. For example, a mother might flatly reject her child's request for a product while they are walking through a toy store together. The child may, as a consequence, acquire an incremental learning "bit" about classes of products, appropriate or inappropriate product attributes, purchase-request strategies, etc. However, *what* and *how* the child has learned depends less on the reinforcement pattern—how often the mother refuses requests—than on how the child interprets what has transpired. The child may interpret his mother's refusal as occurring because the toy is an inappropriate gift, because the child already has one, or because a product feature might be dangerous. All—or only some—of these aspects of the situation may be interpreted by the child, and, depending on the interpretations that are made, different learning processes may be involved. In any case, it is far more complex than simply asserting that children's consumer learning occurs simply as a function of reinforcement histories.

As should be clear to the reader by this point in the book, a child's interpretation of situations—such as discussed in the preceding paragraph—will depend upon his cognitive abilities, or cognitive stage. Younger, preoperational children, for example, should be less able than older children to infer motives to the mother in order to interpret why she turned down his purchase request. *Thus, the same parental behavior will have differential impact on the child, depending upon his stage in cognitive development.*

How can the impact of these parental behaviors best be understood? What are the ways families influence consumer socialization? At a conceptual level, family influences may function in various ways.

First, as developmental theorists have pointed out, families can influence the pace and quality of cognitive development by providing an enriched environment or, conversely, a relatively sterile environment. In this process, families influence *general cognitive abilities,* which in turn influence the child's development of consumer skills.

Second, families may help (or hinder) the child's application of an already-developed cognitive ability in specific consumption situations. For example, a child may be able to decenter his attention to examine multiple dimensions of objects. However, whether he applies this ability in a consumer situation, such as in selecting a cereal, may depend on family influences.

Third, families may have an impact relatively directly on children's consumer behavior, teaching a specific skill. For example, a parent may teach a child that the doll clothes shown in a TV commercial are bought separately from the doll itself. This may result in the learning of a specific skill, e.g., asking about all the items included in a purchase, such as batteries, premiums, etc.

Besides cognitive ability, another factor which determines how children interpret family influences is the situation in which particular kinds of influence occur. Parents can opportunistically use situations to teach their child consumer skills—as in encouraging children to select Christmas gifts from store catalogues, for example (Caron and War, 1975). Conversely, situations may occur in which parents have no explicit goals but, from the child's perspective, form important opportunities for learning. For example, simply by overhearing parents discuss the family budget or buying priorities, children may acquire some consumer knowledge and performance skills. Thus, we expect three

kinds of activities to be particularly important in linking family behavior and outcomes in children's learning: (1) children's observation of
parental behavior; (2) parent-child interaction in consumption situations; (3) children's direct consumer experiences, occurring to some
extent under parental guidance.

To summarize this overview, we believe that understanding the way
the family influences consumer socialization best proceeds from (1) a
cognitive perspective, indicating that children differentially select and
interpret various parent behaviors as a basis for learning; (2) a developmental perspective, indicating that what and how children learn—the
"quality" of learning—varies by cognitive ability level; and (3) a situational perspective, suggesting that the quality of learning depends upon
the situation in which opportunities for learning occur.

PAST APPROACHES TO UNDERSTANDING HOW THE
FAMILY INFLUENCES CHILD DEVELOPMENT

The preceding discussion has attempted to provide the reader with a
brief understanding of our view of how parents have an impact on
consumer socialization. We are explorers in this area, since few previous
theorists have attempted to examine family influences from a cognitive
developmental perspective. Our view is that the family rarely "teaches"
a child new behaviors; rather, parents provide what we call "support"
for children's performance of various skills and behaviors. Parental
support may increase a child's motivation to utilize an existing skill in a
consumption situation ("you choose which product is best") or encourage a child to learn a new consumption-related skill ("how can you tell
which product is the best buy for the money?"). As we argued in the
preceding section, parental support can occur explicitly, when parents
set out to teach their child a skill, or it may occur only implicitly, when
children select and observe some aspect of a parent's behavior which is
useful to them in some aspect of consumer information processing.

Our viewpoint regarding parental support for consumer socialization
is shaped by past research in the area of family influences on child
development. Past research can be grouped according to: (1) family-
variables studied; (2) basis of impact; (3) family patterns. We briefly
review each of these approaches, and explain how research in these
areas was helpful in developing our conceptualization of how family
influences interact with cognitive abilities and ultimately affect the
course of consumer socialization.

Family-Variables Studied

Many socialization studies attempt to correlate parental character-istics and practices with attitude and behavioral outcomes among children. These studies can be viewed along a continuum. At one end are studies which attempt to relate causally distant "global" variables to child development. At the other end of the continuum are studies involving more specific variables, causally "closer" to the child's personality and behavior.

At the most global level are "structural variables," which examine the influence of such characteristics or dimensions as parental background (e.g., educational history, ethnic background), current family setting (e.g., social class), and family composition (e.g., size of family, ordinal position of children, etc.).

More specific family dimensions are examined in studies of parental characteristics which indirectly influence children, such as husband/wife power in decision making, their affective relationship, and social attitudes. In the present context, for example, parents may never discuss their approach to budgeting with their children, but children may indirectly learn some things by observing parents discuss the checking account, savings, and buying plans.

Finally, some studies have examined family dimensions which are conceptually "close to" outcomes in children. These include studies of parent-child interaction, child-rearing practices, and so on.

The specific variables selected for a study generally depend upon assumptions the investigator makes regarding influence processes. For example, researchers assuming a reinforcement-learning model will choose variables assessing rewards and punishments, e.g., affection, types of punishment, etc. Researchers assuming a vicarious-learning model will choose variables assessing the parental behaviors which are modeled for the child. Psychoanalytic researchers will assess children's identification with parents. Role-learning researchers will select variables assessing the norms and expectations parents have for children.

Two conclusions can be offered about these studies which attempt to relate general or more specific family dimensions to outcomes in child development. First, it is generally found that stronger relationships occurred in studies involving variables which are more specific to parent-child relations than in studies attempting to relate more global, conceptually ' distant" variables to child outcomes.

Second, the frequent findings of low correlations between family dimensions and child behavior is probably due to the fact that some conceptual mechanism is necessary to link parent variables with child variables: the "leap" between cause and effect is considerable.

These conclusions clearly point to the need to link parent behaviors to child-development outcomes. Our linkage in this research is to consider the *situation* in which learning can occur. Moreover, we postulate that children actively select situations, and aspects of situations, to attend to rather than simply assuming that all relevant parental behaviors influence a child. Thus, we selected a variety of consumption situations and examined parental behavior and parent-child interaction in those situations.

Basis of Impact

Studies of family or parental influences can be classified into two categories in terms of the basis for the impact assumed to occur.

Studies in the first category view the impact of a parental response on the child's behavior as essentially a function of the frequency of the child's exposure to the response. Therefore, conceptualization of parental behaviors, such as physical or psychological punishment, protection, restrictiveness, or affection (Sears, Maccoby, and Levin, 1957), or more recently such interactional variables as socio-oriented and concept-oriented communication, (Chaffee, McLeod, Wackman, 1973), treat them as *general-response tendencies.* This approach does not deny that situational variations may occur; rather, it treats these variations as unimportant. Sheer frequency of exposure to the parental response is seen as most important in determining its impact on the child.

The impact of some parental behaviors on the child may be similar across many situations, but we would expect that the situational context is important for most.

For example, the impact of parental punishment or reward (measures of reinforcement in S-R learning models) will depend on *what* child behavior is being rewarded or punished. Yet in many studies, including some of the authors' own research, punishment and reward (affection) have been viewed as general parental-response tendencies with no linkage made to the situations in which these responses occur. It is little wonder that most of these studies show little or no impact of parental punishment or affection on children's or adolescents' behavior.

A second approach to conceptualizing family variables is the *situational approach.* In this approach, parental behaviors are viewed as situation-based responses rather than as general-response tendencies. In this view, whatever impact a parental behavior may have is seen as depending upon the context in which it occurs. Therefore, in using this approach the researcher must keep a clear focus on the situational context and examine situational variation empirically in order to assess the generality of parental-response tendencies.

In the present study, we have generally used the situational approach to examine mothers' behaviors relevant to children's consumer socialization. We have done this because the situational approach is more consistent with the cognitive development perspective regarding the impact of the child's experiences on his development. However, we have also used the general-response approach for measuring several mother behaviors.

Family Patterns

A final way of classifying studies of family influence on child development is in terms of conceptualizations of family patterns. The most common approach is to conceptualize and assess family patterns in terms of a single broad conceptual continuum. This *unidimensional* approach often involves categorizing families in terms of a number of "ideal types" (often only two) which conceptually represent the ends of a continuum involving a set of highly correlated specific behavioral dimensions. Miller and Swanson's (1958) entrepreneurial and bureaucratic families, and Burgess and Locke's (1953) institutional and companionship family types, are examples of the "typology" view.

The evidence for high relationships among the various dimensions that make up the major continuum is not impressive. Furthermore, when researchers have correlated various parental behaviors they have found little evidence of high relationships. For example, in a longitudinal study, Kagan and Moss (1962) found only two of twelve correlations among maternal behaviors to be statistically significant in both the infancy to three-year-old period and the three- to six-year-old period. Only for the six-to-ten age range were maternal behaviors reasonably consistent, with seven of twelve correlations significant.

The generally low correlations between family dimensions spurred investigators to a second analytic approach. In this view, combinations of two or more dimensions are conceptualized and measured as distinct influences on child development. For example, Williams (1958) used the variables of extent of parental love and parental authority to identify four family socialization types: authoritarian to exploitative, democratic to overprotective, permissive to overindulgent, and ignoring to self-centered. And Chaffee, McLeod, and Wackman (1973) used socio-oriented and concept-oriented communication patterns to identify four types of family communication environments: pluralistic, consensual, laissez faire, and protective.

The development of these *two-dimensional* typologies is based on the idea that specific combinations of the two (or more) underlying dimensions represent qualitatively distinct and meaningful environments for the child. Research does indicate that, in some instances, the typology predicts somewhat better than a simple linear combination of the two underlying variables (Chaffee, McLeod, and Wackman, 1973). But the improvements in prediction are not very large. Furthermore, when the researcher moves beyond two dimensions, the number of possible types becomes very large and, as a consequence, very difficult to deal with conceptually.

The third *multi-dimensional* approach actually involves an implicit view of family patterns. This conception emerges when a set of measures of various family or parent behavior dimensions is included in multi-variate analysis, such as a regression analysis. In this kind of analysis each family is viewed as a vector of responses, e.g., frequency of punishment, affection, parental power, maternal restrictiveness, etc.

Although this notion of pattern has only been an implicit one in research, it need not remain implicit. In fact, there are good reasons to suggest that pattern as a vector of response tendencies be conceptualized explicitly. First, the view that behavior is substantially influenced by the situation suggests, for example, that a mother's use of information in buying products would vary from situation to situation. Similarly, if one accepts a transactional view of social behavior—that one actor's behavior influences the other's—then one would expect, for example, a mother's response to her child's purchase request would vary depending upon how the child asks for the product. Both of these propositions suggest that we should expect substantial variation in parent's behavior, depending on characteristics of the situation and on the dynamics of interaction processes.

In the present study, we have explicitly conceptualized mother's behavior and mother-child interaction as a *set of situational-response tendencies*. Thus, we have tried to assess the variation in the mother's behavior across a variety of specific examples of situations (e.g., product purchases, purchase requests by the child) and develop a series of measures of her tendencies to use alternative responses in the situation.

CONCEPTUALIZING FAMILY INFLUENCES FROM A COGNITIVE DEVELOPMENT PERSPECTIVE

Against the backdrop of literature we have reviewed, we developed a different theoretical view of socialization processes—a view of socialization *from a cognitive development perspective*. What this view means theoretically, and its implications for conducting socialization research, are discussed in this section.

Cognitive development theory is sometimes criticized for its emphasis on intra-individual processes. However, as we have noted, most cognitive development theorists and researchers stress the importance of the environment in the progress of cognitive development. Nevertheless, since most cognitive development theories are structural theories which specify the course of development in terms of the cognitive abilities that succeed one another, discussions of the specific processes occurring in development are not well developed.

Cognitive development theories' general explanation of how development occurs stress that changes are due to both maturation and experience. In our research, sampling children at three-year intervals insured that our three age groups would differ substantially both in maturation and in the *quality* of the children's experiences. Age differences alone do not guarantee that the *quality* of the learning experiences will differ, however. Rather, the quality of the learning experience depends on two factors: (1) the richness of the child's environment; (2) the child's ability to interpret this environment appropriately. These two factors are important concepts in the newer, functional cognitive development theory advanced by the "neo-Piagetians," chiefly Pascal-Leone (1970) and Case (1974).

The functional neo-Piagetian view of cognitive development suggests that development can proceed more rapidly when the learning environment appropriately matches the child's current level of cognitive ability. When this occurs—when the environment provides new experiences which can be assimilated and accommodated to the child's cognitive level—then new cognitive abilities can be developed at a much earlier age (cf. Case, 1974).

This view contains two crucial assumptions. First, it assumes that the child's interpretation of his experience is central in determining what he learns from the experience. Since the child's cognitive abilities have a major impact on the interpretations the child does make, this implies that his level of cognitive development itself has a major impact on both *what* he learns and *how* he learns.

For example, telling a child that he should buy product X instead of product Y because "Uncle Joe will really like it" will have considerably more meaning for an older child, who is more likely than a younger child to be able to take the role of another and infer emotional responses of others. The older child may learn the general principle of taking others' wants into account when buying gifts. The younger child, on the other hand, is likely to simply learn that Uncle Joe likes product X.

The second crucial assumption is closely related to the first. It is that learning occurs in specific situations, and the cumulative impact of learning on development results from appropriate matching of children's cognitive abilities and environmental factors. When the sequence of situations which the child experiences provides an appropriate match for his developing cognitive abilities, development can proceed rapidly. When the situations are not appropriately matched—being either too simple for the child or so complex that he cannot meaningfully interpret the situation—development can be slowed down, or even hindered.

Case's research (1974) illustrates the impact of appropriate matching of cognitive ability and environmental factors on increasing speed of learning. In this study, eight-year-olds with high cognitive ability went through a four-day training program designed to teach them a complicated logical procedure which Piaget said could not be learned until a child was fourteen or fifteen! On a separate criterion test two months later nine of ten high-level eight-year-olds passed the test. In contrast, only two of eight low-level eight-year-olds passed the test, and none of the high-level six-year-olds. These results clearly indicate that a match between the child's cognitive ability and the environment (training program) is necessary to produce development of a new cognitive ability.

These results, and the more general functional view of cognitive development, suggest that learning processes for children with different cognitive abilities may be quite different. Furthermore, research concerning the development of noncognitively based behavior indicates similar differences in learning processes.

Crandall, Orleans, Preston, and Rabson (1958) studied the relationship between parental training of compliant behaviors and actual compliant behavior toward peers and adults among three- to five-year-olds and six- to eight-year-olds. Results showed nonsignificant correlations between mothers' behavior and children's behavior for the nursery schoolers, but correlations in the .40-.60 range for older, grade-school children. This suggests that mothers' rewards and punishments may have substantially different impacts on children's learning of a behavior at different ages.

In Kagan and Moss' (1960) landmark longitudinal study, four maternal behaviors—protection, restrictiveness, hostility, and acceleration— were correlated with a large number of children's behaviors. Measures of both mother's and child's behaviors were taken in three of the five time periods for which measurements were made in the study: 0-3, 3-6, 6-10.

When a correlation between a specific maternal behavior and a specific child behavior was substantial (.35 or higher) in one age group, it was also substantial in both of the older age groups only 14 percent of the time. In another third of the cases, the initial relationship was also large in a second time period, but not in the third. On the other hand, in over half of the cases the relationship was substantial in only *one* time period; in the other two time periods, the relationship was not statistically significant. These results indicate that even for behaviors which are not cognitively based (e.g., passivity, independence, aggressiveness, spontaneity, conformity, etc.), the relationship between maternal behaviors and the child's behavior changes from one age group to another.

Thus, both functional development theory and research by Crandall, et al., and Kagan and Moss indicate that we should expect variation in the kinds and processes of learning that children of differing ages experience. However, neither theory nor research is well enough developed to suggest which family variables will be important or which learning processes are most likely to occur for children in different age groups.

Nevertheless, it is clear that the cognitive development view of socialization carries a number of conceptual and methodological implications for how the researcher approaches the family as a socialization environment:

(1) Conceptualization and measurement of family variables should not be of a global nature; rather, they should be more situational since children's interpretations of learning experiences occur in the context of specific situations.

(2) Major analyses of the impact of family variables should be conducted within a relatively small age range in order to increase the chances that different children's interpretations of the same situation are similar.

(3) Because of the cognitive ability differences between younger and older children, the researcher should expect that children's learning at the two ages may be the result of quite different family variables and, by implication, of different learning processes.

(4) The researcher should expect that the same variable might have quite different impacts on different-aged children's learning.

The remainder of the chapter will discuss how these implications were adopted in our conceptual and empirical approach to examining the family's role in children's consumer socialization.

CONCEPTUALIZING THE FAMILY CONSUMER CONTEXT

We have focused on the family as a key context for grade-school children's consumer socialization. But the specific aspects of this context likely to be of particular significance to the child's consumer socialization are not immediately apparent. From our analysis of the cognitive development literature, we thought it necessary to conceptualize and measure the family context in ways consistent with the situational view of learning. But this provided no guidelines for the specific aspects of the family context we should be examining. However, Kohlberg (1969) offered a suggestion that provided some direction for our conceptualization of the family context.

In analyzing the effect of experience upon cognitive development, Kohlberg (1969) points to several kinds of conceptual analyses that are, unfortunately, often omitted in discussion of learning. One of these is analysis of the relation of the structure of the child's specific experience to the structure of the child's behavior. Too often, as we pointed out earlier, investigators sought to relate global or general family variables to outcomes in child development which were conceptually distant from the specific dependent variables of interest. The prevalance of null results in early research strongly suggested to us that we should attempt to relate children's consumer skills to independent variables in the family context which can be expected to be functionally related to these skills. Since our major focus is on the child's information-processing skills, we decided to concentrate on aspects of the contexts in which information is—or may be—used.

In the family context, there appear to be three main ways in which a child can learn information-processing skills relevant to consumer behavior: (1) by observing his parents' behavior; (2) by interacting with his parents in a consumption situation; and (3) by acting as a consumer himself, perhaps under parental guidance.

Obviously, a child's ability to learn from his parents' consumer behavior depends a great deal on what kind of behavior it is. Some behaviors may not be highly observable to children, e.g., budgeting, accounting, long-term insurance, etc. Much of this activity may be carried out by one parent only or through husband-and-wife discussion. In either case, children are probably not present.

Information-search activities, such as looking through newspaper advertisements or catalogues or calling stores, are somewhat more likely to be conducted in the presence of children. However, the *kinds* of information sought in these information searches typically are not observable by the child. When they are, such as when the child overhears a parent asking questions about a product over the phone, the child is not likely to pay much attention to the specific information being sought. On the other hand, when the child accompanies a parent shopping, he is often able to observe quite a bit concerning the parent's use of information. The child can see whether or not the parent compares prices and whether the parent purchases different kinds of products at different stores; he can hear the kinds of questions the parent asks sales personnel about different products. Thus, in-store shopping experiences are likely to provide the child with the potential for observing a great deal about the parent's shopping behavior and the kinds of information the parent seeks.

Interaction between parent and child about consumption is likely to occur in one of two situations. In some cases the parent will initiate the interaction, for example, when he sees a television commercial and comments to the child about it, when he asks the child what he would like for a birthday gift, and so forth. At other times the child will initiate interaction, most often when he asks his parents to buy a product. Child-initiated interactions may also occur in situations less directly related to buying products, for example, when the child asks the parent for help in deciding what to do with his money. In any case, the parent has an opportunity in both kinds of situations to "teach" the child something about using information in consumption situations.

A child's own experiences as a consumer are likely to be largely under the control of his parents, although this control decreases as the child begins to develop his own sources of income and relative independence to spend as he chooses. Parents can limit the child's opportunity to exercise any independence in purchasing products by not providing him with any money and by insisting on selecting all products for him. However, most parents provide even young children with opportunities to select products by giving them small amounts of money and by allowing them to choose such products as cereals, candy, etc. Thus, even with a young child, personal consumption experiences may play an important role in determining what he learns about using information in making consumption decisions.

In Chapter 7 we focus on these parental inputs to the child's consumer socialization experiences. We attempted to develop a series of measures that would (1) tap parental and parent-child consumption-related behaviors that occur frequently; (2) provide indices of information-processing aspects of the parental behaviors; and (3) show some promise of affecting children's consumer learning. The measures we developed do not constitute a tight theoretical structure. Rather, they represent a sampling of parental consumer behaviors, parent-child interactions about consumption, and children's consumption opportunities that will provide a description of the family context for consumer socialization.

The major purpose of Chapter 7 is to develop a general description of the family context of children's development of consumption skills, particularly their consumer information-processing skills. In this chapter we first examine the *goals* mothers have for their children's consumer learning. Then we describe *mothers' behavior as consumers,* focusing on their use of information in consumption decisions. Next *mother-child interaction* about consumption is reviewed in mother-initiated learning situations and in child-initiated learning situations. The chapter closes with an examination of the child's opportunities for *independent consumer behavior.*

Our analysis plan in Chapter 7 involves examining all family-context variables for differences related to socio-economic status. In general, we expect greater use of information by higher-status mothers and greater communication with their children by high-status mothers. We examine all variables except the mother's own consumer behaviors by the age of the child. We expect to find somewhat greater communication between mothers and older children and more opportunities for older children to operate as independent consumers. Analyses of sex differences produced no major differences; therefore, we do not report these results. The chapter closes with a section describing an analysis of family patterns.

FAMILY IMPACT ON CHILDREN'S CONSUMER SOCIALIZATION: HYPOTHESES

Cognitive development theories hypothesize that an enriched environment will generally facilitate children's cognitive development. In the present study, we expect that an enriched family consumer context will help children to learn consumer skills more rapidly. Chapter 8 presents our analysis of the impact of the family context on children's consumer socialization. We began this analysis with some general expectations concerning the relationship between each class of family context variable and the child behavior variables.

Skill Behaviors[3]

1. We expect a *positive* relationship between the child's skill behavior and three classes of family context variables—mother-child interaction, mother's own behavior, and mother's consumer-education goals.

We based this hypothesis on an expectation that direct attempts by parents to monitor and teach consumption behaviors (mother-child interaction) and having specific goals for the child's learning (mother's consumer-education goals) will have their intended impact on the child's behavior, at least to some extent. Further, we expect that the modeling of effective consumer behaviors (mother's own behavior) will have impacts similar to that found in other observational learning research (Bandura and Walters, 1963).

2. We expect rather *mixed* relationships between child's skill behaviors and the child's independence-opportunity variables.

We think that the child is just as likely to learn ineffective consumption behaviors when utilizing his opportunities for independent consumption as he is to learn effective behaviors.

Nonskill Behaviors

3. We expect that reduced control over the child's consumption by parents (indexed by mother-child interaction) and increased independence-consumption opportunities are *positively* related to the performance of the nonskill behaviors.

These predictions are based on the learning-theory assumption that engaging in behaviors which are usually rewarding (buying or receiving products) will increase the frequency of these behaviors.

4. We expect *mixed* relationships between the child's nonskill behaviors and both mother's own behaviors and mother's consumer-education goals.

Our reasoning is that a mother's own consumer behavior and her consumer-education goals might be expected to have an impact on *how* the child made purchases or asked for products, but they would probably have little impact on the sheer frequency of the child's spending or requesting of products.

In addition to these general hypotheses, we expect substantial age differences in how the family-context variables are related to children's consumer behaviors. As indicated earlier, this expectation derives from functional-development theories' assumption that the impact of a learning experience on the child is dependent on his interpretation of that experience. This clearly implies that we should expect the same family-context variable to have different impacts for different-aged children.

Data in Chapter 8 are used to test our general hypotheses and expectations. At the outset of that chapter, we analyze the relative impact of age compared to all other independent variables. To anticipate the findings, the results show that grade level is a better predictor of virtually all of the dependent-child behaviors than are any of the family-context variables. We feel that this finding reinforces our view of the importance of focusing on within-age-group processes. We believe it would be quite misleading to interpret these findings as cognitive development versus family influences.

Consequently, within-age analyses occupy the bulk of Chapter 8. The analyses will show that the factors which account for variation in the use of consumer skills within the three age groups in our study are quite different. These results suggest that children in the three age groups may learn consumer skills through somewhat different learning processes. Data will be presented to try to specify more clearly the function of family inputs in the overall development of children's consumer skills.

NOTES

1. We recognize that other influences—school, peer groups, etc.—may also have an impact, but the family group would seem to be a particularly important external influence on consumer socialization. Parents control children's resources

to varying degrees, provide opportunities for consumption, and are models for a wide range of consumer behaviors. Furthermore, we refer to "family" influences in this chapter, while actually referring to mother-child relations. The primacy of the mother in child development during the ages included in this study is well documented (Zigler and Child, 1969). We do acknowledge the importance of assessing sibling and father influences more explicitly in future research.

2. Following Belk (1974), we conceive of the "situation" as factors particular to a time and place of observation which do not follow from a knowledge of personal, stimulus, or interpersonal attributes and which have a demonstrable and systematic effect on behavior.

3. For purposes of this analysis, we have grouped together all three types of child skill behaviors—higher-level information-processing skills, lower-level information-processing skills, and money use skills.

Chapter 7 ▓▓▓▓▓▓▓▓▓▓▓▓▓▓▓▓▓▓▓▓▓▓▓▓▓▓▓▓▓▓▓▓▓▓▓▓▓▓▓

THE FAMILY CONTEXT FOR
CHILDREN'S CONSUMER LEARNING

▓▓

Our review of pertinent literature in the past chapter suggests that there
are three primary ways that families influence the consumer-
socialization process: (1) children may observe and imitate parent
behaviors; (2) parent-child interaction occurring in consumption situation may affect learning; and (3) children may engage in independent
consumer behaviors, with some degree of parental guidance.

The data presented in this chapter focus on the kinds of parental
inputs to these three learning processes. The measures we developed
represent a sampling of parental consumer behaviors, parent-child interaction pertaining to consumption, and children's consumption opportunities. Taken together, these measures comprise our view of the
family context for consumer socialization.

The first analyses in this chapter focus on family dimensions which
are conceptually "distant" from specific consumer-socialization outcomes in children. However, these variables—mothers' consumer goals
for children and patterns of information-processing in consumer situa-

tions—form a framework in which socialization occurs. At the very least, they may reflect subtle learning processes which are occurring in the family, and cannot be measured directly.

Other data in the chapter are 'conceptually closer," i.e., parent-child interaction patterns occurring in both parent-initiated and child-initiated situations, and children's opportunities for independent consumption. We close the chapter with a review of patterns in the data and what they suggest about the family context for consumer socialization.

MOTHERS' CONSUMER-EDUCATION GOALS
AND TEACHING METHODS

Parents transmit social norms, notions of good and bad, and other values to their children. Sometimes they do so consciously, but probably more often unconsciously. Nevertheless, parents are usually aware of their role in preparing their children for adulthood. Whether this role includes educating their children for consumer activities was our first concern in examining the family as a context for consumer socialization.

We expected that most mothers want their children to develop some kinds of positive consumer habits or orientations and to avoid others. Mothers may play a consumer-educator role in order to transmit desired goals. We sought to identify the kinds of things mothers want their children to learn relevant to consumer behavior and to examine the methods they use to "teach" or achieve these consumer-education goals. Two open-ended questions addressed these goals mothers have for their children. The first item explored long-range goals: "What kinds of things do you do as a consumer that you would like your child to learn?" This question was designed to ascertain the kinds of consumer behaviors mothers wanted their children to learn by the time they were adults. A second question attempted to determine the short-range goals mothers might have for their children: "What kinds of things do you want him to learn now, at his age?" Additionally, responses to this question should reveal the different kinds of goals mothers have for different-aged children.

Long-term and short-term goals were coded into three categories which were constructed inductively from analysis of open-ended responses. *Money-related* goals refer to the mother's concern that her child learn how to use money wisely. Typical responses include "saving money," "learning the value of the dollar," or "learning how to budget."

The second category, *price/bargain* goals, emphasizes the price of products and bargain shopping; price/bargain includes "learning to shop around and compare prices," "watching for bargains and reading ads," and "learning to buy items by price per unit weight."

Concern for learning to shop for *quality products* makes up the third category as exemplified by such answers as "learning to buy quality products," "learning it's better to spend a little more for better quality," and "reading *Consumer Reports.*"

The findings show that mothers express more long-term goals than short-term goals. Sixth-graders' mothers mention more short-term goals than mothers of children in the two younger age groups. Mothers of children in these younger age groups report about the same number of long-term goals.

Perhaps these patterns reflect age-related differences in marketplace involvement. As we will see, sixth-graders are the most active consumers, having more money available to them and spending more often than younger children. It may be that mothers of sixth-graders feel more urgent needs to impart consumer-education goals than do mothers of kindergartners and third-graders. On the other hand, the data may simply indicate that mothers of sixth-graders are more alert to their children's behavior as consumers.

A look at the *specific consumer goals* mothers have for their children shows that the major short-term objectives are money-related and quality goals (see Table 7-1). It would appear that mothers are particularly concerned that their children learn how to handle money and be able to identify quality products. However, over the long term, mothers place equal emphasis on bargain and quality goals. This suggests that mothers generally believe that money-handling skills will be learned early but that skills involved in effective shopping will take longer to acquire. It is interesting to note that there are no differences among age groups in mothers' short-term or long-term goals. Perhaps this indicates little discrimination by mothers in terms of what they think different aged children are capable of learning about consuming. There were no social-class differences among mothers for either short-term or long-term goals.

After determining the kinds of consumer goals mothers have for their children, we inquired into the methods they use to impart these goals. We asked mothers, "How do you try to teach your child these

TABLE 7-1

Mothers Mentioning Various Consumer Goals by Grade Level[*]

	K %	3 %	6 %	Total %	x^2
Short-Term Goals					
Money-related goals	54	52	57	55	1.18 (2 d.f.) n.s.
Price/bargain goals	21	24	31	26	5.72 (2 d.f.) p<.05
Quality goals	56	61	58	58	1.14 (2 d.f.) n.s.
N =	(195)	(198)	(205)	(598)	
Long-Term Goals					
Money-related goals	27	34	39	33	6.44 (2 d.f.) p<.05
Price/bargain goals	69	61	64	64	3.02 (2 d.f.) n.s.
Quality goals	72	73	73	73	0.17 (2 d.f.) n.s.
N =	(195)	(198)	(205)	(598)	

[*] Cell entries add up to more than 100 percent in each column because respondents often gave multiple responses to this question.

things you would like him/her to learn about being a consumer?" The methods mothers use were coded into five categories, varying in terms of the amount of supervision over the child's consumer transactions. They are: (1) prohibiting certain acts; (2) giving lectures on consumer activities, i.e., "one-way" talks by mother to child; (3) holding discussions with the child about consumer decisions; (4) acting as an example; and (5) allowing the child to learn from his own experience.

Most mothers use only one teaching method, but an appreciable number of mothers of sixth-graders use two. The only statistically significant difference between age groups is that sixth-graders' mothers are less likely to teach by prohibiting actions. Perhaps of most interest is the considerable variation among mothers in how they teach their child consumer skills.

We are struck by the mothers' lack of attention to socialization. The typical mother in our sample described a few general goals and mentioned just one method of teaching her child. Possibly, consumer training in the home is more likely to result indirectly through parents' modeling behaviors or from responding to children's pleas for products. The child is also likely to learn when parents shop and take him along.

In any case, we find few mothers who actively attempt to train children as "good" consumers.

MOTHERS' CONSUMER BEHAVIOR

Mothers' own consumer behavior should be examined against the backdrop of few goals and little direct teaching. These behaviors serve as a model for the child, although, as we indicated earlier, the behaviors vary in observability to the child and in effectiveness as good examples. Nonetheless, our data indicate that many mothers recognize that the example they set may have an impact on the child's subsequent consumer behavior—one-fourth of them mentioned this as a principal teaching method. The importance of this essentially passive method may be even greater in light of the mothers' limited use of active teaching methods.

Our perspective in examining mothers' consumer behavior is once again the information-processing orientation, although we will be discussing other behavior aspects as well. We will look first at the kinds of information sources mothers use in preparing for product decisions. Next we will examine mothers' shopping behaviors. Finally we will consider the budgeting and accounting practices families use.

Mothers' Use of Information Sources in Product Purchases

Consumer marketing practices in the United States have institutionalized several sources of information about products: advertising through the mass media of television, radio, and newspapers; sales promotion devices, such as coupons and premium offers; and personal selling efforts by salesmen. The functions which marketing vehicles perform for consumers and for marketers depend on the characteristics of media vehicles, the product, and the consumer. For example, a major purpose of advertising is to bring certain products and brand names to the attention of consumers (see Bucklin, 1965, on the information role of advertising). Television advertising can effectively introduce many consumer products or "remind' consumers, i.e., keep a well-known brand name salient. Products that are complex and involve extensive consumer decision processes are typically promoted through multiple marketing vehicles, including those which are capable of imparting a lot of information, e.g., print advertisements and brochures. Salesmen and other individuals provide an opportunity for interactive consumer information processing. Consumer-oriented guidebooks, such as *Consumer*

Reports and *Consumer Media,* also provide information, often in rebuttal of information disseminated by manufacturers of products.

The role of personal influence in shaping attitudes toward political affairs, moviegoing, fashions, and marketing early on received much attention by communication researchers. Katz and Lazarsfeld (1955) found that opinion leaders in the community were more influential than mass media in shaping attitudes. Interpersonal communication appeared to be an important ingredient in the persuasive communication process and as a potential source of information about the world (see Chaffee, 1972, for an updated discussion of the interpersonal context of mass communications).

In order to gauge mothers' use of both mass media and interpersonal sources of information about products, we asked them: "When you have made a major purchase, such as a washing machine, automobile, or refrigerator, how often have you consulted the following sources of information about that product: newspaper ads, consumer guidebooks, friends, relatives, and salesmen at stores other than where you made the purchase?" Respondents then checked a four-point Likert scale to indicate the frequency with which they use these basic sources of information.

Consistent with research findings of Rich and Jain (1968) and Carman (1965), newspaper ads have a greater frequency of use than other sources. Nearly two-thirds of the mothers report using newspaper ads usually or sometimes. Other sources are consulted with less frequency in the following order—salesmen (61 percent), friends (54 percent), consumer guidebooks (51 percent), and relatives (40 percent).

Two patterns in source use emerge when we compare mothers of differning socio-economic status. Frequency of using consumer guidebooks, friends, and salesmen increases with socio-economic status. In contrast, there are differences in use of newspaper ads or relatives by socio-economic status.

These data diverge from earlier findings indicating that housewives of high socio-economic status consult friends less frequently than do housewives of lower social status (see Rich and Jain, 1968, and Hollingshead, 1965). However, these differences between findings may be due to the fact that we based our question on durable-goods purchases. Other kinds of products may lead to different class-related patterns of information source use.

Another aspect of information source use is the *range* of different information sources consulted in purchasing durable goods. Such an analysis is presented in Table 7-2, which shows that the higher social-status mothers use more sources of information. One explanation of this pattern is that increased social status brings an expanded "life space" for the individual.

Communication researchers have also used the life-space notion to explain the frequent finding that use of print media and knowledge of public affairs increase with education and socio-economic status (see Tichenor, Donohue, and Olien, 1970; and Wade and Schramm, 1969).

Although data in Table 7-2b confirm this relationship between number of media sources and socio-economic status, use of mass-media

TABLE 7-2

Mothers' Sources of Information by Socio-Economic Status

		Low %	Medium %	High %	Total %
a.	*Total Number of Sources*				
	1	21	17	5	15
	2-3	35	34	30	33
	4-5	44	49	65	52
		100	100	100	100
	N =	(215)	(227)	(170)	(612)
		$x^2 = 25.46$ (4 d.f.) $p < .001$			
b.	*Number of Mass Media Sources*				
	0	21	12	8	14
	1	44	37	25	36
	2	35	51	67	50
		100	100	100	100
	N –	(215)	(227)	(170)	(612)
		$x^2 = 45.40$ (4 d.f.) $p < .001$			
c.	*Number of Interpersonal Sources*				
	0	17	16	4	13
	1	21	20	19	20
	2	25	23	30	26
	3	37	41	47	41
		100	100	100	100
	N =	(215)	(227)	(170)	(612)
		$x^2 = 19.34$ (4 d.f.) $p < .001$			

sources is relatively high at each status level: even among low-status mothers, four out of five report consulting at least one media source for product information.

The relationship between socio-economic status and use of interpersonal sources for product information is more difficult to explain in terms of an expanded life space. One could argue, for example, that the higher education levels of high-status individuals equip them for efficient information processing (from media sources), so they use few interpersonal sources in the decision process. Conversely, less-educated individuals might lack information-processing skills, or perhaps self-confidence, and therefore they consult a relatively high number of interpersonal sources.

Research by Dervin and Greenberg (1971) on the communication environment of urban residents found middle-class residents were more likely to use institutional sources of information (including the media) than were lower-class residents. Lower-class persons were more likely to rely on interpersonal sources (particularly friends and relatives). Gans also observed high use of interpersonal sources for a wide range of consumer decisions among lower-class families in an ethnic neighborhood in Boston (Gans, 1962).

Our findings do not agree with these earlier results. In comparing the use of interpersonal sources by mothers of different socio-economic status (Table 7-2c), we find that the number of sources increases with social level. Nearly half of the mothers with high status report using all three interpersonal sources frequently, while only slightly more than a third of the mothers with low socio-economic status do so. Our data might be explained by the fact that a considerable number of the low-status mothers work, which limits the time available to them for seeking information.

In general, the mothers' reports of the number of media and interpersonal sources used to decide about durable goods indicate an increase in the number of different sources with higher socio-economic status. Furthermore, when comparisons are made within status levels (not shown), there is a positive relationship between use of mass media and interpersonal sources. Both sets of data indicate that higher-status mothers tend to be more thorough when seeking information from various sources about durable goods. Whether they are also more thorough in seeking various *kinds* of information will be discussed in the next section.

Mothers' Use of Information in Choosing Products

Marketing and consumer researchers have examined the role of information in consumer evaluations of products (Hemple, 1970; Cox, 1963; Chaffee and McLeod, 1973; Hughes and Ray, 1974). Models of consumer decision making have tried to predict the probability that certain kinds of information will be used in product evaluation. We attempted to measure the kinds of information mothers consider "important" when evaluating particular products. Specifying the product is necessary because cost characteristics, for instance, are less important when deciding which brand of salt to buy than when considering the purchase of a new winter coat.

For each of nine products (TV set, laundry soap, ice cream, pair of children's shoes, hair dryer, good winter coat, dining room set, paper towels, and a purse), mothers were presented with a list of seven types of information which might be considered during purchase. The different kinds of information fell into three categories: (1) information on *cost/appearance* attributes—the price of the brand as compared to other brands of that product, the cost of the product in terms of the mother's own budget, and how the product looks; (2) information relating to *advertising* content—the brand name and claims for the product made in advertisements; and (3) two kinds of information about the decision-making situation, or *contextual* attributes—the quality of the store where the product is purchased and friends' experiences with the product.

Mothers clearly differ by socio-economic status in the number and kinds of information they use. As Table 7-3 indicates, high-status

TABLE 7-3

Total Number of Attributes Mentioned by Socio-Economic Status

		Low %	Medium %	High %	Total %
Low (6-13)		34	23	19	25
Medium (14-17)		25	27	22	25
High (18-21)		26	29	26	28
Very High (22+)		15	21	33	22
		100	100	100	100
	N =	(212)	(226)	(170)	(608)
		x^2 = 25.22 (6 d.f.) p < .001			

mothers use substantially more kinds of information than do middle-status or lower-status mothers. Apparently high-status mothers are more thorough in product decisions, both in using more information sources and in using more kinds of information.

Whether high-status mothers are more likely to use *all* kinds of information or whether they are selective is the next question to ask.

Table 7-4 give the percent of mothers within each status level who mention the different types of attributes frequently. In this analysis, a mother is included in the "frequent mention" category if she selects the attribute at least one-third of the time. For the nine products tested, mothers are most likely to pay attention to cost/appearance attributes and least likely to mention contextual attributes.

The data indicate a positive relationship between status level and both cost/appearance and contextual attributes. In contrast, differences in the number of advertising attributes mentioned are not statistically significant, although medium-status and high-status mothers are a bit more likely to mention them.

A second analysis examined mothers' *efficiency* and *effectiveness* in using information to make a product decision. Not all types of information presented to the mothers may be considered either necessary or useful in choosing a particular product. Therefore, for this second analysis, each kind of attribute information was screened for its usefulness in making a decision about the nine products by means of an elaborate procedure.

First, for each product, the authors made a subjective judgment about which of the seven types of information would be relatively

TABLE 7-4
Mothers Frequently Mentioning Use of Various Types of Attributes by Socio-Economic Status[*]

	Low %	Medium %	High %	Total %	x^2
Cost/Appearance	43	52	60	51	11.18 (2 d.f.) p <.01
Contextual	9	10	18	12	8.82 (2 d.f.) p <.05
Advertising	20	26	26	24	2.92 (2 d.f.) n.s.
N =	(212)	(226)	(170)	(608)	

[*]Cell entries add up to more than 100 percent in each column because respondents selected multiple attributes for each product considered.

useful. Then, our subjective judgments were matched against the distribution of mothers who chose each kind of information for that product. If 40 percent of the mothers checked the same type of product information as we did, that piece of information was classed as "useful." In this manner the following sets of attribute information for each product was labeled useful, i.e., important for effective decision making:

1. TV set—price of the brand as compared to other brands; cost of the product in terms of your own budget; brand name; friend's experience; quality of the store.

2. Laundry soap—price of the brand as compared to other brands; brand name.

3. Ice cream—price of the brand as compared to other brands; brand name.

4. Children's shoes—cost of the product in terms of your own budget; brand name; quality of the store.

5. Hair dryer—price of the brand as compared to other brands; cost of the product in terms of your own budget; brand name.

6. Good winter coat—cost of the product in terms of your own budget; how the product looks; quality of the store.

7. Dining room set—cost of the product in terms of your budget; how the product looks; quality of the store.

8. Paper towels—price of the brand as compared to other brands.

9. Purse—cost of the product in terms of your budget; how the product looks.

The list discloses several features of our judgment—and of mothers. First, advertised claims did not satisfy the criterion for "useful" information for any of the nine products. Obviously, advertising does play a role in purchase decision making, but this role is complex, depending on product and consumer characteristics. The fact that fewer than 40 percent· of the mothers indicated advertising was useful in purchase decisions probably reflects the inability of consumer to make valid assessments of advertising's impact on their decisions. The mothers may feel that the role of other types of information in purchase decisions is more clearly identifiable.

Second, this designation of useful types of information should not be generalized beyond this sample and study. Since the mothers were supplied a list of types of information from which to choose, not all kinds of information they actually use in making product decisions were available to them. For instance, one might assume consumers would be interested in warranty guarantees or service agreements when deciding about major purchases. This alternative was not presented to the mothers for consideration. Consequently, the designation of each of the above kinds of information as useful for "effective" decision making is only *relative* to the other kinds of information presented.

Third, the 40-percent criterion enabled us to develop a scale to measure the *relative* effectiveness and efficiency with which mothers use information in considering a product purchase. We define *effectiveness* in decision making as the total number of useful types of information each mother mentions for the nine products. *Efficiency* in decision making is operationally defined as a difference score: the total number of types of information checked for each product minus the number of useful kinds of information checked.

The highest possible score on the relative effectiveness scale (i.e., if mothers choose each useful type for each product) is 24. The actual scores for the sample range from 4 to 20. Effectiveness in using information for product decision making increases with status level, with nearly one-third of the high-status mothers "very high" on the effectiveness scale compared to only 13 percent of the low-status mothers and 17 percent of the medium-status mothers.

The efficiency scale ranged from a low score of eight or more "extra" items of information to a very high score of zero to two extra items. There are no significant differences by status level in the relative efficiency of the mothers. Overall, the mothers in each status group are fairly evenly distributed across the scale.

By combining the effectiveness and efficiency scales, we are able to develop a more complete picture of the information use patterns of mothers in the different social classes. Information use patterns were constructed by dichotomizing both scales, then assigning each mother to one of four classifications: high effectiveness/high efficiency, high effectiveness/low efficiency, low effectiveness/high efficiency, and low effectiveness/low efficiency. Results of this analysis are presented in Table 7-5.

A large proportion of high-status mothers have high effectiveness/ low efficiency. Since high-status mothers use more information in product decisions than the other two groups, it is not surprising that a substantial number of them are relatively inefficient in their informa-

TABLE 7-5

Information Use Efficiency/Effectiveness by Socio-Economic Status

	Low %	Medium %	High %	Total %
High Effectiveness/High Efficiency	15	19	20	18
High Effectiveness/Low Efficiency	25	31	41	32
Low Effectiveness/High Efficiency	39	30	26	32
Low Effectiveness/Low Efficiency	21	20	13	18
	100	100	100	100
N =	(212)	(226)	(170)	(608)

$$x^2 = 17.60 \text{ (6 d.f.) } p < .01$$

tion use. In contrast, many low-status mothers have low effectiveness/ high efficiency. Medium-status mothers frequently have high effectiveness/low efficiency and low effectiveness/high efficiency.

Perhaps the most striking aspect of these data is that substantial numbers of mothers at each status level fall into each information use pattern.

We have now examined mothers' use of various information sources and various kinds of information relevant to product decision making. Both behaviors are clearly related to consumer effectiveness. Another behavior, to which we now turn, is also useful as an index of consumer effectiveness. This is a measure of mothers' shopping behavior.

Mothers' Shopping Behavior

Some consumers travel among several stores when grocery shopping to take advantage of advertised specials and price and quality differences. These consumers can be thought of as more effective grocery shoppers. To index this behavior, we inquired how frequently mothers stopped at more than one store when they were grocery shopping. We also asked mothers their reasons for doing this.

Although differences in multiple-store shopping between status groups are statistically significant ($p < .01$), they are not very large and are not linear. Rather, there appears to be a slight curvilinear trend, with low-status mothers shopping around most regularly and medium-status mothers least regularly. High-status mothers generally fall in between.

Surprisingly, the reasons given for multiple-stop grocery shopping do not differ among mothers from the various status levels. Although we might expect low-status mothers to be price-conscious, and high-status mothers with more money to be quality-conscious, neither expectation is supported by the data.

In general, the data indicate that a large proportion of mothers at each status level shop around for groceries frequently. They want to take advantage of advertising specials and low prices. In short, many women at each status level are rather effective grocery shoppers.

Budgeting and Accounting

The mothers' behaviors we have just considered can be observed by children and can provide models for their use of information when acting as consumers. Family budget planning and accounting practices are probably less observable to the child and, in most instances, bear little relation to his consumer information processing. Nevertheless, careful budgeting and close accounting of family finances may serve as a model for other aspects of children's consumer behavior (e.g., how they should handle their own money) even though the specifics of these activities may not be highly observable to the child.

We attempted to index both planning and accounting by asking how money was managed in the family. Mothers were able to choose from six alternative responses, varying on the dimensions of planning and accounting: (1) We have a written budget, and we stick to it closely almost every month. (2) We have a written budget, and we stick to it much of the time. (3) We have a written budget, but most of the time we don't stick to it. (4) We don't have a written budget, but we keep careful track of our money through our checking account. (5) We don't have a written budget but, through our checking account, we pretty well know what we're spending. (6) To tell you the truth, we really don't manage our money at all.

Two separate measures were developed from this question, reflecting planning and control, activities which are separated in time. Mothers who checked number 1 or 2 were categorized as "high" budget *planners,* since written budgets indicate anticipation and organization. All other mothers were categorized as low planners.

A measure of budget *accounting* was constructed in a similar way: mothers who checked number 1, 2, or 4 were categorized as high in budget accounting; all other mothers were categorized as low.

Mothers from the three socio-economic status levels are similar in terms of budget planning, with about one in five using a written budget. There is a slight trend toward higher budget planning among lower-status mothers, perhaps reflecting their tighter financial situations, but this trend is not statistically significant.

On the other hand, the trend toward closer *accounting* in higher-status families is statistically significant (p<.05). These data suggest that higher-status families keep somewhat tighter control over their money, primarily by keeping a close eye on their checkbook. Perhaps such an accounting procedure is not so relevant in low-status families where checkbook balances may not be high enough to require careful accounting of allocations. Instead, a small but steady balance may be their principal device to regulate their spending.

Summary

Mothers' own consumer behaviors display some differences related to social class. Information use increases directly with social class, with high socio-economic status mothers typically using the most sources of information and paying attention to the most kinds of information in product decisions. However, some information sources (e.g., relatives) are used equally by mothers in all social classes, as are some kinds of information (e.g., advertising attributes).

Mothers in each social class are alike in the relative efficiency of their information use. Grocery-shopping behavior of mothers in the different social classes is quite similar. So is budget planning. However, we find a positive linear relationship between social class and budget accounting.

MOTHER-CHILD INTERACTION ABOUT CONSUMPTION

Although modeling behavior can help children learn consumer skills, a more direct method of teaching involves interaction with the child. Mothers appear to acknowledge the importance of this contact. Thirty-five percent say that lecturing is their principal teaching method, and another 38 percent claim they teach by "discussing" things with their child. Some of this interaction about consumption undoubtedly follows the child's request for products.

Parent-Initiated Situations

We focused on two kinds of interaction the parent might initiate about consumption—discussion about products and discussion of TV commercials. Both kinds of communication afford clear opportunities for the parent to teach specific consumption skills to the child. Parents can teach which attributes are important in brand choice, the relative costs of different products and brands, the availability of products in different stores, and ideas about the quality of products and stores.

We gauged the frequency with which mothers talk to their children about products by having mothers report how often they (1) talked about the cost of products; (2) talked about where different products can be purchased; (3) asked the child's preference when buying things for him or her; (4) told the child he or she could not buy certain products. Mothers were asked to respond on a five-point scale—often, pretty often, sometimes, not too often, or never. The mothers' responses were summed to create a scale of product discussion. Frequency of mothers' discussion distributed evenly with no apparent effect of age or social class upon frequency.

TABLE 7-6

Discussion of TV Commercials with Children by
Grade Level and by Socio-Economic Status

Number of comments		K %	3 %	6 %	Total %
By Grade Level					
0		48	39	36	41
1		39	48	46	44
2-3		13	13	18	15
		100	100	100	100
	N =	(205)	(202)	(208)	(615)

$x^2 = 8.15$ (4 d.f.) $.05 < p < .10$

Number of comments		L %	M %	H %	Total %
By Socio-Economic Status					
0		46	46	29	41
1		41	42	51	44
2-3		13	12	20	15
		100	100	100	100
	N =	(212)	(226)	(170)	(608)

$x^2 = 16.09$ (4 d.f.) $p < .005$

Parents can increase children's understanding of the purpose of commercials and help them to learn to assess the value of the information they contain by talking with them about commercials. We measured this form of interaction by asking mothers whether they talked about commercials with their child, and if so what kinds of things they discussed. Topics of discussion were divided into two types: *General* comments were those made about TV commercials as a category, e.g., "commercials are not honest," "you cannot buy everything you see." *Specific* comments referred to those made about a particular commercial, e.g., statements about the good or bad points of a commercial, and statements about absurdity or humor in a commercial.

Three-fifths of all mothers report that they talk with their children about commercials; kindergartners' mothers report somewhat less frequent discussion than other groups. High-status mothers report more frequent discussion of commercials than middle-status or low-status mothers.

We found that mothers typically make general comments about commercials more often than specific comments. However, sixth-graders' mothers are equally likely to make both kinds. As we saw above, discussion of commercials increases slightly with age, but the data show that this change is confined to specific comments. About two-fifths of the mothers in each age group make general comments about commercials. The great majority—over 85 percent—of these comments are negative.

Mothers' dislike of commercials directed toward children is also evident in their answers to a series of opinion statements concerning commercials for children. We asked how strongly they agreed or disagreed with the following statements: (1) "Commercials on children's shows are often deceptive (that is, untrue in ways which mislead children in important ways)." (2) "There are too many commercials on shows children watch." (3) "Commercials are a fair price to pay for the entertainment children receive" (reversed item). (4) "Commercials to children should be regulated by the government." (5) "Commercials often make my child want the thing advertised."

Responses to these five statements were summed to create a measure of mothers' attitudes toward commercials directed at children.

Nearly one-fourth of the mothers have a strongly negative attitude, compared to only 4 percent with a slightly positive attitude. Mothers of kindergartners hold somewhat more negative attitudes than mothers of third-graders or sixth-graders, but there are no differences among the attitudes of mothers in the three socio-economic groups (Table 7-7).

Child-Initiated Situations

Parents can take the lead in interacting with their children to teach them about being good consumers, but such teaching opportunities occur more frequently in situations initiated by the child. As we saw in Chapter 5, children of all ages request products often, especially food products, toys, and games. Teaching opportunities may also arise when the child asks for advice about a product or about using his own money.

A mother can adopt a number of different strategies in responding to her child's purchase requests. She can yield to the request or she can simply refuse to buy the product without explaining the basis for

TABLE 7-7

Mothers' Attitude Toward Commercials Directed at Children by Grade Level and by Socio-Economic Status

		K %	3 %	6 %	Total %
By Grade Level					
Strongly negative		28	20	21	23
Negative		54	48	48	50
Neutral		15	28	27	23
Positive		3	4	4	4
		100	100	100	100
	N =	(205)	(202)	(208)	(615)
		$x^2 = 13.03$ (6 d.f.) $p < .05$			

		L %	M %	H %	Total %
By Socio-Economic Status					
Strongly negative		24	21	24	23
Negative		51	47	54	50
Neutral		21	27	20	23
Positive		4	5	2	4
		100	100	100	100
	N =	(215)	(227)	(170)	(615)
		$x^2 = 4.99$ (6 d.f.) n.s.			

refusal. If a mother responds in either of these ways, she loses an opportunity to teach something about consumption.

Alternatively, a mother might yield to the child's request after discussing the purchase with him, perhaps negotiating an arrangement to share the cost. Or she could refuse the request but explain reasons for her refusal. These more complex responses enable the parent to teach something quite specific about consumption.

We measured mothers' response strategies in two ways. First we inquired how frequently each mother's child asked for twelve products. For each product the child requested, the mother was asked how often she bought it. She could answer (1) most of the time, (2) some of the time, or (3) not too often. A scale indicating the mother's *general yielding behavior* was derived by summing across these responses and dividing by the number of items which the child requested.

Frequency of yielding is positively related to children's age. As can be seen, the biggest jump occurs between third and sixth grade. It may

TABLE 7-8

Mothers' General Yielding to Children's Product Requests by Grade Level and by Socio-Economic Status

		K %	3 %	6 %	Total %
By Grade Level					
High		22	27	39	30
Moderate		32	33	34	33
Low		46	40	27	37
		100	100	100	100
	N =	(204)	(202)	(207)	(613)

$$x^2 = 21.30 \text{ (4 d.f.) } p < .000$$

		L %	M %	H %	Total %
By Socio-Economic Status					
High		33	30	27	30
Moderate		36	31	33	33
Low		31	39	40	37
		100	100	100	100
	N =	(213)	(227)	(170)	(610)

$$x^2 = 4.85 \text{ (4 d.f.) n.s.}$$

be that this change in yielding is largely a consequence of sixth-graders' greater skill in approaching their mothers with product requests. It is not simply due to more more frequent requests by sixth-graders since, as we saw in Chapter 5, all age groups are the same in frequency of requests.

Our measure of general yielding fails to portray the kind of interaction that might have occurred during request situations. A second measure is needed for this. Accordingly, we posed twelve hypothetical purchase-request situations to mothers. These varied according to source for the request (TV commercial, peers, siblings, or self), location of the request (home or store), time of day, and type and cost of product. (See Appendix A for a more detailed description of situations.)

We provided six response alternatives and asked each mother to indicate her most likely response in each situation. She was allowed to add a second response if she used it rather frequently. The alternatives were: (1) I buy the product my child wants; (2) I'll agree to pay for the product if my child will do his share—pay part of the cost, do chores, etc.; (3) I'll agree to allow the purchase with the understanding my child will use his own money; (4) I refuse to buy the product, but I give an explanation of why my child can't have the product; (5) I just say no, and that's that; and (6) My child never asks for this product. For purposes of analysis, we grouped the second and third responses together as a "negotiation" strategy.

Extensive pretesting indicated that these six response strategies covered almost all the ways mothers respond to purchase requests. The realism of these situations in the questionnaire is also confirmed by the main survey. Forty percent of the mothers never selected the response "my child never asks for this product" in any of the twelve situations and another 30 percent chose this alternative only once.

As Table 7-9 indicates, mothers of children in all age groups are similar in their frequency of using strategies 1 and 5, i.e., simply buying what the child asked for or refusing the request without explanation. Mothers of varying status levels do not differ, either.

However, we found substantial differences by age and by social class in the frequency of using the other two strategies. For example, mothers of older children are much more likely to negotiate with their child about purchase requests. This finding may be due in part to the older children's greater ability to negotiate on the basis of their capacity to do meaningful chores or pay money from their greater incomes. This interpretation is supported by the data on socio-economic status,

TABLE 7-9.
Mothers' Response Strategies to Children's Specific Purchase Requests
by Grade Level and by Socio-Economic Status

Frequency of Choosing Response Strategy	a. By Grade Level			b. By Socio-Economic Status		
	K %	3 %	6 %	Low %	Medium %	High %
Mother buys what children ask for						
0-3	20	16	14	14	16	22
4-6	42	52	53	50	49	47
7-12	38	32	33	36	35	31
	100	100	100	100	100	100
	$x^2 = 5.96$ (4 d.f.) n.s.			$x^2 = 4.59$ (4 d.f.) n.s.		
Mother and Child discuss and negotiate						
0	51	30	23	40	35	25
1-3	34	43	41	41	37	40
4-12	15	27	36	19	28	35
	100	100	100	100	100	100
	$x^2 = 44.77$ (4 d.f.) $p < .000$			$x^2 = 17.78$ (4 d.f.) $p < .005$		
Mother refuses but explains why						
0-2	15	26	40	39	23	28
3-5	35	34	33	34	38	29
6-12	50	40	27	27	39	43
	100	100	100	100	100	100
	$x^2 = 41.14$ (4 d.f.) $p < .000$			$x^2 = 20.42$ (4 d.f.) $p < .000$		
Mother refuses with no explanation						
0	21	15	18	19	18	19
1-3	36	44	41	39	39	45
4-12	43	41	41	42	43	36
	100	100	100	100	100	100
	$x^2 = 4.71$ (4 d.f.) n.s.			$x^2 = 2.26$ (4 d.f.) n.s.		
N =	(205)	(202)	(208)	(215)	(222)	(170)

which indicate increases in the use of this response strategy by higher-income mothers.

These data may also shed some light on the greater yielding by sixth-graders' mothers. We suggested above that this yielding may be due to the greater persuasion skills of the sixth-graders. Yielding may also involve the mothers' willingness to negotiate purchases with the sixth-graders, who frequently have the resources needed to conduct meaningful negotiations.

The "refuse but explain" response strategy displays the opposite trend, decreasing with age. Fifty percent of the kindergartners' mothers use this response in at least half of the purchase-request situations, compared to only about one-fourth of the sixth-graders' mothers.

It would appear from examining the various response patterns that mothers of all age groups often prefer to refuse purchase requests. However, in many cases the older children have substantial resources for assuming some or all of the cost and hence are able to convince their mothers that they should allow the purchase. On the other hand, younger children, who have few resources for negotiation and perhaps few skills in negotiating, are not able to bargain effectively with mothers. Instead, the younger children's mothers frequently deny the request, at the same time explaining to the child why the purchase cannot be made.

Both the negotiation and "refuse but explain" strategies are used more often by higher-status mothers. This is not because their children have greater financial sources. As will be seen shortly, middle-status and high-status children have lower incomes than low-status children, except for sixth-graders. Perhaps high-status mothers have greater expectations regarding the child's sharing of responsibility for purchases.

Differences by social class in using the "refuse but explain" strategy may simply indicate a greater willingness on the part of high-status mothers to explain things to their child. An alternative interpretation is that middle-status and high-status mothers may find it more necessary to justify their refusal than do low-status mothers with less money. Whatever the basis for the communication, there is a clear increase by social class in mothers' explanations of their denials.

We performed a second analysis of mothers' responses to determine their flexibility in handling purchase requests under different circumstances. We felt that mothers who shifted responses between situations would have greater effectiveness in teaching consumer skills.

To measure flexibility, we classified the mother's use of each response strategy into high use (four times or more) or low use (three times or less). We then totaled the number of response strategies that had high use to obtain a scale from low flexibility (only one response strategy with high use) to high flexibility (three or four response strategies with high use).

About 30 percent of the mothers demonstrate high flexibility in their responses to purchase requests. There are no differences according to the child's age. On the other hand, the mother's flexibility differs by social status in a curvilinear fashion, with medium-status mothers more flexible than low-status or high-status mothers.

To summarize, we find few age differences affecting mother-child interaction about consumption. However, the differences which do occur are probably important, particularly those regarding the substantially greater negotiation that occurs between older children and their mothers.

Differences in mother-child interaction by social class are more frequent, though usually smaller than age differences. Social-class differences indicate a pattern of increased interaction about consumption as status increases, with high-status mothers particularly likely to communicate frequently with their child about consumption.

CHILDREN'S OPPORTUNITIES FOR INDEPENDENT CONSUMPTION

A final way parents can have an important impact on their children's consumer learning is by providing them with opportunities to engage in consumer behavior. Indeed, one-fifth of the mothers say they use this method for teaching consumer skills. These independent consumption opportunities may not teach consumption skills, however, since they may reinforce poor consumer behavior. Whether these consumption opportunities result in the acquisition of consumer skills will be discussed in the next chapter. Here we will focus on how often parents provide independent consumption opportunities.

Children's Purchase Opportunities

One way a parent can provide consumption opportunities is to take her child along on shopping trips. During these trips the child may be able to purchase items. In most cases, the mother will be able to supervise. Shopping trips also enable the child to observe the mother's consumer behavior and to interact with her about products and reasons for buying.

To measure frequency of mother-child shopping, we asked mothers how often they took their child with them on three kinds of trips during the preceding two weeks—grocery shopping, general family shopping, and shopping for the child. We summed the mothers' responses.

Seventy percent of the mothers had taken their child on at least one shopping trip during the preceding two weeks; almost one-third had taken the child on two or more shopping trips. There were no differences by age of the child or social class. These results indicate that children frequently accompany their mother on shopping trips.

A second way parents can provide consumption opportunities is by allowing children to select products on their own. Parents can supervise even when granting purchase authority by discussing purchases before the child makes them.

To index this kind of consumption opportunity, we developed a measure of a child's *power in making purchases.* We asked mothers to indicate how each of nine child-related products—including candy, a snack food, a magazine or book, a game or toy, a ticket to a movie, and sports equipment—was selected when either the mother's or child's money was used. We provided four response alternatives: (1) child

TABLE 7-10

Child's Power in Making Purchases by Grade Level and by Socio-Economic Status

		K %	3 %	6 %	Total %
By Grade Level					
High		18	39	61	40
Medium		39	37	28	34
Low		43	24	11	26
		100	100	100	100
	N =	(204)	(201)	(208)	(613)
		$x^2 = 94.62$ (4 d.f.) $p < .000$			
By Socio-Economic Status					
High		47	37	35	40
Medium		30	36	39	34
Low		23	27	26	26
		100	100	100	100
	N =	(214)	(226)	(170)	(610)
		$x^2 = 7.33$ (4 d.f.) $.05 < p < .10$			

chooses for himself; (2) child chooses but talks to parents first; (3) parent chooses but talks to child first; (4) parents choose without talking to child. Mothers' responses were summed across the nine items as our measure of child's purchase power.

The data show a major linear increase in children's purchase power as they grow older. One-fifth of the kindergartners are given substantial power in making purchase decisions, compared to two-fifths of the third-graders and three-fifths of the sixth-graders. This increase may reflect mother's belief in the greater competence of older children. Perhaps it also indicates their greater willingness to allow older children to spend their money as they choose.

Low-status mothers gave their children somewhat greater purchase power than mothers at the other two status levels.

Children's Income

Parents also provide consumption opportunities for their children by supplying them with money. We asked mothers a series of questions to determine how often they gave money to their children and how much money was provided. Mothers' responses are shown in Table 7-11; these data are comparable to results on children's sources of income as measured in a recent national survey (Reilly, 1973a).

Providing an allowance increases substantially with age, although only one-half of the sixth-graders receive an allowance. Allowance giving also increases slightly with social class.

About half the children in each age group get money as needed—more than the percentage that receive a regular allowance. This form of providing money *decreases* with social class. Two-thirds of the low-status mothers report giving nonallowance money to their child weekly, compared to only two-fifths of the high-status mothers.

Children also earn money by working outside the home. As would be expected, outside earning increases substantially with age, with the biggest jump occurring between third and sixth grade. There are no differences by social class in children's working outside the home.

Combining the various sources of money, we find that almost all children receive money on a regular basis from at least one source. However, the number of sources increases substantially with age, mainly due to an increase in allowances for older children and sixth-graders' outside work. Perhaps surprisingly, children from low-status homes have slightly more sources of income than the other children.

Parents can provide additional consumer-learning opportunities for

TABLE 7-11

Children's Money Opportunities by Grade Level and by Socio-Economic Status

	K %	3 %	6 %	Low %	Medium %	High %
a. Allowance						
Yes	28	46	52	36	43	49
No	72	54	48	64	57	51
	100	100	100	100	100	100
	$x^2 = 26.43$ (2 d.f.) p<.001			$x^2 = 6.77$ (2 d.f.) p<.05		
b. Money Just Given to Child						
Yes	55	51	52	66	55	41
No	45	49	48	34	45	59
	100	100	100	100	100	100
	$x^2 = 2.08$ (2 d.f.) n.s.			$x^2 = 23.74$ (2 d.f.) p<.001		
c. Child Earns Outside Home						
Yes	6	8	29	14	18	11
No	94	92	71	86	82	89
	100	100	100	100	100	100
	$x^2 = 54.28$ (2 d.f.) p<.001			$x^2 = 3.23$ (2 d.f.) n.s.		
d. Number of Money Sources						
0	18	14	5	10	10	18
1	59	54	52	52	59	53
2-3	23	32	43	38	31	29
	100	100	100	100	100	100
	$x^2 = 30.28$ (4 d.f.) p<.001			$x^2 = 10.56$ (4 d.f.) p<.05		
e. Bank Account						
Yes	50	48	63	43	57	64
No	50	52	37	57	43	36
	100	100	100	100	100	100
	$x^2 = 11.16$ (2 d.f.) p<.05			$x^2 = 16.42$ (2 d.f.) p<.001		

TABLE 7-12

Amount of Child's Weekly Money by Grade Level and by Socio-Economic Status

	K %	3 %	6 %	Low %	Medium %	High %
a. Allowance						
$.01–.50	81	61	31	37	59	63
$.51 +	19	39	69	63	41	37
	100	100	100	100	100	100
N =	(58)	(98)	(105)	(78)	(98)	(83)
	$x^2 = 41.68$ (2 d.f.) p<.001			$x^2 = 11.35$ (2 d.f.) p<.01		
b. Just Given						
$.01–.50	67	51	35	44	52	63
$.51 +	33	49	65	56	48	37
	100	100	100	100	100	100
N =	(118)	(103)	(108)	(137)	(124)	(67)
	$x^2 = 24.12$ (2 d.f.) p<.001			$x^2 = 6.05$ (2 d.f.) p<.05		
c. Total Weekly Income						
None	19	14	5	9	10	20
$.01–.50	50	35	11	25	35	34
$.51–1.00	17	23	23	26	18	19
$1.01 +	14	28	61	40	37	27
	100	100	100	100	100	100
N =	(205)	(202)	(208)	(215)	(227)	(170)
	$x^2 = 141.46$ (6 d.f.) p<.001			$x^2 = 24.18$ (6 d.f.) p<.001		

children by establishing a bank account for them (Table 7-11e). The proportion of children having a bank account increases with age and, again, the major jump occurs between third and sixth grade. Nevertheless, half of the kindergartners have bank accounts too; this result is not surprising, since 43 percent of all the bank accounts were established when the children were infants.

Having a bank account increases substantially with social class, rising from about two-fifths of the low-status children to almost two-thirds of the high-status children. This result reflects the greater financial resources of the higher-status families, but it may also be indicative of a greater emphasis on savings by high-status parents.

Data on the amounts of allowance, other money given to the child, and total weekly income are presented in Table 7-12. Older children have substantially larger incomes than younger children. For example, only about one-fifth of the kindergartners with an allowance receive more than 50 cents weekly, compared to two-fifths of the third-graders and two-thirds of the sixth-graders.

Data on social-class differences indicate a consistent pattern of lower-status children receiving more money. This relationship is observed for both kindergartners and third-graders on all income measures. However, among sixth-graders total weekly income is approximately equal for all three status groups. This would seem to indicate that medium-status and high-status parents lessen their restrictiveness— or increase their generosity—as their children near the completion of grade school.

Children's Exposure to Television Advertising

Our final measure of children's independent consumption opportunities is the amount of time children spend viewing television. Children (and adults) seldom watch television to learn about new products or to gain more information about products. Nevertheless, for children, television advertising is a significant point of contact with the marketplace. Thus, we felt exposure to television represents a consumption-related experience for children.

We asked mothers how many hours their children spend watching television on an average weekday after school, on an average weekday evening, and on Saturday. We summed these measures, with appropriate weighting, as an index of the children's exposure to commercials.

Data indicate a slight, nonsignificant increase in television viewing time by age, probably reflecting the older children's somewhat greater opportunity to watch television at night. On the other hand, amount of TV viewing decreases with status level. This result is consistent with a pattern of less supervision and restriction of the child by low-status mothers.

To summarize the data on children's consumption opportunities, older children have a substantially greater opportunity to engage in independent consumer behaviors. They are granted more power to choose products, and the financial resources they have available for purchasing products and for saving are larger. Lower-status children also have consistently greater opportunities for independence as consumers, although the status differences are quite a bit smaller than the age differences. This increased independence for lower-status children is consistent with data on mother-child interaction, which indicated there was less communication—and probably less supervision—concerning children's consumer activities among lower-status families.

PATTERNS IN THE FAMILY CONTEXT FOR CONSUMER SOCIALIZATION

To complete our analysis of the family context for consumer socialization, we were interested in discovering whether the various family-context measures may form a small number of family patterns or types. Research discussed in Chapter 6 indicated this was not likely to be the case, but we were interested in determining whether some patterns might occur in our data. For example, two general dimensions might emerge, such as a mother's general consumer-competency dimension and a mother-child consumption-interaction dimension. If this occurred, we might then be able to construct a fourfold typology of family consumer-socialization contexts.

To investigate this possibility, we conducted factor analyses. First, we randomly split the sample of mothers into two equal groups, then conducted independent factor analyses on each group using principal components analysis with varimax rotation (SPSS Program, 1970). All fifty-two family-context variables discussed in this chapter were included in these analyses. Five factors emerged from these analyses, each of which accounted for at least 5 percent of the total variance in both groups. Further, each factor was structurally similar in terms of the variables included in the factors and the size of the factor loadings for both samples of mothers.

This analysis indicates that a small number of general dimensions do *not* emerge. Only nineteen of the fifty-two family-context variables are included in the five factors, and none of the factors account for much of the variance. It would appear from these analyses that the family consumer socialization context *cannot* adequately be depicted by a small number of family types. Rather, a more meaningful conceptualization views family patterns as a series of response tendencies, in line with our discussion in Chapter 6.

TABLE 7-13
Independent Family Context Variables

Mother-Child Interaction Variables
    1. Frequency of negotiating purchase requests
    2. Frequency of refusal with explanation
    3. *Frequency of not yielding to purchase request
    4. *Frequency of discussing consumption generally
    5. *Number of comments about commercials
    6. Flexibility in responding to purchase requests

Mother's Own Consumer Behavior Variables
    1. Frequency of using contextual attributes in purchases
    2. Frequency of using price/appearance attributes in purchases
    3. Frequency of using advertising attributes in purchases
    4. Relative effectiveness of information use in purchases
    5. Relative efficiency of information use in purchases
    6. Total information use in purchases
    7. Number of sources consulted in major purchases
    8. Budget planning
    9. Budget accounting

Mother's Consumer-Education Goals and Attitude Variables
    1. [+]Number of money goals
    2. [+]Number of quality-shopping goals
    3. [+]Number of bargain goals
    4. Degree of opposition to children's commercials

Child-Opportunity Variables
    1. Number of different sources for money
    2. *Total child income
    3. Frequency of taking child shopping
    4. Child power in making purchases
    5. [+]Frequency of exposure to television commercials

Other
    1. *Family Socio-Economic Status
    2. Grade level of child

    *Selected by means of factor analysis.
    [+]Combination of original variables.

Although the factor analyses did not result in a typology, we used the analysis to reduce the number of family-context variables and eliminate much of the redundancy among variables. Basically, we wished to reduce the independent variable set in order to increase both the ease and meaningfulness of interpretation when examining the relationships between family-context variables and the dependent-child behavior variables.

The five independent factors obtained from the factor analysis (combining nineteen variables) are: (1) frequency of *not* yielding to purchase requests; (2) frequency of discussing consumption generally; (3) number of comments about commercials; (4) total child income; and (5) family socio-economic status.

To reduce the remaining thirty-three variables, we used our judgment to combine variables referring to the same behavior. For example, we summed mother's long-term and short-term goals to form three scales, one each for money, quality shopping, and bargain goals. Similarly, we constructed a new scale of frequency of exposure to television commercials, one of the child-opportunity variables. In each case, when we judgmentally combined variables to form a scale, the correlations among the variables forming the scales were substantial.

We also used our judgment in selecting sixteen unmodified variables to include in subsequent analyses. We chose these variables because they described distinctive aspects of the family-consumer-socialization context and showed some promise of relating to the various children's consumer behaviors. Applying these procedures resulted in the set of twenty-five family context variables, plus child's grade level, shown in Table 7-13. These are the variables we used to examine the relationships between family context and child consumer behavior presented in the next chapter.

SUMMARY: THE FAMILY CONTEXT OF CHILDREN'S CONSUMER SOCIALIZATION

Mothers have few specific goals for their children's consumer learning and few plans for teaching their children consumership. Nevertheless, within the family environment children have the opportunity to learn both effective and ineffective consumer behaviors by observing their parents' consumer practices, by interacting with their parents about products and other consumption activities, and by behaving independently as consumers, with or without parental guidance.

The family context for consumer learning varies in rather consistent ways for different socio-economic status levels. In general, as social status increases, mothers become more active consumers in terms of using more sources of information and more kinds of information in making consumer decisions. Furthermore, interaction with the child about consumption increases as the mother's social status increases. On the other hand, lower-status parents appear to give their children more opportunities to operate as independent consumers by providing higher income levels and more power in making purchases. The greater independence given the low-status children in terms of consumption opportunities is consistent with a pattern of less frequent communication between low-status mothers and their children, particularly in specific product-request situations, and perhaps indicates less supervision of the children's consumer activities.

The family context for consumer socialization differs substantially for children of different ages, too. Although the frequency of interaction about consumption does not differ much by age, the kind of communication that occurs changes markedly, especially in specific purchase-request situations. Mothers of older children are much more likely to negotiate with their child about purchases, whereas mothers of younger children are much more likely to refuse their child's purchase request but explain their reasons for doing so. Furthermore, parents provide older children with substantially greater opportunities for independence as consumers by giving them larger incomes and granting them more authority to make independent purchases.

Lastly, our analysis indicates that it is not meaningful to conceptualize the family consumer-socialization context in terms of either a small number of general dimensions or a small number of family types. Rather, viewing family patterns as a series of response tendencies seems to be more appropriate.

Chapter 8

INFLUENCES ON CHILDREN'S CONSUMER LEARNING

▓▓▓▓▓▓▓▓▓▓▓▓▓▓▓▓▓▓▓▓▓▓▓▓▓▓▓▓▓▓▓▓▓▓▓▓▓▓

In earlier chapters, we have examined changes in children's use of a variety of consumer skills and behaviors (Chapters 4 and 5) and the family context in which children's consumer socialization occurs (Chapter 7). The present chapter examines the relationship between the family context and children's consumer behavior, and provides data relevant to hypotheses stated in Chapter 6. Our intention here is to present a broad picture of our results. Consequently, we have tried to reduce technical discussion in the body of this chapter. Specific regression results used in analyses in this chapter are contained in Appendix C.

OVERVIEW

Our major focus in the present chapter is the relationship between the four classes of family-context variables and the child's skilled and nonskilled behaviors. In conducting the analyses for this chapter, we began with some hypotheses regarding the relationship between each class of family-context variables and the child behaviors. We also expected to find some differences in these relationships across the three age groups, but previous research and theory do not provide a basis for explicit hypotheses regarding the precise nature of age-related differences.

Our hypotheses regarding the relationship between each class of family-context variables and the child's skill or nonskill behaviors are summarized in Table 8-1. For the purposes of this analysis, we have grouped together all three types of child skill behaviors—higher-level information-processing skills and lower-level information-processing skills (both discussed in Chapter 4) and money use skills (discussed in Chapter 5). We expected—and found—few differences among them in their relationship to various family-context variables. On the other hand, we expected—and again found—substantial differences in the relationship between family-context variables and the nonskill behaviors (discussed in Chapter 5). Our hypotheses are:

1. Skill Behaviors

   a. We expect a *positive* relationship between the child's skill behaviors and three classes of support variables—mother-child interaction, mother's own behavior, and mother's consumer education goals.

   b. We expect rather *mixed* relationships between child's skill behaviors and the child independence-opportunity support variables.

TABLE 8-1
General Hypotheses for Relationships Between
Family Context Variables and Child Behaviors

| | Child Consumer Behaviors | |
| | Skill | Nonskill |
Family Context Variables	*Behaviors*	*Behaviors*
Mother-Child Interaction	Positive	Positive
Mother's Own Consumer Behavior	Positive	Mixed
Mother's Consumer Education Goals	Positive	Mixed
Child's Independent Consumption Opportunities	Mixed	Positive

2. Nonskill Behaviors

    a. We expect that reduced control over the child's consumption by parents (indexed by mother-child interaction) and increased independence-consumption opportunities are *positively* related to the performance of the nonskill behaviors.

    b. We expect *mixed* relationships between the child's nonskill behaviors and both mother's own behaviors and mother's consumer-education goals.

TABLE 8-2

Dependent Child Consumer Behavior Variables

Skill Behaviors

A. Higher-level information-processing skills
    1. *Awareness of the purpose of TV commercials
    2. *Asking about performance attributes in TV purchase
    3. *Comparing brands on the basis of performance and ingredient characteristics
    4. Awareness of multiple sources for information about new products
    5. Awareness of brand names

B. Lower-level information-processing skills
    1. Asking about perceptual attributes in TV purchase
    2. Comparing brands on the basis of perceptual characteristics
    3. Awareness of in-store shopping for information about new products

C. Money use skills—savings
    1. *Prescriptive norms—savings
    2. *Proscriptive norms—don't waste money
    3. Proscriptive norms—don't buy specific products
    4. Number of types of prescriptive money norms
    5. Number of types of proscriptive money norms
    6. *Money behavior—savings
    7. Regularity of saving part of child's income
    8. Number of different uses of child's income

Nonskill Behaviors—Spending and Asking for Products
    1. Prescriptive norms—spend
    2. Money behavior—spending
    3. Regularity of spending part of child's income
    4. Asking for food products
    5. Asking for child-related products
    6. Asking for adult products
    7. Asking for brands
    8. Strength of brand preference

*Combination of original variables.

Our analysis plan called for reducing the number of dependent variables utilized in the analysis, since some were redundant, and we thought it desirable to combine a number of dichotomous or trichotomous measures into more reliable scales. Second, we analyzed the relative impact of age compared to all the other independent variables on the child's behaviors. Third, we conducted separate regression analyses for each grade level, regressing the four classes of family-context variables on each dependent variable. Lastly, we conducted several analyses with kindergartners designed to assess several alternative roles the family may play in children's consumer socialization.

In combining scales in order to reduce the number of dependent variables, two or more variables were combined only when · they referred to essentially the same behavior. For example, we initially coded children's reports of their saving behavior into two categories— short-term saving and long-term saving. In the analysis reported here, the two dichotomous variables are combined into a single trichotomous variable. The same combining procedure was used with a number of other variables. In addition, two other variables that were essentially measures of verbal ability were eliminated.

The result of this data reduction was a set of twenty-four dependent-child consumer-behavior variables. These variables are listed in Table 8-2, categorized in terms of the classification scheme discussed in Chapters 4 and 5. The remainder of the analyses in this chapter will focus on these twenty-four variables.

AGE AS AN EXPLANATORY VARIABLE

We began our analysis of the relationships between the family-context variables and child behaviors by focusing again on age as an independent variable. We knew from our analyses in Chapters 4 and 5 that age was a reasonably strong predictor variable for · many child behaviors, particularly higher-level information-processing skills. However, for a number of child behaviors—even for money use skills—age accounted for a relatively small percentage of the variance. Consequently, we were interested in examining the explanatory value of age when other independent variables were also included as potential explanatory variables.

To examine this question, we conducted multiple regression analyses with the total sample of children using the SPSS program (Nie et al., 1970). In these analyses, all twenty-six of the independent variables listed in Table 7-13 were included. Results indicated that age is the best predictor variable for all but four of the twenty-four child variables. Even when the zero-order correlation between age and the dependent-child variable is rather low, age is the best predictor in most instances. There would seem to be three plausible explanations for this result.

First, it may be the case that *none* of the family-context variables we identified and measured has much impact on children's consumer learning. This explanation would lead us to reject the hypotheses listed earlier, or at least to severely question our selection of variables and measures.

Second, it may be that age is strongly related to most family-context variables, and as a consequence age "overpowers" these variables in the regression analyses. However, as we saw in Chapter 7, age is *not* related to most family-context variables; indeed, the average correlation between age and these variables is only .11. Thus, it would appear that we can reject this explanation because of the generally low relationship between age and the independent variables.

A third explanation is that the family-context variables of significance for any particular child behavior may differ for the three age groups. As we noted in Chapter 6, the theoretical literature on socialization research suggests that environmental factors may operate quite differently on children at different ages. If this is the case, the impact of a single family-context variable important in only one age group might be substantially diminished when all three age groups are combined in the analysis. This kind of condition is analogous to an "interaction," but it is difficult to identify adequately using a linear additive model such as a multiple-regression approach. By conducting multiple-regression analyses *separately* for each of the age groups it is possible to determine whether or not this explanation is plausible. At the same time, separate subgroup regressions make possible an evaluation of the first explanation—that none of the family-context variables has much impact on children's consumer learning. All of the remaining discussion in this chapter will involve analyses conducted separately for the three grade levels—kindergarten, third grade, and sixth grade.

PATTERNS OF RELATIONSHIPS WITHIN GRADE LEVEL

To identify possible age differences in relationship patterns, we conducted a separate set of multiple regressions for the twenty-four child-consumer behavior variables for children in each of the three grades. In each regression, all twenty-five of the independent family-context variables were included.

The first question to ask concerning these analyses is whether much of the variance in children's behavior is being explained. About 12 percent of the variance within both the skill and nonskill behaviors is accounted for by the family-context variables (Table 8-3). Further, the variance accounted for at each grade level is essentially the same. Although 12 percent of the variance is not large, it is a reasonable amount in the type of research being discussed here. Translated into other terms, 12 percent of the variance accounted for is equivalent to a multiple R of about .3.6.

The next question to ask concerning the analyses is whether there appear to be meaningful *patterns* among the family-context/child-behavior relationships. For purposes of identifying those family-context variables which provided significant support for the child's performance of a behavior, we utilized a stepwise regression procedure. Our criterion for accepting a family-context variable as an important support variable was that the addition of the variable increased the variance accounted for by at least half of 1 percent. In practice, the number of family-context variables identified as important support variables for each child behavior ranged from five to fourteen, with an average of eight.

Our analysis of the pattern of relationship involved identifying whether a class of family-context variables were generally *positively* related to a set of child behaviors, were generally *negative,* or were *mixed* with some positive and some negative relationships. We hypothesized both positive and mixed patterns, but no negative patterns (see Table 8-1).

TABLE 8-3

Average Percentage of Variance of Child Skill and Nonskill Behaviors Accounted for by Family-Context Variables Within Each Grade Level*

		K %	3 %	6 %
Skill Behaviors		12.6	11.6	12.9
	N =	(16)	(16)	(16)
Nonskill Behaviors		12.9	11.8	12.0
	N =	(8)	(8)	(8)

*N's are the number of regressions conducted for each class of variables within each grade level. The number of respondents included in each regression analysis is as follows: K = 205, 3 = 202, 6 = 208.

In order to categorize a pattern of relationships as positive, mixed, or negative, we first recorded all the beta-values for each significant family-context variable in the sixteen regressions with child-skill behaviors (i.e., those that accounted for at least half of 1 percent of the variance). Then, for each class of family-context variables, such as mother-child interaction, we counted the number of positive relationships and the number of negative ones. If at least *two-thirds* of the beta-values for this class of family-context variables are positive, we categorize the pattern of relationships as *positive.* [1] If between one-third and two-thirds of the relationships are positive, we categorize the pattern as *mixed.* We call this a mixed pattern because such a set of relationships included substantial numbers of both positive and negative values with no clear-cut pattern. We planned to classify patterns as *negative* if less than one-third of the relationships were positive, but none of the patterns in the present research was generally negative.

As an example of these analytic procedures, consider the following patterns for kindergartners. We find that in the sixteen regressions involving skill behaviors, a mother-child interaction variable has a significant positive beta-value thirty-three times and a significant negative beta-value only seven times. Thus, 83 percent of the significant relationships between mother-child interaction variables and children's skill are positive. Therefore, we classify this pattern as *positive.* In these same sixteen regressions, a mother's own consumer-behavior variable has a significant positive relationship eighteen times and a significant negative one nineteen times. Thus, 49 percent of the significant relationships between mother's own consumer behavior and child's skills are positive; we classify this pattern as *mixed.*

Patterns of Relationships Between Family Influences and Children's Skill Behaviors

Let us first examine relationships between the various family-context variables and children's skills. The results indicate *clear differences by age* in terms of the pattern of relationships. Mother-child interaction variables clearly provide positive support for the kindergartner's performance of consumer skills, but not for third-graders and sixth-graders, where the pattern of relationships is mixed. This result suggests that the role of parent-child interaction in supporting the child's performance of various consumer skills decreases with age; for older children, mother-child interaction is equally likely to facilitate or hinder the performance of skills. The same pattern emerges for mother's goals and for children's opportunity variables, i.e., a change from positive support among kindergartners to a mixed pattern among both third- and sixth-graders.

The pattern for mothers' own behaviors is just the opposite; these behaviors are mixed in their impact on kindergartners' performance of consumer skills, but are clearly supportive of third-graders' and sixth-graders' skill performance.

These results are surprising in some respects and not in others. It is hardly surprising that the mother's own consumer behavior does not have a clear positive impact on the kindergartner's behavior. The kinds of consumer information-processing skills we measured among mothers would certainly seem to be more subtle and abstract than those which a kindergartner could be expected to understand. On the other hand, it would not be surprising for the mother's information-processing behaviors to serve as a positive model for older children because of older children's ability to understand their mother's behavior and integrate it with their own.

In addition, it is not surprising that a mother who frequently talks to

TABLE 8-4

Patterns of Relationships Between Each Class of Family Context Variables and Children's Consumer-Skill Variables by Grade Level

		K %	3 %	6 %
Type of Pattern				
Mother-Child Interaction		Positive	Mixed	Mixed
Mother's Own Behavior		Mixed	Positive	Positive
Mother's Goals/Attitudes		Positive	Mixed	Mixed
Children's Opportunities		Positive	Mixed	Mixed
Percentage of Positive Relationships [*]				
Mother-Child Interaction		83	58	53
	N =	(40)	(33)	(36)
Mother's Own Behavior		49	67	68
	N =	(37)	(36)	(41)
Mother's Goals/Attitudes		81	68	52
	N =	(26)	(19)	(23)
Children's Opportunities		68	48	62
	N =	(28)	(23)	(24)

[*] N's refer to the total number of statistically significant regression coefficients within each class of family context variables for the regression runs of the 16 dependent consumer skill variables.

her kindergartner about consumption and explains to him why he can or cannot have products would teach him various consumer skills which he could then perform on his own. What is surprising is that the positive relationship between mother-child interaction and children's skill performance does not continue for third-graders and sixth-graders. Perhaps the impact of this kind of interaction on the children's skill learning simply stops after a certain period of time and the mechanism for the child's learning shifts from interaction to observation of others' behavior. This may be the case, but it is certainly surprising that the positive impact of mother-child interaction on skill learning doesn't extend at least through the third grade.

An explanation for the finding of a relatively mixed impact of mother-child interaction on third-graders' and sixth-graders' skill performance might be that the rather gross kinds of interaction behavior we measured have little utility for children's skill learning after early childhood. At this point, more subtle aspects of parent-child interaction about consumption could begin to have a major impact on children's skill learning.

The decrease in positive impact of mother's goals on skill performance from kindergarten to third and sixth grade may simply indicate that the major way in which these goals are communicated to the child is through interaction; thus, if interaction variables do not have an impact on the child's skill performance it is not surprising that the mother's goals do not have an impact either.

The similar decrease in the positive impact of children's opportunities on skill performance is somewhat surprising. Perhaps providing a child with increased opportunities to play the consumer role facilitates skill learning only when some level of supervision is maintained. We saw in Chapter 7 that parents exert substantially more control over kindergartners' purchases than over third-graders' or sixth-graders' purchases. On the other hand, the relatively less supervised consumer behavior of third-graders and sixth-graders may make skill learning through performance pretty much a matter of trial and error for the older children. It could be that the errors balance out about equally with the successes, at least in terms of learning consumer skills.

Patterns of Relationships Between Family Influences and Children's Nonskill Behavior

Some evidence in support of the trial-and-error interpretation advanced above can be found in Table 8-5, which shows the pattern of relationships between the various family-context variables and the children's nonskill behaviors. For purposes of this analysis, we reversed three of the six mother-child interaction measures, changing them from measures of interaction with the child about purchase requests to measures of *lack* of interaction. Then, in looking at the relationship between the mother-child interaction variables and children's nonskill behaviors, we find that the interaction variables provide positive support for children's performance in all three age groups. These results indicate that lack of communication about the child's purchase requests combined with frequent communication about consumption in general results in higher levels of nonskill behaviors (i.e., spending and asking for products) for children in all age groups. Thus, it would appear that lower levels of supervision of children's purchases results in increased general consumption by the child. This pattern holds for each age group.

Further indication that providing children with consumption opportunities may indeed result in hit-or-miss learning can be seen in the last row of Table 8-5. The pattern of relationships for both third-graders

TABLE 8.5

Patterns of Relationships Between Each Class of Family-Context Variables and Children's Nonskill Consumer Behaviors by Grade Level

		K %	3 %	6 %
Type of Pattern				
Mother-child Interaction		Positive	Positive	Positive
Mother's Own Behavior		Mixed	Mixed	Mixed
Mother's Goals/Attitudes		Mixed	Mixed	Mixed
Children's Opportunities		Positive	Mixed	Mixed
Percentage of Positive Relationships[*]				
Mother-child Interaction		77	82	100
	N =	(22)	(22)	(20)
Mother's Own Behavior		35	56	52
	N =	(17)	(18)	(23)
Mother's Goals/Attitudes		85	70	52
	N =	(6)	(12)	(8)
Children's Opportunities		85	70	53
	N =	(13)	(10)	(19)

[*]N's refer to the total number of statistically significant regression coefficients within each class of family-context variables for the regression runs of the eight dependent nonskill consumer behavior variables.

and sixth-graders is mixed, possibly indicating that increasing older children's consumption opportunities by giving them more money and more power in choosing products for themselves doesn't always result in more frequent spending and asking. On the other hand, increasing consumption opportunities for kindergartners clearly produces an increase in their spending and asking.

The mixed pattern of relationships between nonskill behaviors and both the mother's own behavior and her consumer-education goals for all age groups would appear to indicate that these aspects of the family context neither motivate children to consume nor inhibit these aspects of consumer socialization.

Summary: Patterns of Relationships Within Age Groups

The various classes of family-support variables examined here do appear to have different impacts on children's behavior at the three grade levels examined in this research. Thus, the data suggest that the most plausible explanation of our initial regression analyses with the total sample is the third—the "interaction" prediction. It will be recalled that in these initial analyses, the family-context variables were generally poor predictors of children's behavior. Age was the best predictor for nearly all child-behavior variables, and the family-support variables did not increase explanatory power to any major extent. In the subsequent analyses for the three separate grade levels, family-context variables did increase our explanatory power, but the importance of specific support variables changed between kindergarten and third grade. In particular, mother-child interaction variables were consistently important for the development of kindergartners' consumer skills. On the other hand, mothers' own consumer behavior appeared to be consistently important for older children's skill development.

These results suggest that a change occurs in the learning process of consumer skills between kindergarten and third grade in that younger children learn more through a relatively direct "teaching" process and older children learn more indirectly through observation. Future research should examine this possible change in the learning process underlying consumer socialization. In conducting such an investigation in future research, it should be remembered that the largest changes in children's consumer skills—particularly higher-level information-processing skills—are a function of age-related changes, perhaps primarily those involving the development of more sophisticated cognitive capabilities.

ALTERNATIVE PROCESSES IN THE DEVELOPMENT
OF CONSUMER SKILLS

To say that the largest changes in children's consumer skills are a result of age-related cognitive changes does *not* mean that environmental influences are unimportant. Cognitive development theory suggests that a child's interaction with his environment propels cognitive changes, but an important question concerns how these changes actually occur. This is the broader question of the functional processes by which cognitive development occurs, a question that is only beginning to be answered as cognitive development theories add a functional component to the basically structural orientation adopted by more classical cognitive development theorists (Pascal-Leone, 1970; Case, 1974).

The data in the present study present a limited opportunity for examining possible alternative developmental processes in terms of three sets of variables: general cognitive abilities, consumer skills, and family variables. Although there may be a number of developmental processes which involve these classes of variables, three seem to be particularly plausible.

The first process would occur in the following sequence: the major impact of the family would be on the development of general cognitive abilities which, in turn, would be the major determinant of the child's use of consumer skills. This process can be diagrammed as follows:

(1)   family $- - - \rightarrow$ cognitive ability $- - - \rightarrow$ consumer skills

With this process, we would expect a substantial relationship between the family variables and the child's cognitive abilities. Further, we would expect substantial correlations between the child's cognitive abilities and his use of consumer skills. Finally, we should expect rather low relationships between the family variables and the consumer skills *when the child's general cognitive ability is controlled,* since the impact of the family is assumed to occur *through* its influence on general cognitive development.

The second process involves a substantially different role for the family. In this process, the family may have some impact on the development of the child's general cognitive abilities. However, a more important role for the family is one of influencing the child's *application* of his cognitive abilities in specific situations, as depicted below.

$$\text{(2)} \quad \text{cognitive ability} \; - - - - \overset{\overset{\textstyle family}{\downarrow}}{-} - - - \to \text{consumer skills}$$

If this process is applicable we would expect a substantial relationship between the cognitive ability and the consumer skills, but this would not simply be a linear relationship. Rather, we would expect that cognitive ability is a *necessary condition* for the performance of the consumer skill. Children with low cognitive ability would not be able to perform the skill, but children with high cognitive ability would be able to do so. However, whether they perform the skill would depend upon the family context. In this process, the family's main impact on development would be in motivating the child to use his general cognitive abilities in a specific area of application—in this case, consumer skills.

The third process involves another substantially different role for the family. The family's primary impact is directly on the child's learning of consumer skills. In this process, the performance of consumer skills is not related to the child's general cognitive ability, but it is directly related to the family variables, as diagrammed:

$$\text{(3)} \quad \text{family} \; - - - \to \text{consumer skills}$$

Here we would expect little relationship between the child's general cognitive ability and the consumer skills either as a direct relationship or as a necessary condition. However, we would expect substantial relationships between the family variables and consumer skills.

We assessed which of these three alternative learning processes is most appropriate, utilizing the following data:

cognitive ability– measured by "perceptual boundedness"

family variables–the four classes of family-context variables used in the regression analysis

consumer skills–the five higher-level information-processing skills

We have restricted our analysis to the higher-level information-processing skills because it is for these variables that we would expect the greatest relationship with the child's general cognitive ability. Furthermore, we are limiting our analysis to kindergartners since only with this group are there substantial numbers of children with low cognitive ability. Thus, only the kindergartners will provide an adequate test of the three development processes. We will examine each process in turn.

Family Impact on Development of General Cognitive Ability

When we performed a regression analysis of the family context variables on perceptual boundedness, our measure of general cognitive ability, we find that we are able to account for 17 percent of the variance—a figure comparable to that for the higher level information processing skills themselves. Furthermore, of the seven variables entering the equation, three are mother-child interaction variables and one is socio-economic status. This also is similar to the pattern of family influences on the children's consumer skills. Thus, it is possible that the family's main impact on children's performance of higher-level information-processing skills is indirectly ocurring through its influence on their cognitive ability.

As hypothesized in this process, perceptual boundedness is also substantially related to each of the information-processing skills. The average correlation is .28 with a range from .21 to .43. Thus, both of these sets of data conform to expectations.

When regression analyses are performed on the five skills, with perceptual boundedness included as an explanatory variable, two different pictures emerge. For three skills—understanding the purpose of TV commercials, asking about performance attributes in TV purchase, and awareness of multiple sources of information about new products—both perceptual boundedness and family variables account for substantial amounts of variance. For these three skills, perceptual boundedness accounts for an average of 10.9 percent of the variance and family variables account for an average of 10 percent.

On the other hand, for the remaining two consumer skills—comparing brands on the basis of performance and ingredient characteristics, and awareness of brand names—family variables account for much more variance then perceptual boundedness, an average of 14.8 percent compared to an average of only 3 percent due to perceptual boundedness.

It would seem, then, that family-consumer socialization variables have some impact on the development of children's general cognitive abilities, which in turn influences their performance of consumer skills, at least the first three skills. On the other hand, even for these three skills, the family's impact on the child's performance of skills is not entirely filtered through cognitive ability. Thus, for all of these skills the family's influence may involve other processes as well.

The next question to examine is whether this influence occurs more as a function of family influences on the child's *application* of his general cognitive ability, or as a function of teaching specific consumer skills.

Family Impact on Application of Cognitive Ability

To determine the extent of family influence on motivating children to apply general cognitive ability, we divided the kindergartners into two groups. The first group is comprised of children scoring low in cognitive ability, i.e., in differentiating between common objects in their environment, they did so almost exclusively in terms of physical, or perceptual, characteristics of objects. Children higher in cognitive ability, on the other hand, differentiated between the objects in terms of activities performed and functions as well as perceptual characteristics. We were interested here in determining whether this cognitive ability was a necessary condition for the performance of the consumer skills.

The classic picture of cognitive ability as a necessary condition for skill performance was observed for one of the consumer skills. This is shown in Table 8-6. These data suggest that only children with at least medium cognitive ability have much awareness of commercials. Among children with low cognitive ability (i.e., high perceptual boundedness), fully 92 percent exhibit a low awareness of commercials. Apparently, understanding the persuasive function of commercials requires a higher-level cognitive skill, indicated here by classifying children in terms of their ability to go beyond simply the physical characteristics of objects when comparing them.

For two other consumer skills there appears to be some tendency for cognitive ability to function as a necessary condition for the performance of the skills. These relationships are shown in Table 8-7.

TABLE 8-6

Perceptual Boundness by Awareness of Commercials for Kindergartners

		Cognitive Skill-Perceptual Boundedness	
		Lower %	Higher %
Awareness of Commercials			
Low		92	60
Medium		8	40
	Total	100	100
	N =	(85)	(119)
		$x^2 = 25.95$ (1 d.f.) $p < .001$	

TABLE 8-7
Perceputal Boundedness by (a) Awareness of Multiple-Information Sources
and (b) Asking About Functional Characteristics for Kindergartners

		(a) Cognitive Ability				(b) Cognitive Ability	
		Lower %	Higher %			Lower %	Higher %
Awareness of Multiple Information Sources	Low	74	48	Asking About Functional Characteristics	Low	69	49
	High	26	52		High	31	51
		100	100			100	100
	N =	(85)	(119)		N =	(85)	(119)
		$x^2 = 14.07, p < .001$				$x^2 = 8.66, p < .005$	

Although the pattern is not so strong as it was with awareness of commercials, less than one-third of the low-cognitive-ability kindergartners perform both these skills at more than a low level, compared to half of the higher-ability kindergartners. This suggests that the family may influence the child's *application* of these two skills, in line with the second process, as well as influencing the performance of the skills by having an impact on the development of perceptual boundedness, as our earlier analysis indicates.

For these three skills, the family-context variables have a substantial impact on the performance among higher-cognitive-ability children, as this process implies. Within higher-ability kindergartners, family-context variables account for an average of 24 percent of the variance in performance of these three consumer skills.

Thus, the necessary conditions analysis and the subsequent regression analysis with higher-cognitive-ability kindergartners would appear to provide some support for the second influence process we suggested: the interpretation of the family's major role as one of helping the child to apply his general cognitive ability in the consumer area.

Direct Family Impact on Consumer Skill Development

The direct relationships between perceptual boundedness and the remaining two consumer skills are relatively low. The correlation between perceptual boundedness and awareness of brands is .22, and with use of ingredients and functional characteristics in brand comparisons the correlation is .21. A necessary conditions analysis of the relationship between perceptual boundedness and these two skills indicates that cognitive ability is *not* a necessary condition for performance of these skills. There are essentially no differences between lower- and higher-cognitive-ability kindergartners in their use of these skills. Thus, as the direct-family-impact process predicts, cognitive ability has neither a direct nor a necessary condition relationship with these two consumer skills.

On the other hand, for both of these consumer skills, family variables account for about 15 percent of the variance in kindergartners' performance of the skills. Perhaps it is with these skills that parents most directly "teach" consumer skills, in line with the third developmental process.

Summary: Developmental Processes

The data provide some support for each of the three alternative roles of the family in the development of kindergartners' consumer information-processing skills. But further, it appears that different processes may be involved in learning different skills. In particular, the process involving family impact on general cognitive development which in turn leads to skill performance is perhaps most characteristic of the development of two skills: asking about performance characteristics of products and awareness of multiple sources of information. The second process, involving family impact on application of cognitive ability, seems to characterize development of one skill: understanding the purpose of commercials. The third process, involving a direct family impact on the development of skills, appears to be involved in the development of two skills: awareness of brands and use of ingredients and functional characteristics in brand comparison.

Thus, the family's impact on kindergartners' development of consumer skills functions both in direct and indirect ways. The indirect impact would probably be even greater if other cognitive abilities of the child and other aspects of the family context, which also influence development of general cognitive abilities, had been measured.

Clearly, these results are tentative ones, and they contain some inconsistencies, e.g., the lack of relationship between perceptual boundedness and use of nonphysical attributes in brand comparisons. When combined with results from earlier analyses indicating the shift in the family-context variables of significance between kindergarten and third grade, however, the data suggest a rather complicated role for the family in the child's socialization as a consumer.

It appears, then, that the family's role in the development of children's consumer skills is probably greater than our earlier analyses would have suggested. We had found that family variables accounted for only about 10 to 15 percent of the variance in children's use of consumer skills at each of the three grade levels. Since no measures of cognitive abilities were included, we were essentially examining the family's impact on motivating children to apply cognitive abilities, and its effects on direct consumer skills teaching in these analyses. However, our analysis of the relationship between family consumer-socialization variables and the child's perceptual boundedness indicated that family variables also have an impact on the child's acquisition of a general cognitive ability and, indirectly, on consumer-skill development. In short, these data are suggestive in pointing to a highly important area for further research—the alternative roles the family plays in the child's consumer socialization.

Two developments will be particularly important in helping us to begin to understand the complexity of the process. First are functional conceptualizations of the role of the child's experience in his cognitive and behavioral development. In these functional conceptualizations, the active role played by the child in both creating his experiences and interpreting them must be highlighted.

Second, research designs must be utilized which will capture the changes in cognitive abilities and in consumer behaviors. To some extent, over-time measurements must be taken, but this need not imply only elaborate long-term longitudinal studies. Reasonably short-term longitudinal studies and field and laboratory experiments may be of substantial value in more precisely specifying the interaction of the family and children's cognitive abilities over the process of consumer socialization.

NOTE

1. If the number of entries in a cell was small (i.e., less than twenty), we required that at least 80 percent of the relationships must be positive ones in order to classify that category as positive. This was done to take into account the relative instability of percentages based on rather small frequencies.

PART IV

IMPLICATIONS OF THE RESEARCH

Chapter 9 ░░

PUBLIC-POLICY ISSUES

░░

BACKGROUND

The development and introduction of presweetened cereals over the past two decades signaled a realization among major U.S. marketers that children comprise a distinct market segment. Children have lower disposable income and directly buy goods less frequently than adults, but their influence on some purchases is substantial. Sales in the presweet-cereal category indicate that mothers are often quite responsive to their children's product desires.

The marketing task of reaching child audiences is considerably simpler than defining and reaching adult audiences, since television is clearly the dominant advertising medium to which children attend. This concentration of advertising, accompanied by emerging "consumerist" concerns with the quality of programming during children's prime viewing hours, and questions concerning product quality have combined over the past several years to thrust the question of effects of television advertising on children into the forefront of "consumerism" issues. Questions of appropriate public-policy responses have been raised by federal regulatory agencies such as the Federal Trade Commission and the Federal Communications Commission. Activist groups such as Action for Children's Television initially advocated removal of all advertising from children's programming and recently proposed more moderate steps, e.g., elimination of certain kinds of advertising, such as commercials in which program hosts are also used to promote products. Most recently groups such as the Council of Children, Merchandising, and Media have expressed concern about the products themselves as well as the advertising for them, including products containing significant amounts of sugar and over-the-counter medicines. These groups have also pointed out that most children's television viewing occurs at times other than Saturday mornings. This in turn raises the issue of effects of advertising which is clearly not directed at child audiences but rather at adult market segments.

For their part, advertisers perceive that regulation of advertising practices affecting children is a distinct possibility. Television commercials do not enjoy the same First Amendment protections as programming content; more importantly, advertising issues are obviously appealing to politicians. Advertisers have responded by advocating self-regulation of advertising to children. The National Association of Broadcasters, representing station licensees, and the Association of National Advertisers, representing marketers, both have extensive codes or sets of guidelines defining acceptable and unacceptable practices in advertising to children. Recently, a Children's Review Unit was formed within the National Council of Better Business Bureaus to perform a watchdog role.

Defining the Issues

Probably all reasonable parties to the controversy would agree that it is difficult to identify and specify exactly what are the issues concerning effects of television advertising on children. The primary reason for the difficulty is that positions have been taken which are deeply rooted in personal values. For example, some argue that skepticism about advertising claims among older children is a healthy "cognitive filter"; others argue that this skepticism is part of a larger syndrome of "breeding a generation of cynics." As another example, critics of advertising charge that cumulative exposure to commercials results in "materialistic" orientations; others feel that it is exactly this long-term exposure which results in positive integration of children into the

American free enterprise system: one man's "materialism" is another's "consumer socialization."

A National Science Foundation-sponsored study team surveyed literature and individuals in government, consumer groups, and industry in an attempt to define the issues (Adler et al., 1976). The study team argues that the most practical way of specifying the issues is in terms of advertising characteristics, since these can be identified and changed directly, if necessary. Particular characteristics identified as issues include premium offers and contest promotions, self-concept appeals, host selling, food and medicine advertising. However, the study team also specifies three "mediating effects" as issues: effects of volume and repetition of commercials, effects of television advertising on consumer socialization, and effects on parent-child relations.

The Role of Research

It is probably safe to conclude that the pace of the controversies surrounding advertising to children have outrun the ability of researchers to undertake sound research pertaining to the issues. Obviously, research and theory in child development and socialization is pertinent, and some research has explored children's responses to advertising through survey and laboratory methods. Few studies have directly focused on specific issues, however, or even included particular commercials as stimulus materials.

In 1975, a conference convened by three foundations identified research on television advertising effects as a top priority for funding in the area of television effects on children.[1] The conference identified three approaches to research in this area: research targeted on specific policy issues (e.g., effects of premium offers in advertising to children); more theoretical research which is basic to a number of issues (e.g., relationship of children's conceptual abilities to questions of understanding advertising content); and longitudinal research among large samples of families to observe various effects of advertising as they develop in the natural environment and the mediating role of other influences on children.

ANALYSES

Our approach to the research reported here falls within the category of "basic" research applications to policy issues. We were particularly interested in some questions which we feel are basic to a range of issues concerning advertising and children. We focused on the following questions:

1. Does a general understanding of the persuasive intent of commercials provide children with a "cognitive filter," which in turn is related to their desires for products?

2. Can parents or others provide children with some kind of training which would result in increased understanding of the intent of commercials?

3. What impact does exposure to television advertising have on the development of consumer skills?

Analyses in preceding chapters have touched on these questions. In this chapter, we examine them explicitly, because of their importance to current issues of public policy. In the concluding chapter, we offer some further thoughts concerning the role of research in this area.

Understanding of the Intent of Commercials

There is little doubt that commercials motivate children to buy products or to ask their parents to buy products for them. Perhaps the most convincing data regarding the effectiveness of commercials in motivating children's purchase behavior are data concerning brand-asking behavior. For the four product classes we asked about (soft drinks, soup, candy, and cereals), at least 40 percent of the children in each age group asked for specific brands of the product. In most instances, two-thirds or more asked for specific brands. This is the case even though the vast majority of kindergartners cannot read. Clearly advertisers wish to have children learn their brand name and to use it in asking for products, and they are often successful.

The question remains, however, whether children may have some sort of "cognitive filter" which may lessen the persuasive effects of commercials. Such a filter might operate in several ways. First, it might help children to recognize that commercials are trying to sell products and, therefore, they should carefully evaluate advertising messages and their own wants. Second, a cognitive filter might lead children to be skeptical of advertising claims. Indeed, our data show that only among kindergartners do appreciable numbers of children believe that commercials *always* tell the truth. Third, this filter might have the impact of reducing the frequency of children's asking for products. Finally, the cognitive filter may serve the function of directing the child *away from* advertising-oriented attributes of a product (such as brand name or product symbols) and *toward* performance and functional attributes in product-choice decisions.

To assess these possibilities, we divided our sample into two groups in terms of their responses to the question, "What is a TV commercial?" Children who explicitly stated that commercials tried to sell products were assumed to have a "cognitive filter" in that they clearly understood advertisers' selling intent. Children who did not explicitly mention this selling intent were assumed to not have the filter. In the following analyses, we refer to these groups as "filters"

TABLE 9-1

Frequency of Purchase Requests for Kindergartners With and Without a Cognitive Filter

		No Filter %	Filter %
Food			
High		46	22
Medium		46	67
Low		8	11
		100	100
	N =	(167)	(37)
		$x^2 = 7.48$ (2 d.f.), $p < .05$	
Nonfood Grocery			
High and medium		21	0
Low		47	49
Very low		32	51
		100	100
	N =	(167)	(37)
		$x^2 = 10.84$ (2 d.f.) $p < .05$	
Child-Relevant			
High		16	8
Medium		48	46
Low		36	46
		100	100
	N =	(167)	(37)
		$x^2 = 1.81$ (2 d.f.), n.s.	

and "nonfilters." Only 18 percent of the kindergartners were classified as filters, but 73 percent of the third-graders and 90 percent of the sixth-graders we classified so. Since so few of the sixth-graders were nonfilters, we do not include them in the analyses to follow.

To determine whether knowledge of the selling intent of commercials serves as a cognitive filter to reduce frequency of product requests, we analyzed purchase requests for food, nonfood grocery, and child-relevant products. Among kindergartners, filters asked for food products and for nonfood products *less* frequently than nonfilters (Table 9-1). However, they show little tendency to ask for child-relevant products less frequently. Among third-graders, children do not differ in frequency of purchase requests for any of the three product types.

These data suggest that a "cognitive filter," indexed here by degree of understanding the selling intent of commercials, does reduce the frequency of purchase requests, but only for the youngest children in our sample. In order to determine whether it serves a different function for the third-graders, we examined whether the filter serves to direct children's attention to performance and functional attributes in product-choice decisions. First, we analyzed the kinds of information children sought in the hypothetical television-buying situation. Second, we looked at the kinds of information they used in differentiating between brands in the brand-choice situations.

As data in Table 9-2 indicate, among both kindergartners and third-graders filters were *more* likely to inquire about performance characteristics of the product (television) than nonfilters. Similarly, in comparing two brands of three different products (toothpaste, peanut butter, and a milk additive), filters were *more* likely to use performance and ingredient attributes in comparing the brands than were nonfilters.

For both the youngest children and third-graders, cognitive filtering appears to direct children toward performance and functional attributes. It should be remembered from the last chapter that a necessary condition for the acquisition of a "filter" is that the child reach a general level of cognitive ability enabling him to decenter his attention to consider nonperceptual characteristics of objects. This suggests that perhaps teaching even young children who have reached a higher level of cognitive ability about the general purpose of commercials and the intent of advertisements may facilitate early development of more skillful consumers. How this might be done in the family is discussed in the next section.

TABLE 9-2

**Number of Performance Attributes in TV Purchases for Children
With and Without a Cognitive Filter**

	Kindergarten			Third Grade	
	No Filter %	Filter %		No Filter %	Filter %
0	37	25		31	20
1	38	27		49	45
2	25	48		20	35
	100	100		100	100
N =	(168)	(37)		(55)	(147)
	$x^2 = 9.57$ (2 d.f.), $p < .05$			$x^2 = 5.12$ (2 d.f.), $.05 < p < .10$	

TABLE 9-3

**Use of Performance and Ingredients Attributes in Brand Comparisons
for Children With and Without a Cognitive Filter**

	Kindergarten			Third Grade	
	No Filter %	Filter %		No Filter %	Filter %
High	21	48		35	59
Medium	36	25		36	21
Low	43	27		29	20
	100	100		100	100
N =	(168)	(37)		(55)	(147)
	$x^2 = 11.94$ (2 d.f.), $p < .01$			$x^2 = 9.70$ (2 d.f.), $p < .05$	

Teaching Young Children the Purposes of Commercials

Results presented in Chapter 4 indicated that kindergartners have a generally low level of understanding of commercials and their purpose. Indeed, only 18 percent of these young children are aware of the selling intent. On the other hand, nearly three-fourths of the third-graders have an understanding of the persuasion function of commercials. Can children be taught to more adequately comprehend and evaluate television commercials?

Data concerning the relationship between family-context variables and children's understanding of commercials indicate that parents can help their children to learn about the selling intent of commercials by talking with them. The top three variables in explaining kindergartners' level of understanding commercials were mother-child interaction variables—discussing purchase requests with children, *not* yielding to children's purchase requests, and talking about commercials with children. On the other hand, the mother-child interaction variables were *not* important in explaining third-graders' and sixth-graders' level of understanding. Among third-graders none of the interaction variables accounted for more than half of 1 percent of the variance, and among sixth-graders only one interaction variable did so, and this variable was negatively related to level of understanding.

These data indicate that parents can have a substantial impact on young children's understanding of commercials by talking with them about commercials and about products they request. For older children who generally have an understanding of commercials' intent, such interaction would probably do little to increase their already-developed understanding. However, as we saw in Chapter 7, only about half of the kindergartners' mothers talked with their children about commercials, compared to more than 60 percent of the older children's mothers. Many kindergarten mothers appeared to be missing an opportunity to teach their children to understand the intent of commercials, an understanding that can help them to begin to function as effective consumers.

The Impact of TV Commercials on
Children's Consumer-Skill Learning

A third issue concerns the effects of television commercial viewing on children's consumer learning. A surrogate measure of exposure to commercials—amount of time viewing television—was included in the category "child opportunities for consumption" because we felt that increased exposure to commercials provided the child with greater opportunity to learn about the availability of products and brands. We examined the input of exposure to TV commercials on consumer learning by examining all the regressions discussed in the last chapter and presented in Appendix C. For this analysis, we focused only on the single independent variable, exposure to TV commercials.

When the relationship between this variable and the children's skill and nonskill behaviors is examined more specifically, we find a generally mixed pattern. For example, with the sixteen skill variables, exposure to commercials is positively related to skill learning four times and negatively related four times for kindergartners; for third-graders there are also two positive and three negative relationships. With the nine nonskill behaviors, exposure to commercials is positively related three times and negatively related five times for the three age groups combined.

These data suggest that increased exposure to commercials neither consistently facilitates nor consistently hinders children's skill learning. Also, it does not appear to motivate children consistently toward increased spending or asking for products. Further, exposure to commercials generally enters the regression equations rather late, indicating this variable has a rather small impact on children's consumer learning.

Implications

These analyses have shown that children can "filter" advertising messages and that this ability extends even to children in the youngest age groups. Most importantly, the data suggest that this ability can be taught by parents, even to kindergarten-aged children. Cognitively filtering advertising messages need not imply rejection of legitimate advertising claims. Children and parents are sometimes dissatisfied with advertised products and they may hold negative attitudes toward advertising to children. The roots of these kinds of dissatisfactions are undoubtedly often a result of children's failure to critically evaluate advertising messages and their own product desires. To the extent that children can be taught to filter advertising claims, more rigorous evaluations of products should result in fewer "mistakes" in product purchases, as when children buy products and find they are not what they expected from the commercial. Additionally, if cognitive filtering implies that children can evaluate products against their wants, then greater selectivity should result in more appropriate requests for products. This in turn may reduce complaints pertaining to children's urging parents to buy products. It seems to us that it is in the best interests of advertisers as well as parents to encourage the development of children's abilities to filter advertising—abilities which our data show can be developed at a very early age.

N O T E

1. The conference was sponsored by the Ford, Markel, and National Science Foundations to help them in determining funding priorities. See *Television and Children: Priorities for Research* (1976) for a report of this conference.

Chapter 10 ▓▓▓

SUMMARY AND IMPLICATIONS

▓▓▓

Our overall objective in this book has been to increase our understanding of how children acquire knowledge and skills relevant to consumer behavior. We have defined the most important of this knowledge and skill in terms of how children process information relevant to consumer decisions. We feel that information processing is a basic and crucial aspect of consumer behavior. Finally, we have been particularly interested in identifying how two major influences on consumer socialization operate: the influence of television advertising and the influence of the family. Our approach to research has been shaped by cognitive development theory, and we have attempted to extend its usefulness to consumer-behavior research and, hopefully, our results will "feed back" to enrich developmental notions. We have also attempted to conduct research and analysis which will be of practical usefulness to various parties—principally those interested in designing communication and education campaigns for preadolescents and those who must make policy decisions in the corporate or regulatory-agency context.

In this chapter we first summarize the principal findings of the research. Second, we discuss implications of our research for practice in three areas: (1) *policy decisions*, e.g., corporate and/or regulatory-agency decisions relevant to current public-policy issues regarding marketing practices affecting children; (2) *education strategy decisions*, i.e., suggestions for the design and implementation of educational programs aimed at improving consumer skills among children; (3) *marketing decisions*, i.e., implications for the design and execution of communication programs aimed at preteenage audiences. Finally, we evaluate the information-processing model used in this analysis in terms of its utility for future research and for policy decisions relating to the general area of consumer socialization.

PRINCIPAL FINDINGS

The theoretical basis for our analysis is cognitive development theory, particularly the notions advanced in the work of Jean Piaget. Since Piaget theorizes that there are important differences between children at the preoperational and concrete-operational stages of cognitive development, we interviewed children from three different grade levels spanning these two stages—kindergartners, third-graders, and sixth-graders.

We conclude from our research that cognitive development theory is highly relevant to the study of consumer socialization in that it can account for younger children's tendencies to respond more to the immediate perceptual aspects of stimuli (e.g., in television advertising or sources of new-product information) and to be less flexible and more constrained in their selection of amounts and kinds of information relevant to consumption decisions than older children. Furthermore, cognitive development theories provide a basis for explaining changes in consumer skills over the grade-school period as young children develop from what might be characterized as "perceptual, narrow information decoders" in their earliest consumer acts to "abstract, flexible, broad information processors" by early adolescence.

A general finding of the research is that chronological age provides only a loose indication of children's capacity to learn various consumption-related skills. In fact, we found considerable variation within each age group in how children apply skills. The results further indicate that certain consumption-related skills can be taught to very young children, but the data suggest that the processes of learning and, consequently, the most appropriate teaching methods change as children develop. While mothers do not usually have well-thought-out teaching strategies, kindergartners whose mothers often engage in direct interaction with them about consumption tend to do better in developing elementary consumer skills. On the other hand, older children appear to acquire consumer skills through the more subtle process of observing parental models of consumer behavior.

A second general finding of this research concerns the efficacy of television advertising directed to children and the mediating role played by children's cognitive abilities and interpersonal communication within families. Among kindergartners the most important factors explaining their level of understanding of commercials related to interaction with parents, including the mother's failure to yield to purchase influence attempts. Among older children family interaction is less prevalent and probably does not have much impact in increasing understanding of commercials; apparently, increased cognitive skills, increased experience with commercials, and, perhaps, earlier interaction with parents led to relatively high levels of understanding of commercials and their purposes among older children.

Other results show that amount of exposure to television is *not* consistently related to consumer-skill development among older children. Further, even a number of the youngest children in our sample appear to have developed somewhat skeptical attitudes toward many commercials, often based on unsatisfactory experiences with advertised products. Such negative experiences and subsequent attitudes may serve as a cognitive defense against future advertising persuasion, although there is little evidence on this point.

Children's Consumer-Skill Development

Information Selection and Initial Processing. The data indicate that even children as young as five or six discriminate between television programs and commercials but, as predicted from developmental theory, these children are likely to base discriminations largely on perceptual cues. This finding supports the recently introduced network television practices of providing a visual cue to separate programs and commercials.

The importance of perceptual cues as a basis for information selection and initial processing is also seen in data regarding information desired by children in hypothetical buying situations. Again, kindergart-ners were most likely to desire information about only perceptual features of a product (e.g., "how big is it?"). On the other hand, even young children are aware of a considerable number of brand names of products (a less perceptual attribute), although this is particularly true when the products are relevant to the child (e.g., food products) and are highly advertised during children's viewing times.

Central Processing. In this study, central processing refers to chil-dren's interpretation, comprehension, structuring, evaluation, and use of information related to consumption. A primary communication input is television advertising, and the data confirm findings of our own and other prior research that older children (i.e., third-graders and sixth-graders) are more likely to understand the purpose of advertising and to discriminate puffery which bends the literal truthfulness of messages. Again, these differences are predicted by cognitive develop-ment theory.

Central processing activities are also seen in children's use of product-related information. Our data indicate that by third grade, children use a greater number and more kinds of attributes to discrimi-nate and evaluate different brands within product groups. On the other hand, kindergartners use few attributes in making discriminations be-tween brands. The differential pattern of attribute use may partially explain the difference in strength of brand preference of the younger and older children. Among older children the increased number of attributes used to evaluate brands may indicate that they use a "com-pensatory" model of brand choice which results in their perceiving fewer differences between brands than do the younger children.

Children's Money Norms and Consumption Behaviors. Children dis-play some understanding of money use norms regardless of age; how-ever, only sixth-graders exhibit any consistency between money norms and behavior, although the relationship is a slight one. In addition, these older children are more flexible in their use of money—saving some for long-term and short-term goals as well as spending.

Perhaps the most prevalent kind of consumer behavior among children consists of buying requests directed to parents. In this study, no significant differences were found in the frequency with which children of varying ages make requests to their parents to buy products except in the case of "child-relevant" products. Older children were more likely to request these kinds of products (record albums, clothing) than were younger children.

Significant intercorrelations between requests for different types of products among children at all age levels suggest that some children are more likely to be general "requesters" for all product types. Further analyses indicates that this finding is not a yea-saying artifact.

The Family Context for Consumer Socialization

We reasoned that parents influence children's consumer socialization in three primary ways:

1. by providing a model for various behaviors;

2. by directly interacting with children in various parent-initiated and child-initiated consumption situations;

3. by providing children with independent opportunities for consumption and for exposure to the marketplace.

Children can learn a great deal about consumption by observing their parents' behavior. We examined several consumer-related activities of mothers which may serve as models for their children's consumer behavior. Although these variables are conceptually "distant" from more specific ways parents can influence consumer socialization of their children, we reasoned that mother's consumer-behavior patterns may underlie more specific socialization activities; at least some of these behaviors may provide a model for children's observational learning.

The major independent variables in analyses of mothers' consumer behavior were family socio-economic status and age of child. We found that relative to working-class mothers, higher-status mothers used more sources and kinds of information in product decision making. Social-status differences were also found in money management, as higher-status mothers were more likely to report greater budget accounting relative to middle-low-status mothers. On the other hand, we found no social status differences in other aspects of mothers' consumer activity: grocery-shopping behaviors and budget planning.

Different parental modeling behaviors vary in the extent to which they are observable to the child. But parent-child interaction about consumption represents a potentially more direct form of parental influence on children's consumer learning. Parent-initiated interaction includes both purposive consumer training, such as lectures about spending and how to choose products, and training that may occur indirectly, as when parents and children discuss commercials they see on television. The data show that few mothers engage in purposive "consumer training," but about half the mothers report frequent discussions about products and about commercials, which they view as a relatively informal means of imparting consumption-related knowledge to their offspring. The incidence of these discussions increases with age, especially among higher-status families.

Children frequently initiate interaction when they request products, and the kinds of responses parents give may affect children's consumer learning. We found that parental responsiveness to children's purchase requests increase among older children, perhaps reflecting parent's perceptions that older children have more competence to make consumer judgments.

In a related question, we attempted to gauge the type and amount of communication that occurs in child-initiated situations by measuring the frequency with which mothers make different kinds of responses to their children's purchase requests. Across several products, it was found that mothers of kindergartners were more likely to respond by "refusing to buy but explain why not," while mothers of older children were more likely to report "negotiating" concerning the purchase request. Both these strategies were used more often by higher-status mothers than lower-status mothers. About one-third of the mothers report frequent use of a "refuse without explanation" response, and about one-half report frequently "buying what the child asks for," without much parent-child communication. The incidence of these latter two response strategies varied little by age of child or socioeconomic status. However, examination of the flexibility of mothers in using the four responses shows that mothers in the middle-status category were most flexible.

Finally, data were gathered concerning the number and kinds of opportunities families provide for children's independent consumption behavior. Mothers were asked how each of nine child-related products were typically chosen, e.g., child buys for himself, parent chooses without talking to child, etc. As would be expected, mothers of older children are likely to report more child-independent purchases ("child power") compared to mothers of younger children. Interestingly, low-status mothers were slightly more likely to report high "child power" compared to mother's in middle-status and upper-status families.

Parents also provide their children with opportunities for consumption by giving them money. More older children than younger children are given regular allowances, but about half of the children in each age group are simply given money each week (as opposed to a fixed, regular allowance). More low-status mothers than high-status mothers simply give money to their children, and lower-income children have more spending money than middle- and upper-income children up to the sixth grade, when amounts are comparable regardless of socio-economic status. On the other hand, middle- and upper-income children are more likely to have a wider range of experiences with money, e.g., more of them have bank accounts, they obtain money from a wider range of sources, etc., as compared to children in lower-income homes.

Family Influences on Consumer Learning

The most important factor in the development of skills between kindergarten and sixth grade appear to be age-related changes in children's cognitive abilities. However, within age groups, different kinds of family-support variables operate to increase children's consumer learning. Our analyses in Chapter 8 attempted to identify the primary, supporting influences on aspects of children's consumer learning. Independent variables were conceptualized as representing four sets of family-context influences: mother-child interaction; mother's own consumer behavior; mother's consumer-education goals and attitudes; and children's independent opportunities (see Table 7-13). The dependent (child) variables were classified in terms of our information-processing conceptualization: higher- and lower-level information-processing skills, money use and savings skills, and nonskill behaviors of spending and asking for products (see Table 8-2).

Regression analyses conducted within each age group suggest that for kindergarten children, mother-child interaction is the most important factor contributing to consumer-skill development. However, by third grade such direct interaction is less important than the mother's own behavior. It seems likely that kindergarten children learn consumer skills more easily as a function of direct, purposive parental teaching than through the observation of parental behaviors. The data certainly suggest that even these young children can learn basic consumer skills through such interaction. On the other hand, older children seem to learn best by modeling parental consumer behaviors. These two sets of findings perhaps suggest that changes occur in the consumer socialization process as children grow older.

Finally, results indicate that simply increasing children's opportunities for consumption—e.g., giving them more money—does not in and of itself lead to greater skill learning. It seems likely that super-

vision and other kinds of parental communication and behavior are
necessary for effective skill development in children.

IMPLICATIONS FOR PRACTICE

Although the consumer-socialization process is a relatively new area
of social research and subsequent investigation should provide a more
complete basis for action, we offer some tentative suggestions for
practice in three areas: (1) policy decisions; (2) educational programs;
and (3) marketing and communication activities.

Policy Decisions

By "policy decisions" we refer to activities which could be under-
taken by industry or government agencies in response to perceived
concerns of significant sectors of society. Policy decisions involve the
"posturing" of corporations across a range of activities, i.e., beyond
tactical decisions involved in, say, a single advertising campaign.

We address three questions: Is there a need for changes—for new
policy decisions? What kinds of changes do the data in our research
suggest? How can changes best be brought about?

Are Any Changes Indicated? We feel that current social trends in
America suggest the need for changes in advertising policies relating to
child audiences. It has sometimes been said in defense of the status quo
that previous generations of children do not seem to have been harmed
by far less-controlled advertising in the past in radio, comics, and other
advertising media. But this point is irrelevant if one takes the position
that children, like adults, have a right to fairly evaluate advertising
messages designed to appeal to them; the fact that earlier generations of
children may have been misled but "recovered" from the experience
does not bear on the issue of fairly dealing with children *as* children.
Secondly, the tolerance of earlier generations for many aspects of
American society and its institutions has changed. For whatever reasons
(see Chapter 9), many Americans today seem to be concerned about
advertising practices affecting children.

Some also question whether significant proportions of Americans
really are concerned with advertising to children. Contradictory results
emerge in various surveys which have probed the extent of concern
among Americans. Our view is that concern in this area can be viewed
along a continuum. Admittedly, few Americans are active members of
advocacy groups. But we feel that many people do have latent concerns

which may not be elicited in response to attitude-survey questions but can be tapped if consumers are provoked by a salient issue. The widespread controversy following the allegation that breakfast cereals contain "empty calories" is a case in point. Latent concern and potentially "anti-business" attitudes also exist, since advertising is a highly visible corporate activity and advertising to children, in particular, invites the emotionalism attending salient political issues.

In any case, recent cases generated by the Federal Trade Commission and recent activities of businesses themselves in promoting codes and guidelines through self-regulatory mechanisms demonstrate the concern of government and industry and suggest the need for policy changes.

What Kinds of Changes are Called for? We feel that data presented here suggest possible policy changes in two areas: (1) changes in advertising practices which may affect children's comprehension of advertising messages; (2) initiation of policies which would encourage effective parental mediation of children's television viewing and consumer behavior.

Our view of consumer behavior as an aspect of information processing leads us quite naturally to focus our concern on children's comprehension (i.e., central processing) of advertising messages. We view consumption as a legitimate activity for children, but we argue that advertising techniques should take children's information-processing abilities and characteristics into account so that they can accurately comprehend advertising messages and accurately perceive advertised products.

There is a problem, however, since children's comprehension abilities vary markedly by age and since children of all ages watch television throughout the broadcast day. It is impractical to attempt to create appeals and design messages which are "age-related." We will address this problem below, when we consider how changes might be brought about.

A second major area for possible policy initiatives stems from our finding that parent-child interaction can effectively augment the development of a "cognitive filter" that even very young children can use in comprehending and evaluating advertising. We feel that opportunities exist for exploiting this apparently underutilized mode of helping children to evaluate advertising. It should be a particularly appealing alternative for policy makers in industry, since they have long argued that parents are the ultimate mediators of their children's viewing and consumer behavior.

How Could Policy Changes Best Be Brought About? We can see three different scenarios: (1) government regulation via the case-by-case approach; (2) self-regulation; (3) advertiser initiatives.

Government regulatory agencies can bring complaints against particular advertisers. The most prominent agency is the FTC, which has recently expressed concern with advertising practices affecting children under their mandate in the FTC Act of 1932 to guard against unfair, deceptive, or misleading business practices. For example, the FTC recently charged a bread manufacturer's ads as, among other things, misleading children about the product's unique abilities to promote physical growth. The FTC can also effect changes via proposed rules—Trade Rules and Regulations.

A principal problem with both the trade-rules and the case-by-case approaches is that they involve large costs in time and money. Changes in advertising may occur only after years of deliberation. More importantly, these approaches make it difficult to effectively use research and theory in both the selection of cases and their resolution. Rules and cases are often conceived without regard for research and theory, but research which is done after charges are brought or rules are initiated is open to suspicion.

It is a moot point whether behavioral research can ever make significant impacts on litigative proceedings. Empirical research has historically not been very productive in litigation, although significant advances have recently been made (Gerlach, 1972). Additionally, the FTC has initiated a policy of bringing behavioral scientists into the FTC for varying lengths of time to assist in issue selection, definition and resolution.

A final problem with the case-by-case or rule-making procedure was touched on earlier: almost any advertising practice singled out by the FTC (e.g., premium advertising) varies in its impact depending on the level of cognitive ability—indexed by age—of children. It would seem grossly unfair to define questionable practices only in terms of very young children—for example, infants!

Self-regulation obviously holds considerably more appeal to policy makers in industry. Advertisers have pursued this policy approach by supporting various industry mechanisms (e.g., the National Association of Broadcasters code and the Children's Review Unit of the National Council of Better Business Bureaus). The principal problem with self-regulation is that enforcement of code or guideline provisions is not always clearly demonstrated or effective. For example, some small advertisers avoid the NAB code stipulations by advertising on television stations which are not affiliated with the NAB. And while the code proffered by the Association of National Advertisers is based on developmental concepts and seems responsive to pressing issues, there is no way of actually knowing whether the individual commercials conform to the guidelines.

One possible solution to the enforcement problem could be to actually test children's responses to commercials—or at least test potentially troublesome commercials. This would be a variation of an institution such as Underwriters Laboratory, which tests certain electrical products and gives a sort of "seal of approval" to adequate products.

Aside from many technical problems which could be raised about such an enforcement mechanism (e.g., sample size, what proportion of children who might be misled would be unacceptable, etc.), the basic flaw is that it would involve asking advertisers to demonstrate that their advertising does *not* do certain things. It is as impossible for the advertiser as it is for the researcher to "prove" the null hypothesis.

Nonetheless, it may be advisable for advertisers to test some questionable techniques when commercials are still in less-than-finished form so that data from children could be a guide to avoiding some kinds of problems.

A third method of bringing about policy changes would call for individual advertisers to undertake some positive steps to improve advertising practices affecting children.

Data reported here suggest some points of departure. The fact that children can develop "filtering" skills suggests that advertisers could contribute to educational efforts. The data reported here, and other data and broadcaster experiences (e.g., *Sesame Street*), clearly indicate that children can learn extensively from television (Lesser, 1974).

We feel that dissatisfaction with the quality of advertising directed to children underlies much consumer dissatisfaction with advertisers appealing to children. Moreover, we feel that significant improvement in the quality of advertising is possible. Advertisers could incorporate prosocial elements into commercials without sacrificing marketing effectiveness. For example, the plethora of animated characters used to promote breakfast cereals, fast food outlets, and other products and services could effectively promote positive values and behaviors and at the same time continue to be effective marketing tools. Alternatively, separate advertising campaigns could encourage the development of positive habits and values among children, as in the case of a major cereal corporation's campaign to encourage children to eat a complete breakfast.

We do not mean to imply that research can never be useful in regulatory/public-policy affairs or that positive initiatives by advertisers will automatically "resolve" the consumerism issues surrounding advertising practices affecting children. We do argue, however, that our data suggest opportunities for marketers to undertake positive programs which could effectively respond to many of the concerns of all but the most extreme individuals. As a first step, we feel that advertisers should undertake and encourage basic research to aid in the development of higher-quality commercials and/or technical campaigns to assist parents in consumer training. Advertisers currently engage in much copy testing to develop and select effective commercials; it is quite possible to extend the use of research to develop directions in advertising to children.

Research for Policy Decisions. We mentioned earlier (Chapter 9) that the joint foundation-sponsored conference on research priorities in children's television suggested that funding priorities should go to more "basic" kinds of research and to longitudinal investigations rather than to proposals for studies of highly specific "hot" issues, e.g., effects of premium offers, host selling, etc. Yet it would seem that the more specific kinds of studies would be most relevant to policy makers, who are likely to be the least patient with more basic, "theoretical" kinds of investigations. Policy makers want specific answers to highly focused questions and frequently lack the training (and the time) to extract the most appropriate interpretation for their specific tasks from research addressed to more general phenomena.

On the other hand, the "technology" for uses of behavioral research in public policy and legal proceedings is far from developed. The advocacy system is designed for presentation of singular points of view and is ill-equipped to deal with the ambiguities and limitations of empirical research. For their part, researchers are generally not inclined to define and carry out research in terms of the needs of policy makers. There are myriad limitations to research itself. For example, questions can be raised about the external validity of, say, laboratory studies of highly focused phenomena. Studies which use particular commercials as stimuli are open to attack on the grounds that the sampling characteristics of the commercials used are unknown. Even research conducted under ideal conditions—large samples, reliable and valid measures, etc.— will certainly be attacked in emotionally charged public-policy arenas.

For all of these reasons, we are skeptical of the ability of "hot issues" research to make much lasting impact on public policy. The longer-term payoffs seem to us to be in further research in more basic areas and continuing efforts to more effectively use research in public-policy deliberations.

Basic research could also be useful to the advertiser. Judging from testimony by advertisers at the FTC's hearing on Modern Advertising Practices (Howard and Hulbert, 1973), it would appear that advertisers have only encouraged the development of copy-testing research. We acknowledge the need of marketers to develop methods to create and select effective communications. But the thrust of the discussion to this point should make it clear that advertisers who wish to be responsive to consumer concerns and to seriously pursue policy changes will require considerably more information of a "basic" sort about how children select, evaluate, and use advertising information. We argue that it is clearly possible for advertisers to incorporate considerably more information in advertising than is typically incorporated currently. And improving the quality of advertising to children will necessitate knowledge about how to effectively build in additional kinds of information.

Educational Programs

Frequently consumer-education curricula designed for preadolescents consist of descriptions of various institutions (i.e., banks) and their functions and arguments for certain consumer practices which are virtual truisms (e.g., it's good to budget). Such lessons reflect adult perceptions of what children ought to know. We would argue for alternative approaches to education based on the information-processing notions discussed in this research. The framework used here provides guidelines for educators to gear activities to the child's level of cognitive development and his abilities to understand and use information. For example, explanations of the persuasive intent of advertising can be understood by kindergarten-age children; it might also be possible to teach these younger children how to find out information about products. But understanding of abstract attributes or different strategies for evaluating products may be too difficult for younger children. Perhaps teaching of these skills should be deferred to the later grade-school years. Thus, the information-processing perspective provides a basis for identifying the most salient kinds of consumption-related skills for children at various age levels as well as a basis for gearing the content of educational programs to age-related abilities to comprehend.

Our research indicates that consumer education can work. The considerable variance within age groups suggests opportunities for education, but apparently parental "consumer training" of offspring is most often a hit-and-miss proposition, leaving gaps that schools could fill. The fact that increased mother-child interaction improves kindergartners' consumer-skills development suggests that education could be effective even within this age group.

Some of the findings suggest the need for consumer education particularly among families in the low socio-economic status. Mothers from low-status households were least effective in some aspects of consumer behavior, yet children from these households had more money to spend and more consumer independence compared to children from middle-status and high-status households. It might be that consumer education among low-status children could contribute a great deal to improvements in the next generation's consumer behavior.

In summary, we think that consumer-education efforts directed at children might profitably proceed from a basis of understanding children's cognitive abilities and consumer-behavior patterns. The data suggest how education also could supplement parental training, which typically occurs indirectly and irregularly, particularly among low-income families. However, the research reported here does not bear only on classroom consumer education. Indeed, the importance of various kinds of parental behaviors suggests that intervention programs might be devised in which parents directly undertake some consumer-training activities, perhaps in conjunction with schools. Such family-based educational programs could be tested in large-scale field experiments which would monitor children's developing cognitive skills and consumer behaviors.

Marketing Practice

The earlier discussion of implications of this research for policy decisions focused on an important contemporary issue relating to marketing to children—that of advertising's effects. In addition to this policy issue, the data suggest some other implications for marketing practice. Perhaps most important, the significance of parent-child interaction, particularly for younger children, implies that marketers might do well to coordinate promotions to children with related communications directed at parents, particularly mothers. Such efforts could inform mothers of a company's efforts to insure responsible communication practices aimed at children as well as provide mothers with product-related information to reinforce child-directed communications. Such coordinated communications might help reverse mothers' generally negative attitudes toward children's advertising.

The data also suggest that marketers should consider the amounts and kinds of attributes to which different-aged children are most likely to respond. Kindergarten children, for example, may be most interested in store displays which feature products; moreover, these young children are quite likely to be responsive to product demonstrations featuring perceptual characteristics of products.

The data suggest that brand loyalties are established very early but may decrease with age as children learn to use other product attributes. Consequently, marketers should *position* brands to young children and introduce new dimensions of products in advertising designed to appeal to older children.

It is probable that some critics of marketing to children will not accept anything short of a total cessation of advertising to children. However, we take the position that consumption is as legitimate an activity for children as it is unavoidable. Rather than making cumbersome attempts to protect children from all marketing stimuli, which is in all probability futile, efforts should be made to *prepare* children for efficacious, satisfying consumer behavior. The major issues concern particular practices in marketing stimuli and children's net impressions of products as a function of exposure to advertising. Our data suggest that marketing efforts to children should be geared to their level of cognitive ability in order to insure that they can fairly evaluate promotional activities designed to influence them. Marketers who take such steps demonstrate responsiveness to current public-policy concerns. Moreover, one could argue that systematic improvements in advertising to children may ultimately contribute to the emergence of more efficacious, less skeptical consumers—a very positive outcome for marketers.

IMPLICATIONS FOR THE COGNITIVE DEVELOPMENT, INFORMATION-PROCESSING APPROACH

The information-processing perspective that is the basis for this research was chosen as our conceptual orientation to children's consumer learning for several reasons. First, various streams in cognitive developmental research are organized around notions of information processing (Farnham-Diggory, 1972; Simon, 1972; Baldwin, 1969). Second, the current theoretical literature on consumer behavior is also largely concerned with information processing (Hughes and Ray, 1974; McGuire, 1973; Ray and Ward, 1975). Third, many of the most important current questions and issues about children's consumer behavior involve information-processing notions—policy issues relating to children's abilities to interpret information in commercials correctly, and marketing issues concerning children's abilities to recall and use information in discriminating between brands, forming attitudes about them, and taking action on the basis of brand evaluations. In short, both theoretical-research areas and consumer-policy issues were the sources of our interest in examining how consumer behavior changes throughout childhood.

We believe that the cognitive development approach utilized here is an appropriate one for research on children's consumer socialization. The research focused on several major aspects of children's consumer activities which undergo developmental changes in ways that can be described by cognitive development theorists. Indeed, as we discussed earlier, cognitive development theories provide a basis for predicting specific age-related changes. The data in the present study conform quite closely to the developmental predictions. We think the data support our view that the cognitive development perspective is highly appropriate for examining changes in consumer-learning processes as children progress through the various stages of cognitive development. However, other approaches may be more appropriate for examining other kinds of questions which do not primarily focus on age-related changes in consumer activities.

In the present study we have advanced some conceptual notions regarding selected aspects of initial and central information processing of children of different ages. In doing so, we have also attempted to show the utility of information-processing models in suggesting research questions regarding important cognitive activities involved in consumer learning. We feel that our model of information processing has directed our attention to a closer examination of the specific *aspects* of the consumer environment children at different age levels attend to, conceptualize, and use to direct their behavior. In important ways, this approach has forced us to examine actual cognitive processes rather than to infer processes from outcomes.

Clearly, future research should be devoted to examining other aspects of children's consumer-information processing. For example, our research virtually ignores such questions as how children structure information and how they modify these structures after receiving information. Further theoretical development will depend on clearer specification of the interrelationships among the various aspects of information processing described in the model we have advanced. This in turn will depend on development of more precise concepts to describe processing activities and more adequate measures of these concepts.

More precise concepts are emerging, and future investigators will have a considerable advantage in using developmental concepts in specifying research problems. This is because very recent work holds the promise of considerably advancing Piagetian theory. We are referring to the work of the functionally oriented neo-Piagetians, such as Pascual-Leone (1969; 1970) and Case (1974). Essentially, these theorists have supplemented Piaget's work by extending "the purely structural (competence) models to process models; that is, models which allow us to represent temporally, step by step, the subject's actual mental or behavioral process" (Pascual-Leone, 1970). These new theories hold the promise of providing greater explanatory power than currently exists in the primarily structural notions in Piaget's theory.[1]

We think the time is ripe for experimentation designed to examine the model and to elaborate upon it, hopefully integrating neo-Piagetian notions advanced recently. The field research reported in this volume has suggested a number of directions for experimental research and, possibly, field experiments. For example, experiments could be conducted to examine more closely cue selection, information source selection, and selection and use of product-related attributes among children. Field experiments could be useful in assessing the impact of alternative educational efforts in the natural environment. We do not believe that long-term longitudinal research is one of the most pressing needs. Although changes in information processing among children is an important topic, the potential payoff from such longitudinal research does not seem to be so great as the potential rewards from experimentation and theoretical development of specific aspects of the model. However, it may be that a combination of short-term longitudinal and cross-sectional research is advisable, i.e., tracking five-year-olds for two years, seven-year-olds for the same time period, etc.

Finally, we would hope that future investigators take into account the practical problems and concerns expressed by potential users of research results—policy makers in government and in corporations which market to children, educators, and planners of communication campaigns. Perhaps the current practices and implicit "hypotheses" of these practitioners will be useful in future attempts to examine children's consumer-information processing.

NOTE

1. Space considerations preclude extended discussion of neo-Piagetian theory. Suffice it to say here that Pascual-Leone has introduced the concept of "M Space" as a measurable construct underlying development. The concept refers to the size of an individual's central processing space. In addition, the theory posits constructs representing learning, affective, and stylistic influences on cognitive processing. The importance of neo-Piagetian theory is that it states testable propositions concerning the interactions of these constructs in determining subject performance. Additionally, the neo-Piagetian theory holds the promise of integrating learning theory and developmental approaches. The interested reader should see Pillemer, 1976; Pascual-Leone (1969, 1970) and Case (1974).

BIBLIOGRAPHY

Adler, Richard, et al., "The Effects of Television Advertising on Children: An Evaluation of the Literature," Interim Report to National Science Foundation, March, 1976 (Cambridge, Mass.: Harvard University Laboratory of Human Development).

Atkin, C.K. (1974), "The Impact of Premium Offers in Children's Commercials," unpublished paper, Michigan State University.

Atkin, C.K. (1975a), "Effects of Television Advertising on Children—First Year Experimental Evidence," Report #1, Michigan State University.

Atkin, C.K. (1975b), "Effects of Television Advertising on Children—Second Year Experimental Evidence," Report #2, Michigan State University.

Baldwin, A.L. (1969), "A Cognitive Theory of Socialization," in D. Goslin (ed.), *Handbook of Socialization Theory and Research.* Chicago: Rand McNally and Co., pp. 325-345.

Bandura, A., and R.H. Walters (1963), *Social Learning and Personality Development.* New York: Holt, Rinehart, and Winston.

Barcus, Earle F., "Saturday Children's Television," unpublished paper, Action for Children's Television, Newton, Mass., July 1971.

Bauer, R.A. (1967), "Application of Behavioral Science" in *Applied Science and Technological Progress,* report to the Committee on Science and Astronautics, U.S. House of Representatives, by the National Academy of Sciences.

Bettman, J.R. (1971), "Methods for Analyzing Consumer Information Processing Models," in D.M. Gardner (ed.), *Proceedings.* Second Annual Conference, Association for Consumer Research, pp. 197-207.

Bilk, R.W. (1974), "An Exploratory Assessment of Situational Effects in Buyer Behavior," *Journal of Marketing Research,* 11, 156-163.

Bucklin, L.P. (1965), "The Informative Role of Advertising," *Journal of Advertising Research,* 5, pp. 11-15.

Burgers, E.W., and J. Locke (1953), *The Family.* New York: American Book.

Carman, J.M. (1965), *The Application of Social Class in Market Segmentation.* Berkeley, California: University of California.

Caron, A., and S. Ward (1975), "Gift Decisions by Kids and Parents," *Journal of Advertising Research,* 15, 4, pp. 15-20.

Case, Robbie (1974), "Structure and Stricture: Some Functional Limitations on the Course of Cognitive Growth." *Cognitive Psychology* 6, pp. 544-574.

Chaffee, S.H. (1972), "The Interpersonal Context of Mass Communication" in F.G. Kline and P.J. Tichenor (eds.), *Current Perspectives in Mass Communication Research.* Beverly Hills: Sage, pp. 95-121.

Chaffee, S.H., J.M. McLeod, and D.B. Wackman (1973), "Family Communication Patterns and Adolescent Political Participation" in J. Dennis, (ed.), *Socialization to Politics*. New York: John Wiley and Sons, pp. 349-364.

Chaffee, S.H., and J.M. McLeod (1973), "Consumer Decisions and Information Use" in S. Ward and T. Robertson (eds.), *Consumer Behavior: Theoretical Sources*. Englewood Cliffs. N.J.: Prentice-Hall, pp. 385-415.

Cox, D.F. (1963), "The Measurement of Information Value; A Study in Consumer Decision-Making" in W.S. Decker (ed.), *Emerging Concepts in Marketing*. Chicago: American Marketing Association, pp. 413-421.

Crandall, J.J., S. Orleans, A. Preston, and A. Rabson (1958), "Development of Social Compliance in Young Children," *Child Development* 29, pp. 429-443.

Dervin, B., and B.S. Greenberg (1972), "The Communication Environment of the Urban Poor," in F.G. Kline and P.J. Tichenor (eds.), *Current Perspectives in Mass Communication Research*. Beverly Hills: Sage, pp. 195-235.

Faber, Ronald (1975), "Children's Television Viewing Patterns," unpublished paper, Marketing Science Institute, Cambridge, Mass.

Farnham-Diggory, S. (ed.) (1972), *Information Processing in Children*. New York: Academic Press.

Fishbein, M. (1967), "A Behavior Theory Approach to the Relations Between Beliefs About an Object and the Attitude Toward the Object" in M. Fishbein (ed.), *Attitude Theory and Measurement*. New York: John Wiley and Sons, pp. 257-266.

Flavell, J.H. (1963), *The Developmental Psychology of Jean Piaget*. Princeton: Van Nostrand.

Gans, H.J. (1962), *The Urban Villager*. New York: Free Press.

Gerlach, G. C. (1972), "The Consumer's Mind: A Preliminary Inquiry into the Emerging Problems of Consumer Evidence and the Law." Working Paper, Marketing Science Institute, Cambridge, Mass.

Ginsburg, H., and S. Opper (1969), *Piaget's Theory of Intellectual Development*. Englewood Cliffs, N.J.: Prentice-Hall.

Hemple, D.J. (1970), "An Experimental Study of the Effects of Information on Consumer Product Evaluation" in S.H. Britt (ed.), *Psychological Experiments in Consumer Behavior*. New York: John Wiley and Sons, pp. 329-336.

Hoffman, Lois W., and Robert Lippitt (1960), "The Measurement of Family Life Variables" in Paul H. Mussen (ed.), *Handbook of Research Methods in Child Development*. New York: Wiley, pp. 945-1014.

Hollingshead, A.B. (1965), "Class Differences in Family Stability" in R. Bendix and S.M. Lipset (eds.), *Class, Status, and Power*. New York: Free Press, pp. 284-292.

Howard, J.A., and J. Hulbert (1973), "Advertising and the Public Interest," a staff report to the Federal Trade Commission, Washington, D.C.

Hughes, G.D., and M.L. Ray (eds.) (1974), *Buyer/Consumer Information Processing*. Chapel Hill: University of North Carolina Press.

Inhelder, B., and J. Piaget (1958), *The Growth of Logical Thinking from Childhood to Adolescence*. New York: Basic Books.

Jacoby, J. (1975), "Perspectives on a Consumer Information Processing Research Program," unpublished paper, Purdue Papers in Consumer Psychology, No. 147.

Kagan, Jerome, and H. Moss (1960), *Birth to Maturity*. New York: Wiley.

Katz, E., and P.F. Lazarsfeld (1955), *Personal Influence*. New York: Free Press.

Kohlberg, L. (1969), "The Cognitive-Developmental Approach to Socialization" in Goslin (ed.), *Handbook of Socialization Theory and Research*. Chicago: Rand McNally and Company, pp. 347-480.

Leifer, A.D., A.W. Collins, B. Gross, P. Taylor, L. Andrews, and E. Blackmer (1971), "Developmental Aspects of Variables Relevant to Observational Learning," *Child Development*, 42, pp. 1509-1516.

Lesser, G.S. (1974), *Children and Television: Lessons from Sesame Street*. New York: Random House.

Lyle, J. (1972), "Television in Daily Life: Patterns of Use Overview" in E.A. Rubinstein, G.A. Comstock, and J.P. Murray (eds.), *Television and Social Behavior*. Volume 4: *Television in Day-to-Day Life: Patterns of Use*. Washington, D.C.: Government Printing Office, pp. 1-32.

Marshall, H.R., and L. Magruder (1960), "Relations Between Parent Money Education Practices and Children's Knowledge and Use of Money," *Child Development*, 31, pp. 253-284.

McGuire, W.J. (1973), "Persuasion, Resistance and Attitude Change," in I. Pool et al. (eds.), *Handbook of Communication*. Chicago: Rand McNally, pp. 216-252.

McNeal, J.R. (1964), *Children as Consumers*. Austin, Tex.: University of Texas Bureau of Business Research.

Miller, D.R., and G.E. Swanson (1958), *The Changing American Parent*. New York: Wiley.

Nie, N.H., D.H. Hull, J.G. Jenkins, K. Steinbrenner, and D.H. Bent (1970), *Statistical Package for the Social Sciences*. New York: McGraw-Hill, Vol. 1.

Pascual-Leone, J. (1970), "A Mathematical Model for the Transition Rule in Piaget's Developmental Stages," *Acta Psychologica* 63, pp. 301-345.

Pascual-Leone, J., and J. Smith (1969), "The Encoding and Decoding of Symbols by Children: A New Experimental Paradigm and a neo-Piagetian Model," *Journal of Experimental Child Psychology* 8, pp. 328-355.

Piaget, J. (1928), *The Child's Conception of the World*. New York: Harcourt, Brace.

Piaget, J. (1950), *The Psychology of Intelligence*. London: Routledge and Kegan Paul Ltd.

Piaget, J. (1952), *The Origins of Intelligence in Children*. New York: International Universities Press.

Piaget, J. (1954), *The Construction of Reality in the Child*. New York: Basic Books.

Pillemer, D.B. (1976), "The Prediction of Human Performance: An Analysis of Juan Pascal-Leone's neo-Piagetian Theory," unpublished paper, Cambridge, Mass., Harvard Graduate School of Education.

Ray, M.L., and S. Ward (eds.), "Communication with Consumers: The Information Processing Approach," *Communication Research*, 2, 3.

Gene Reilly Group, Inc. (1973a), *The Assumption by the Child of the Role of Consumer*. Darien, Conn.: The Gene Reilly Group, Inc.

Gene Reilly Group, Inc. (1973b), *The Child*. Vol. II, unpublished report, Darien, Conn.

Rich, S., and S.C. Jain (1968), "Social Class and Life Cycle as Predictors of Shopping Behavior," *Journal of Marketing Research,* 5, 1, pp. 41-49.

Robertson, T.S., and J.R. Rossiter (1974), "Children and Commercial Persuasion: An Attribution Theory Analysis," *Journal of Consumer Research,* 1, 1, pp. 13-20.

Rosenberg, M.J. (1956), "Cognitive Structure and Attitudinal Effect," *Journal of Abnormal and Social Psychology,* 53, 3, pp. 367-372.

Rubin, R.S. (1972), "An Exploratory Investigation of Children's Responses to Commercial Content of Television Advertising in Relation to Their Stages of Cognitive Development," unpublished doctoral dissertation, University of Massachusetts.

Schuessler, K., and A. Strauss (1950), "A Study of Concept Learning by Scale Analysis," *American Sociological Review,* 15, pp. 752-762.

Sears, R.R., E.E. Maccoby, and H. Levin (1957), *Patterns of Child Rearing.* Evanston, Ill.: Row, Peterson.

Shimp, T.A., R.F. Dyer, and S.F. Divita (1975), "Advertising of Children's Premiums on Television: An Experimental Evaluation of the FTC's Proposed Guide," unpublished paper, School of Government and Business, George Washington University.

Simon, H.A. (1972), "On the Development of the Processor" in S. Farnham-Diggory (ed.), *Information Processing in Children.* New York: Academic Press, pp. 3-22.

Television and Children: Priorities for Research (1975) New York: Ford Foundation.

Tichenor, P.J., G.A. Donohue, and C.N. Olien (1970), "Mass Media Flow and Differential Growth in Knowledge," *Public Opinion Quarterly,* 34, 2, pp. 159-170.

Wade, S.E., and W. Schramm (1960), "The Mass Media as Sources of Public Affairs, Science, and Health Knowledge," *Public Opinion Quarterly,* 33, pp. 197-209.

Wells, William D., "Communicating with Children," *Journal of Advertising Research,* 5, June, 1965, pp. 2-14.

Ward, S. (1972), "Effects of Television Advertising on Children and Adolescents," in E. Rubinstein, G. Comstock, and J. Murray (eds.), *Television and Social Behavior.* Volume 4: *Television in Day to Day Life: Patterns of Use.* Washington: Department of Health, Education, and Welfare, pp. 432-451.

Ward, S., and M.L. Ray (1974), "Cognitive Responses to Mass Communication: Results from Laboratory Studies and a Field Experiment," Working Paper, Marketing Science Institute, Cambridge, Mass.

Ward, S., and D.B. Wackman (1972), "Children's Purchase Influence Attempts and Parental Yielding," *Journal of Marketing Research,* 9, 3, pp. 316-319.

Ward, S., and D.B. Wackman (1973), "Children's Information Processing of Television Advertising" in P. Clarke (ed.), *New Models for Communication Research.* Beverly Hills: Sage, pp. 119-146.

Wartella, E., and J.S. Ettema (1974), "A Cognitive Developmental Study of Children's Attention to Television Commercials," *Communication Research.* 1, 1, pp. 44-69.

Williams, W.C. (1958), "The PALS Tests: A Technique for Children to Evaluate Both Parents," *Journal of Consulting Psychology*, 22, 487-495.

Wohlwill, J.F. (1962), "From Perception to Inference: A Dimension of Cognitive Development," in W. Kessen and C. Kuhlman, (eds.), *Cognitive Development in Children, Five Monographs of the Society for Research in Child Development*. Chicago: University of Chicago Press, pp. 73-94.

Wright, P.L. (1974), "On the Direct Monitoring of Cognitive Response to Advertising" in G.D. Hughes and M.L. Ray (eds.), *Buyer/Consumer Information Processing*. Chapel Hill: University of North Carolina Press, pp. 220-248.

Zigler, E., and I.L. Child (1969), "Socialization" in G. Linzey and E. Aronson (eds.), *The Handbook of Social Psychology*. Second Edition, Volume 3, *The Individual in a Social Context*. Reading, Mass.: Addison-Wesley, pp. 450-490.

THE INTERVIEW SCHEDULES AND QUESTIONNAIRE

CHILD INTERVIEW

1. When you watch TV you must see a lot of commercials. What is a TV commercial? (PROBE HARD: "Is there any other way you can tell me what a commercial is?")

2. Why are commercials shown on television? (PROBE: "Is there any other reason they're shown on TV?")
   2a. What do commercials try to do? (PROBE: "Anything else they try to do?")

3. What is your favorite TV commercial—the one you like the most?
   3a. Tell me what happens in this commercial (PROBE: "Anything else?")
   3b. Why do you like it? (PROBE: "What do you like about it? What's in it that you like?")

4. When you watch TV you see both programs and commercials. What is the difference between a TV program and a TV commercial? (PROBE HARD: "Anything else?")

4a. Let's see if you can tell me about differences between other things:
   (1) school—house
   (2) car—truck
   (3) father—mother

5. Let's talk about TV again, do you think TV commercials always tell the truth?
   _____Yes (ASK Q. 6)
   _____Sometimes, No (SKIP TO Q. 7)

6. How do you know they tell the truth?
   6a. Why do you think commercials tell the truth? (PROBE: "What do you think is the reason commercials tell the truth?"– THEN SKIP TO Q. 8)

7. How often do they lie—most of the time, some of the time, or just once in a while?
   7a. How do you know when they lie?
   7b. Why do you think they don't tell the truth? (PROBE: "What do you think is the reason commercials don't tell the truth?")

8. Suppose somebody gave you $15 for your own. What would you do with the money? (PROBE: IF SAYS, "PUT IN BANK OR SAVE," ASK: "Would you save it to buy something later? What?")

9. Now, let's pretend that you want a new bike. And let's pretend I'm your mother and you have to try to talk me into buying this new bike for you. Now you have to try really hard to make me buy it. OK, what are you going to say to me? (PROBE A FEW TIMES: "Is there anything else you would say 'cause you have to try real hard to make me buy it?")

10. Now guess *exactly* how much each of the following things cost?
   a. a Hershey bar $_____
   b. a small doll $_____
   c. a jacket to wear this spring $_____
   d. a bottle of Bayer aspirin $_____
   e. a bottle of shampoo $_____
   f. a new washing machine $_____
   g. a pair of tennis shoes (sneakers) $_____
   h. a can of soda pop (tonic) $_____
   i. a can of Campbell's soup $_____

    j. a new Chevrolet car $_____
    k. a baseball bat $_____

11. What is an advertisement? (PROBE HARD: "Do you know what an ad is?")

    11a. Where do you see advertisements? (PROBE HARD: "Do you see them anywhere else? Think real hard now—have you seen them anywhere else?")

12. What are some different brands of toothpaste? (IF ANSWER IS "DON'T KNOW" OR "WHAT'S A BRAND," SKIP TO Q. 12a) (IF ANSWER INCLUDES BRAND NAMES, PROBE HARD: "Can you think of any more?"—THEN SKIP TO Q. 13)

    12a. What are some different kinds of toothpaste? (IF ANSWER IS "DON'T KNOW" OR TYPES SUCH AS WHITE, GREEN, ETC.—BRAND NAMES NOT MENTIONED, SKIP TO Q. 12b.) (IF ANSWER INCLUDES BRAND NAMES, PROBE HARD: "Can you think of any more?"—THEN SKIP TO Q. 13)

    12b. OK, now what are the names of some different toothpastes? (PROBE HARD: "Can you think of any more?")

13. That's right, that's what a brand is. It's the name of a certain kind of product. Now what are some different brands of (INSERT ____a,b,c,d____)? Can you think of any more? (PROBE HARD FOR EACH)

    a. Chewing gum (PROBE IF NONE: "What is your favorite kind of gum?")
    b. Gasoline (PROBE IF NONE: "Where do your mom and dad get gas?")
    c. Soft drinks (PROBE HARD: "What's your favorite kind?")
    d. Cameras

14. Who decides to give products different brands or brand names—like calling toothpaste "Crest" toothpaste? (PROBE)

    14a. Why do you think they do that? (PROBE)

15. When people go shopping, why do they look for different brands? (PROBE: "How does the brand name help you when you go shopping?")

16. (SHOW 2 PRODUCTS—CREST TOOTHPASTE AND COLGATE TOOTHPASTE) If you could pick one of these, which one would

you choose—Colgate or Crest? (ALTERNATE BRAND NAME YOU READ FIRST) (IF NO DECISION, PROBE HARD TO TRY TO GET A DECISION.)

_____ Crest

_____ Colgate

_____ Really indifferent (SKIP TO Q. 18)

_____ Can't decide (SKIP TO Q. 18)

17. How much better is (BRAND PREFERRED) than (OTHER BRAND)—is it a lot better, a little better, or are they just about the same?

_____ a lot better

_____ a little better

_____ about the same (SKIP TO Q. 18)

17a. Why is (BRAND PREFERRED) better; what is it about (BRAND PREFERRED) that makes it better? (PROBE: "Anything else?" (IF FLUORIDE IS MENTIONED, ASK Q. 17b; OTHERWISE SKIP TO Q. 19)

17b. Did you know both of these toothpastes have fluoride in them? Which one do you pick now?

_____ Crest

_____ Colgate

_____ Indifferent (SKIP TO Q. 18)

17c. Why do you choose that one? (PROBE—THEN SKIP TO Q. 19)

18. In what ways are they about the same? (PROBE: "Any other ways?")

19. How did you learn these things about toothpaste? (PROBE: FROM WHERE?)

_____ .

20. What kind of toothpaste do you use at home? (PROBE FOR BRAND)

_____ .

21. How much does Crest cost in the store?

$_____ .

21a. How much does Colgate cost in the store?

$_____ .

22. SHOW 2 PRODUCTS—SKIPPY PEANUT BUTTER AND JIF PEANUT BUTTER) If you could pick one of these, which one would

you choose—Skippy or Jif? (ALTERNATE BRAND READ FIRST) (IF DON'T KNOW, PROBE HARD TO TRY TO GET A DECISION)

_____ Skippy

_____ Jif

_____ Really indifferent (SKIP TO Q. 24)

_____ Can't decide (SKIP TO Q. 24)

23. How much better is (BRAND PREFERRED) than (OTHER BRAND)—is it a lot better, a little better, or are they just about the same?

_____ a lot better

_____ a little better

_____ about the same (SKIP TO Q. 24)

    23a. Why is (BRAND PREFERRED) better; what is it about (BRAND PREFERRED) that makes it better? (PROBE: "Anything else?")

24. In what ways are they about the same? (PROBE: "Any other ways?")

25. How did you learn about peanut butter?

26. What kind of peanut butter do you eat? (PROBE FOR BRAND)

27. How much does Skippy cost in the store?

    $_____.

    27a. How much does Jif cost in the store?

        $_____.

28. Did you ever have something, like a toy, and it broke?

    28a. Why did it break?

    28b. Would you buy that (toy) again?

29. Did you ever see something on TV that you got and then when you got it, it wasn't as good as you thought it would be? Tell me what happened?

_____ yes

_____ no (SKIP TO Q. 30)

    29a. Tell me what happened. (PROBE)

30. (FOR KINDERGARTNERS) I'm going to ask you some questions. Tell me if your answer is yes or no. Let's try one. "Is brushing your teeth good for you?" Let's try another one. "Is it OK to tell lies?"

(FOR 3RD AND 6TH GRADERS) Now I'm going to read you some questions and I want you to tell me if you think they're right or wrong. Let's try one. "Is brushing your teeth good for you?" (GET "YES" OR "NO") Do you really think _____ or sort of think _____ ? (PROBE AT THIS POINT, MAKE SURE CHILD UNDERSTANDS)

	YES		NO	
	Really Think	Sort of Think	Really Think	Sort of Think
a. Do you think commercials on TV make you want to have things?	_____	_____	_____	_____
b. Do you think people would be lots happier if they had more things like color TVs and big cars?	_____	_____	_____	_____
c. Can you tell how good something is from the TV commercial?	_____	_____	_____	_____
d. When I grow up, the most important thing is to have lots of money.	_____	_____	_____	_____
e. Do you think the things they show in TV commercials are the *best* you can buy?	_____	_____	_____	_____
f. Do you think that to *really* be happy when you grow up you *have* to have lots of money?	_____	_____	_____	_____
g. Would you like to have *most* things they show on TV commercials?	_____	_____	_____	_____
h. Are all the products you buy safe? (PROBE)	_____	_____	_____	_____

_____
_____ .

    i. Are all the products your
mom buys safe for you
to use? (PROBE) _____ _____ _____ _____

_____

_____ .

31. Do you get an allowance each week? PROBE: "Do you receive any money each week?")

    _____ Yes

    _____ No (SKIP TO Q. 32)

    31a. How much? $_____ Any other money each week? _____

    31b. What do you do with your allowance? (IF _____ SAYS "I SPEND IT," ASK: "What do you buy?")

    31c. Is there anything you aren't allowed to buy? (SKIP TO Q. 33)

32. Do you ever get money of your own?

    _____ Yes

    _____ No (SKIP TO Q. 33)

    32a. What do you do with this money? (IF SAYS "I spend it," ASK: "What do you buy?") (IF SAYS "I save it," SKIP TO Q. 33)

    32b. Is there anything you aren't allowed to buy?

33. Did you ever save money to buy something? (PROBE: "Well did you ever put money in a piggy bank and later take some of it out to buy something? Are you saving money right now to buy something?")

    _____ Yes or tried to save

    _____ No (SKIP TO Q. 34)

    33a. What were you saving your money for? (PROBE: "What are you saving your money for?")

    33b. How much did it cost? $_____ (PROBE: "How much will it cost?")

    33c. About how long did it take you to save enough money to buy it? (PROBE: "How long do you think it will take to save enough money to buy it?")

34. Now I'm going to read you a list of things you might try to get your mother or father to buy. I want you to tell me *how often* you try to get your parents to buy each thing—that might be often, or

sometimes, not too often, or never. (IF CHILD ANSWERS IN
TIME DIMENSIONS, USE GUIDELINES–OFTEN–ONCE OR
MORE/WEEK: SOMETIMES–ONCE OR MORE/MONTH: NOT
TOO OFTEN–LESS THAN 1/MONTH.)

	Often	Some-times	Not Too Often	Never
a. cereal	___	___	___	___
b. snack food	___	___	___	___
c. shampoo	___	___	___	___
d. candy	___	___	___	___
e. toothpaste	___	___	___	___
f. a game or toy	___	___	___	___
g. aspirin	___	___	___	___
h. soft drinks	___	___	___	___
i. clothing	___	___	___	___
j. record album	___	___	___	___
k. household cleanser	___	___	___	___
l. soup	___	___	___	___

35. Sometimes when kids ask for a product, they ask for certain kinds
or brands. How about you? Do you ask for certain kinds or brands
of:

35a. Soft drinks _____Yes   Which ones? _____
                 _____No   _____

35b. Soups   _____Yes   Which ones? _____
                 _____No   _____

35c. Candy   _____Yes   Which ones? _____
                 _____No   _____

35d. Toothpaste _____Yes   Which ones? _____
                 _____No   _____

35e. Cereal   _____Yes   Which ones? _____
                 _____No   _____

36. (SHOW 2 PRODUCTS–HERSHEY'S AND QUIK) If you could
pick one of these, which one would you choose? (IF "DON'T
KNOW," PROBE HARD TO TRY TO GET A DECISION)

_____Hershey's Instant
_____Nestles Quik
_____Really indifferent (SKIP TO Q. 38)
_____Can't decide (SKIP TO Q. 38)

37. How much better is (BRAND PREFERRED) than (OTHER BRAND)—is it a lot better, a little better, or are they just about the same?

_____ a lot better

_____ a little better

_____ about the same (SKIP TO Q. 38)

    37a. Why is (BRAND PREFERRED) better: what is it about (BRAND PREFERRED) that makes it better? (PROBE: "Anything else?")

38. In what ways are they about the same? (PROBE: "Any other ways?")

39. How did you learn these things about Hershey's Instant and Nestles Quik?

    39a. How much does Hershey's Instant cost in the store $_____ .

    39b. How much does Nestles Quik cost in the store? $_____ .

40. What kind do you usually get, Hershey's Instant or Nestles Quik?

_____ .

41. Suppose you wanted to buy a new TV set. What would you want to know about it? (PROBE HARD: "Is there anything else you'd want to know?")

42. Suppose you wanted to buy a new toy. How would you find out what new toys there were to buy? (PROBE HARD: "Are there any other ways you could find out what toys there were to buy?")

43. Suppose you wanted to buy something new to wear. How would you find out what new clothes there were to wear? (PROBE HARD: "Are there any other ways you could find out?")

44. How about a new snack to eat? How would you find out what new snacks there were to eat? (PROBE HARD: "Are there any other ways you could find out?")

45. Like you did before, try to guess exactly how much each of the following things cost:

a. a candy bar $ _____

b. a pair of Keds tennis shoes (sneakers) $ _____

c. a bottle of Johnson's shampoo $ _____

    d. a bottle of aspirin $ _____

    e. a new car $ _____

    f. a can of soup $ _____

    g. a Maytag washing machine $ _____

    h. a can of Pepsi $ _____

46. Now, let's pretend that you want a new bike again. This time pretend that I'm your father. You have to try to talk me into buying this new bike for you. Now you have to try really hard to make me buy it. OK, what are you going to say to me? (PROBE: "Is there anything else you'd say 'cause you have to try really hard to make me buy it?")

47. Pretend you're a mother/father and you gave your child $25. Now you're going to have to tell him what he should do with the $25. What would you tell him? (PROBE HARD: "Anything else?")
    47a. What would you tell him *not* to do with the money? What things? (PROBE HARD: "Anything else?")

48. (SHOW AEROSOL CAN) It's a spray can. You press the button and the stuff inside comes out—like paint, deodorant, bug spray.
    48a. Could you get hurt using a spray can like this?
    _____ Yes   How? _____

                         _____

                         _____(SKIP TO Q. 49)_____

    _____ No   How about little kids—could they get hurt using spray cans like this? (IF YES, HOW?)

                         _____

                         _____

49. Has anyone ever told you to be careful when you use spray cans?
    _____ Yes   Who told you and what did they tell you?
                   (PROBE)

                         _____

                         _____

50. You know what a toaster is, don't you? (IF NO, EXPLAIN) Could you get hurt using a toaster?
    _____ Yes   How? _____
                         _____(SKIP TO Q. 51)_____

    _____ No   How about little kids—could they get hurt? (IF YES, HOW?)

                         _____

                         _____

51. Has anyone ever told you to be careful when you use the toaster?

_____ Yes Who told you and what did they tell you? (PROBE)

_____
_____

_____ No What shouldn't you do when you use the toaster?

_____
_____

END OF INTERVIEW   TIME: _____

MOTHER'S INTERVIEW

As you well know, being a consumer today is pretty complicated. With prices increasing as they are, it's probably becoming more difficult to manage your money and to get the best value for your money. This survey will ask two kinds of questions about being a consumer. Some questions will ask how you act as a consumer. Other questions will ask about your child _____. Please try and focus on _____. It may be hard not to think of your other children, but try and focus on just this one child.

1. What kinds of things do you do as a consumer that you would like _____ to learn? (PROBE HARD: Anything else?)

2. What things do you want _____ to learn now at his/her age?

3. How do you try to teach _____ these things? (PROBE: Anything else?)

4. About how many times in the past two weeks have you taken _____ grocery shopping with you? _____

5. About how many times in the past month have you taken _____ shopping to buy clothes for him/her? _____

6. About how many times in the past month have you taken _____ to do general family shopping . . . like going to Rosedale, Harmar, or Northtown (Boston: Porter Square, Union Square, Lechmere, or Davis Square)? _____

7. Does _____ have a bank account of his/her own?

_____ No (SKIP TO Q. 8)

_____ Yes (ASK Q. 7a & 7b)

7a. How old was _____ when this bank account was opened?

_____

7b. How does _____ get money to put in this account?

_____

8. How much allowance does _____ receive each week, if any?
$_____(TO 8b)__ (IF NO ALLOWANCE, ASK 8a)

8a. Does he get paid to do any chores on a weekly basis?

_____ Yes   How much? $ _____

_____ No   (SKIP TO Q. 9)

8b. Is _____ required to work or perform special chores at home to receive this allowance . . . usually, sometimes, never?

_____ Usually

_____ Sometimes

_____ Never

9. About how much money does _____ receive each week from a job outside the home? $_____ .

10. Aside from _____ allowance, about how much money is just given to _____ each week . . . by you or other people?
$_____ .

(IF THE CHILD RECEIVES NO MONEY IN Q. 8, 9, and 10, SKIP TO Q. 12)

11. Which of the following things does _____ do with the money he/she receives each week? For instance, does _____ . . . (READ INSERT) . . . usually, sometimes, not too often, never?

	Usually— At least once a week	Sometimes— About every two weeks	Not too often— Once a month or less	Never
a. . . . spend his/her money on candy or snacks . . .	_____	_____	_____	_____
b. . . . saves his/her money to buy something special . . .	_____	_____	_____	_____

c. ... saves his/her
   money for
   nothing
   special ...   _____   _____   _____   _____
d. ... spends
   money on
   things besides
   candy or
   snacks ...   _____   _____   _____   _____
(IF NEVER TO 11d, SKIP TO Q. 12; OTHERWISE ASK Q. 11e)
e. What things does _____ buy? _____
_____

12. I'm going to read you a list of products you may buy and that
    _____ may ask for. Please indicate how often _____ tries
    to get you to buy that product for himself/herself, or for the
    family. Does _____ ask for (READ ITEM)—very often, pretty
    often, not too often, or never?

	ASKS			
	Very Often	Pretty Often	Not Too Often	Never
a. cereal	_____	_____	_____	_____
b. snack food	_____	_____	_____	_____
c. shampoo	_____	_____	_____	_____
d. candy	_____	_____	_____	_____
e. toothpaste	_____	_____	_____	_____
f. a game or toy	_____	_____	_____	_____
g. aspirin	_____	_____	_____	_____
h. soft drinks	_____	_____	_____	_____
i. clothing	_____	_____	_____	_____
j. record album	_____	_____	_____	_____
k. household cleaner	_____	_____	_____	_____
l. soup	_____	_____	_____	_____

	BUYS			
	Most of Time	Some of Time	Not Too Often	Never
a. cereal	_____	_____	_____	_____
b. snack food	_____	_____	_____	_____
c. shampoo	_____	_____	_____	_____

d. candy   _____   _____   _____   _____
e. toothpaste   _____   _____   _____   _____
f. a game or toy   _____   _____   _____   _____
g. aspirin   _____   _____   _____   _____
h. soft drinks   _____   _____   _____   _____
i. clothing   _____   _____   _____   _____
j. record album   _____   _____   _____   _____
k. household cleaner   _____   _____   _____   _____
l. soup   _____   _____   _____   _____

13. INTERVIEWER: GO BACK OVER THE LIST OF PRODUCTS AND FOR EACH PRODUCT THAT WAS *NOT* ANSWERED *NEVER,* ASK: When _____ asks for (READ ITEM), how often do you buy what he/she asks for—most of the time, some of the time, not too often, never?

14. For some of these products, children ask for a particular kind or brand. How about _____? Does he/she ask for a particular kind or brand of cereal? Yes_____No_____(IF NO, SKIP TO Q. 14b).

    14a. Which ones does _____ask for? _____
_____

    14b. What kinds of brands do you usually buy? _____
_____

    14c. Why do you buy this kind? (PROBE HARD: Any other reason?) _____
_____

15. Does _____ ask for a particular kind or brand of candy? Yes_____No_____(IF NO, SKIP TO Q. 15b).

    15a. Which one does _____ask for? _____
_____

    15b. What kinds of brands do you usually buy? _____
_____

    15c. Why do you buy this kind? (PROBE HARD: Any other reason?) _____
_____

16. Does _____ ask for a particular kind or brand of soft drinks? Yes_____No_____(IF NO, SKIP TO Q. 16b)

    16a. Which ones does _____ask for? _____

16b. What kinds of brands do you usually buy? _____

16c. Why do you buy this kind? (PROBE HARD: Any other reason?) _____

17. Does _____ ask for a particular kind or brand of chewing gum? Yes_____ No_____ (IF NO, SKIP TO Q. 17b)

   17a. Which one does _____ ask for? _____

   17b. What kinds of brands do you usually buy? _____

   17c. Why do you buy this kind? (PROBE HARD: Any other reason?) _____

18. How many TV sets are there in your home? _____ (IF ONE SKIP TO Q. 19)

   18a. Does your child have access to a TV set of his own? _____

19. How often do you place restrictions on _____ (READ INSERT), regularly, sometimes, or never?

	Regularly	Sometimes	Never
19a. Which programs your child can watch on TV	_____	_____	_____
19b. When your child can watch TV	_____	_____	_____
19c. How many hours each day your child can watch TV	_____	_____	_____

20. About how many hours does your child spend watching TV on weekdays?

before dinner _____

after dinner _____

   20a. What programs does he/she watch? (PROBE FOR NAME OR TYPE, e.g., "WESTERN," "CARTOON") _____

21. About how many hours does your child spend watching TV on Saturday? _____

   21a. Does your child watch ZOOM?

      _____ Yes _____ Often—almost everytime it's on.

                 _____ Sometimes—every few shows.

                 _____ Not too often—a few times a month.

      _____ No _____ (SKIP TO Q. 22)

   21b. What does he/she like about it? _____

21c. What do *you* like about it? _____

22. How many hours per day do you usually spend watching TV?
afternoons, noon–6:00 _____
evenings, after 6:00 _____

23. Do you ever talk to _____ about TV commercials?
_____ Yes
_____ No (SKIP TO Q. 26)
23a. What do you talk about? (PROBE: Anything else?) _____

24. How do you feel about TV commercials that are made for children? _____
24a. What else do you like/dislike about TV commercials that are made for children? _____

25. How often do you agree with _____ on the following matters?

	Usually Agree	Sometimes Agree/ Sometimes Disagree	Usually Disagree
a. clothing	___	___	___
b. choice of friends	___	___	___
c. bed time	___	___	___
d. his choice of time of play	___	___	___
e. which TV program to watch	___	___	___
f. amount of time spent watching TV	___	___	___

26. Now here's a card which describes a few different reactions parents might have to their child's request for a product. (HAND CARD A TO MOTHER) Please read it. (WAIT UNTIL MOTHER READS THROUGH)

CARD A:

1. I buy the product he/she wants.
2. I'll agree to pay for the product if my child will do his share—pay part of the cost, do chores, etc.
3. I'll agree to allow the purchase with the understanding that my child will use his own money.

    4. I refuse to buy the product, but I give
       an explanation of why my child can't
       have the product.
    5. I just say no and that's that.
    6. My child never asks for this product.

As I describe some products, please tell me what you *usually* do when _____ asks you for the product . . . just call out the number of the response you are most likely to make. (PROBE: AFTER EACH PRODUCT ASK: "Is there another response you make pretty often?")

		PROBE
a. a certain kind of cereal	_____	_____
b. sports equipment	_____	_____
c. snack foods to be eaten at home	_____	_____
d. a shirt or blouse	_____	_____
e. a book or magazine	_____	_____

AFTER e: Are the responses on this card really like things you do? Is there anything you'd like to add?

These next few questions have to do with situations in which _____ might ask you to buy him/her a product . . . again, indicate the number of your response to him/her (PROBE AFTER EACH SITUATION, ASK: "Is there any other response you might make?")

                                                     PROBE

f. _____ comes home from a
   friend's house and asks you to
   buy a toy costing about $4, like
   the one his/her friend has.   _____   _____

g. You're at home, and _____
   and his brother(s) and sister(s)
   all ask you to buy a game costing
   about $5. It's a safe game, and
   there would be no problems in
   sharing it.   _____   _____

h. You were watching TV last night
   and your child asks you to buy
   him a toy he/she saw on a com-
   mercial costing about $3 or $4.   _____   _____

i. You're in a hurry while shopping with _____, you're just about to leave the store, and _____ asks you to buy a bag of popcorn. It's early afternoon and there's no line at the checkout counter.   _____   _____

j. Your child is at home with one of his/her best friends, and he/she asks for a game which costs about $4. You're pretty sure he/she got the idea to want the game from his/her friend.   _____   _____

k. You're shopping in a grocery store early in the afternoon with your child and he/she asks you for money to buy some candy.   _____   _____

l. You've been shopping for about three hours with _____ and he asks you to buy a toy costing about $2.   _____   _____

27. I'm going to read you a list of products. For each product, please indicate how that product is usually purchased, either with your money or with _____ own money. Choose one of these answers. (HAND CARD B TO MOTHER)

	(1) Child chooses for self	(2) Child chooses but talks to parent first	(3) Parent chooses but talks to child first	(4) Parent chooses doesn't talk to child
a. candy	_____	_____	_____	_____
b. new style shirt	_____	_____	_____	_____
c. new style shoes	_____	_____	_____	_____
d. game or toy	_____	_____	_____	_____
e. record album	_____	_____	_____	_____
f. ticket to movie	_____	_____	_____	_____
g. magazine, comic book	_____	_____	_____	_____

h. snack food   _____   _____   _____   _____
i. sports
  equipment   _____   _____   _____   _____

Now, the next set of questions are going to focus on you . . . not
on _____.

28. How often do you go grocery shopping *at more than one store* . . .
would you say usually, sometimes, seldom, or never?
_____ Usually
_____ Sometimes
_____ Seldom
_____ Never (SKIP TO Q. 29)
28a. For what reasons do you do your grocery shopping at more
than one store? _____

29. What was the last major purchase of a major appliance, new
furniture, or an automobile that you made? _____
29a. When did you buy it? (PROBE FOR SPECIFIC DATE) _____
29b. When did you first think about buying it? (PROBE FOR
SPECIFIC DATE) _____
29c. Why did you buy it when you did? (IF ANSWER IS LIKE,
"MY OLD ONE BROKE DOWN AND I HAD TO GET A
NEW ONE RIGHT AWAY," ASK Q. 29d; OTHERWISE,
SKIP TO Q. 29f.) _____
29d. Had you expected your old one to break down?
_____ Yes
_____ No (SKIP TO Q. 29f)
29e. When you first thought it was breaking down, what plans did
you make to replace it? _____
29f. About how much did it cost? $ _____
29g. How did you pay for it? _____

30. What was the last major purchase before (PRODUCT FROM
Q. 29)? _____
30a. When did you buy it? (PROBE FOR SPECIFIC DATE) _____
30b. When did you first think about buying it? (PROBE FOR
SPECIFIC DATE) _____
30c. Why did you buy it when you did? (IF ANSWER IS LIKE,
"MY OLD ONE BROKE DOWN AND I HAD TO GET A
NEW ONE RIGHT AWAY," ASK Q. 30d; OTHERWISE,

SKIP TO Q. 30f.) _____

30d. Had you expected your old one to break down?
_____ Yes
_____ No (SKIP TO Q. 30f)

30e. When you first thought it was breaking down, what plans did you make to replace it? _____

30f. About how much did it cost? $ _____

30g. How did you pay for it? _____

31. What is the next major purchase you expect to make? (IF NOT PLANNING ANYTHING, SKIP TO Q. 32) _____

31a. When do you plan to buy it? (PROBE FOR SPECIFIC DATE) _____

31b. How much do you plan to pay for it? _____

31c. How do you plan to pay for it? _____

32. When you have made a major purchase such as a washing machine, automobile, or refrigerator, how often have you consulted the following sources for information about that product. (READ ITEM) Would you say usually, sometimes, not too often or never?

	Usually	Some-times	Not Too Often	Never
a. newspaper ads	____	____	____	____
b. your relatives	____	____	____	____
c. your friends	____	____	____	____
d. salesmen at stores other than where you eventually made the purchase	____	____	____	____
e. consumer guidebooks, such as *Consumer Reports*	____	____	____	____

33. I'm going to read you a list of products, and I'd like you to tell me which of these seven things (HAND RESPONDENT CARD C) are the most important when you buy them. Pick only as many as are actually important to you in buying.

CARD C

1. The price of the brand as compared to other brands.

2. The brand name.
3. The cost of the product in terms of your own budget.
4. Claims for the product made in advertisements.
5. Your friends' experience with the product.
6. The quality of the store where you are buying the product.
7. How the product looks.

	1	2	3	4	5	6	7
a. a TV set	___	___	___	___	___	___	___
b. a laundry soap	___	___	___	___	___	___	___
c. ice cream	___	___	___	___	___	___	___
d. a pair of good children's shoes	___	___	___	___	___	___	___
e. a hair dryer	___	___	___	___	___	___	___
f. a good winter coat	___	___	___	___	___	___	___
g. a dining room set	___	___	___	___	___	___	___
h. paper towels	___	___	___	___	___	___	___
i. a purse	___	___	___	___	___	___	___

34. Suppose you had a problem with something you bought that was pretty expensive. You took it back to the store, but didn't get satisfaction. What could you do? (PROBE: What else could you do?) _____

35. Have you ever used information from consumer guides ... like *Consumer Reports* ... to help you choose a product?
_____ Yes
_____ No

36. Have you ever read any books or magazine articles that help you learn *how* to be a better consumer?
_____ Yes
_____ No

37. Have you ever called or written about a store or product to the Better Business Bureau, State Office of Consumer Affairs, Attorney General's Office, or to a newspaper or TV station?
_____ Yes
_____ No (SKIP TO Q. 38)

37a.   For what reason? _____

38. What does your husband do for a living? (PROBE TO GET DE-
    SCRIPTIONS LIKE THIS: He's a sales clerk, waits on customers in
    a department store.) (SUGGESTED PROBES: What is his job
    called? What kind of business or industry does he work in? What
    does he do on his job?) _____

39. Do you hold a job?
    _____ Yes
    _____ No (SKIP TO Q. 40)
    _____ Part-time
    39a. What is this job? (PROBE TO GET DESCRIPTION AS FOR
          HUSBAND) _____

40. What is _____ 's birth date? _____

Thank you for answering these questions. While I'm checking over the
interview to make sure we didn't miss anything, would you please fill
out this questionnaire?

MOTHER'S QUESTIONNAIRE

1. Sometimes children and parents talk about purchases. Below are
   some questions your child might ask about buying three different
   products—tennis shoes, a bike, and candy.

   For each product, please choose which question your child would
   ask *first,* then *second,* then *third.* If you feel your child would not
   ask as many as three questions, just pick one or two.

   Questions:
   a. How much does it cost, or how much should I spend?
   b. Where should I buy it?
   c. What are the differences between brands?/or what brand should
      I buy?
   d. What are the differences between types?/or which type should I
      buy?
   e. SNEAKERS—How long will they last?
      BIKE—How well will it work?
      CANDY—How good does it taste?

Place the *letter* of the first, second, and third question your child would ask about each product in the space provided below. If you feel your child would ask a different question, write it in the space provided next to "Other."

SNEAKERS OR TENNIS SHOES

First question: _____ (or other: _____)
Second question: _____ (or other: _____)
Third question: _____ (or other: _____)

BIKE

First question: _____ (or other: _____)
Second question: _____ (or other: _____)
Third question: _____ (or other: _____)

CANDY

First question: _____ (or other: _____)
Second question: _____ (or other: _____)
Third question: _____ (or other: _____)

2. Below are are a series of statements concerning TV advertising, business, government, and the consumer. For each statement, please check *one* space to indicate how much you agree or disagree with it.

   a. My child understands what commercials on children's shows are trying to do.
      Strongly Agree _____ Somewhat Agree _____
      Strongly Disagree _____ Somewhat Disagree _____

   b. Commercials on children's shows are often deceptive (that is, untrue in ways which mislead children in important ways).
      Strongly Agree _____ Somewhat Agree _____
      Strongly Disagree _____ Somewhat Disagree _____

   c. There are too many commercials on shows children watch.
      Strongly Agree _____ Somewhat Agree _____
      Strongly Disagree _____ Somewhat Disagree _____

   d. Commercials are a fair price to pay for the entertainment children receive.
      Strongly Agree _____ Somewhat Agree _____
      Strongly Disagree _____ Somewhat Disagree _____

e. Commercials to children should be regulated by the government.
    Strongly Agree _____ Somewhat Agree _____
    Strongly Disagree _____ Somewhat Disagree _____

f. My child likes many TV commercials.
    Strongly Agree _____ Somewhat Agree _____
    Strongly Disagree _____ Somewhat Disagree _____

g. Commercials to children should be regulated by advertisers themselves.
    Strongly Agree _____ Somewhat Agree _____
    Strongly Disagree _____ Somewhat Disagree _____

h. Commercials often make my child want the thing advertised.
    Strongly Agree _____ Somewhat Agree _____
    Strongly Disagree _____ Somewhat Disagree _____

i. Advertising often persuades people to buy things they don't need.
    Strongly Agree _____ Somewhat Agree _____
    Strongly Disagree _____ Somewhat Disagree _____

j. Advertising is more effective in influencing the consumer than was the case ten years ago.
    Strongly Agree _____ Somewhat Agree _____
    Strongly Disagree _____ Somewhat Disagree _____

k. The products that are advertised the most are usually the best products.
    Strongly Agree _____ Somewhat Agree _____
    Strongly Disagree _____ Somewhat Disagree _____

l. In general, advertisements present a true picture of the product advertised.
    Strongly Agree _____ Somewhat Agree _____
    Strongly Disagree _____ Somewhat Disagree _____

m. Advertising is a fair price to pay for mass-media entertainment.
    Strongly Agree _____ Somewhat Agree _____
    Strongly Disagree _____ Somewhat Disagree _____

n. Unadvertised brands are generally not as high quality as nationally advertised brands.
    Strongly Agree _____ Somewhat Agree _____

    Strongly Disagree   _____   Somewhat Disagree _____

o. Information consumers really need about products is rarely on the label or instructions.
    Strongly Agree   _____   Somewhat Agree   _____
    Strongly Disagree   _____   Somewhat Disagree _____

p. The government should regulate the advertising, sales, and marketing activities of manufacturers.
    Strongly Agree   _____   Somewhat Agree   _____
    Strongly Disagree   _____   Somewhat Disagree _____

q. Most business firms make a sincere effort to adjust consumer complaints fairly.
    Strongly Agree   _____   Somewhat Agree   _____
    Strongly Disagree   _____   Somewhat Disagree _____

r. Many of the mistakes that consumers make in buying products are the result of their own carelessness or ignorance.
    Strongly Agree   _____   Somewhat Agree   _____
    Strongly Disagree   _____   Somewhat Disagree _____

s. Generally, self-regulation for business can be effective.
    Strongly Agree   _____   Somewhat Agree   _____
    Strongly Disagree   _____   Somewhat Disagree _____

t. The federal government definitely should pass extensive new laws to help consumers get fair deals for their money.
    Strongly Agree   _____   Somewhat Agree   _____
    Strongly Disagree   _____   Somewhat Disagree _____

u. The information needed to become a well-informed consumer is readily available to most people.
    Strongly Agree   _____   Somewhat Agree   _____
    Strongly Disagree   _____   Somewhat Disagree _____

3. Which *one* of these things do you think would offer the best means of avoiding consumer problems in the future:
    _____ More efforts by business to help consumers.
    _____ Consumer legislation by the government.
    _____ Consumer education programs.
    _____ Other (Specify: _____)

4. Which statement below *best* describes how you and your husband manage your money:

_____ We have a written budget and we stick to it closely almost every month.

_____ We have a written budget and we stick to it much of the time.

_____ We have a written budget but most of the time we don't stick to it.

_____ We don't have a written budget but we keep careful track of our money through our checking account.

_____ We don't have a written budget but—through our checking account—we pretty well know what we're spending.

_____ To tell you the truth, we really don't manage our money much at all.

5. Listed below are some things you may do with your child. Please check the space indicating how often you do each thing with your child.

a. Play games with him.

   Often—several times a week   _____
   Pretty Often—about once a week   _____
   Sometimes—about every two weeks   _____
   Not Too Often—once a month or less   _____
   Almost Never   _____

b. Spank him.

   Often—several times a week   _____
   Pretty Often—about once a week   _____
   Sometimes—about every two weeks   _____
   Not Too Often—once a month or less   _____
   Almost Never   _____

c. Tell your child he has been good.

   Often—several times a week   _____
   Pretty Often—about once a week   _____
   Sometimes—about every two weeks   _____
   Not Too Often—once a month or less   _____
   Almost Never   _____

d. Punish him by taking away some of his privileges.

   Often—several times a week   _____
   Pretty Often—about once a week   _____

Sometimes—about every two weeks   _____
Not Too Often—once a month or less   _____
Almost Never   _____

e. Get angry at him.
    Often—several times a week   _____
    Pretty Often—about once a week   _____
    Sometimes—about every two weeks   _____
    Not Too Often—once a month or less   _____
    Almost Never   _____

f. Hug or kiss him.
    Often—several times a week   _____
    Pretty Often—about once a week   _____
    Sometimes—about every two weeks   _____
    Not Too Often—once a month or less   _____
    Almost Never   _____

g. Make him feel guilty when he does something wrong.
    Often—several times a week   _____
    Pretty Often—about once a week   _____
    Sometimes—about every two weeks   _____
    Not Too Often—once a month or less   _____
    Almost Never   _____

h. Take him to movies or things like that.
    Often—several times a week   _____
    Pretty Often—about once a week   _____
    Sometimes—about every two weeks   _____
    Not Too Often—once a month or less   _____
    Almost Never   _____

i. Tell your child he can't buy certain things.
    Often—several times a week   _____
    Pretty Often—about once a week   _____
    Sometimes—about every two weeks   _____
    Not Too Often—once a month or less   _____
    Almost Never   _____

j. Ask your child what his preference is when you are buying something for him.
    Often—several times a week   _____
    Pretty Often—about once a week   _____

          Sometimes—about every two weeks   ————
          Not Too Often—once a month or less ————
          Almost Never   ————

k. Talk to him about how much products cost.
          Often—several times a week   ————
          Pretty Often—about once a week   ————
          Sometimes—about every two weeks   ————
          Not Too Often—once a month or less ————
          Almost Never   ————

l. Talk to him about where different products can be bought.
          Often—several times a week   ————
          Pretty Often—about once a week   ————
          Sometimes—about every two weeks   ————
          Not Too Often—once a month or less ————
          Almost Never   ————

6. In families, decisions are sometimes made by the husband, sometimes by the wife, and sometimes both husband and wife decide together. For each of the decisions listed below, please check the space indicating how you and your husband make the decision.

	Husband More Than Wife	Wife More Than Husband	Both Husband and Wife
a. Who decides what car to get?	————	————	————
b. Who decides whether or not to buy some life insurance?	————	————	————
c. Who decides how much money your family can afford to spend per week on food?	————	————	————
d. Who decides what house or apartment to take?	————	————	————

  e. Who decides
    where to go
    on a vacation? _____ _____ _____

  f. Who keeps
    track of money
    and bills? _____ _____ _____

7. Some people have said that consumers themselves are the primary source of consumer problems, while others feel that business or the government is primarily responsible. Suppose you had 100 points to divide among these three groups—consumers, business, and government. How would you divide up the points in order to indicate how much you think each group is responsible for *causing* consumer problems?

  _____Consumer
  _____ Business
  _____Government

8. Using the same 100-point scale and the same three groups, how would you divide up the points in order to indicate how much you think each group can help to *resolve* consumer problems?

  _____Consumer
  _____ Business
  _____Government

  8a. What is your approximate total family income per year?

    _____$3,000 or less   _____$11,001-$13,000
    _____$3,001-$5,000   _____$13,001-$15,000
    _____$5,001-$7,000   _____$15,001-$20,000
    _____$7,001-$9,000   _____$20,001-$25,000
    _____$9,001-$11,000   _____$25,001 or over

9. How many years of schooling have you had?

  _____Never attended school   _____Bachelor's degree
  _____1-6 years   _____Master's degree
  _____7-8 years   _____Ph.D.
  _____9-11 years   _____Professional graduate (law, medicine, etc.)

  _____High school graduate   _____Other (what?)
  _____Some college   _____

10. How many years of schooling has your husband had?

_____ Never attended school	_____ Bachelor's degree
_____ 1-6 years	_____ Master's degree
_____ 7-8 years	_____ Ph.D.
_____ 9-11 years	_____ Professional graduate (law, medicine, etc.)
_____ High school graduate	_____ Other (what?)
_____ Some college	_____

11. What is your approximate age, and your husband's?

Your Age		Husband's Age
_____	under 21	_____
_____	21-25	_____
_____	26-30	_____
_____	31-35	_____
_____	36-40	_____
_____	41-45	_____
_____	46-50	_____
_____	Over 50	_____

12. What are the ages of all your sons and daughters?

Sons	Daughters
_____	_____
_____	_____
_____	_____
_____	_____

EXCERPTS FROM CODE: CHILD'S INTERVIEW

▬▬▬▬▬▬▬▬▬▬▬▬▬▬▬▬▬▬▬▬▬

1. When you watch TV you must see a lot of commercials. What is a TV commercial? (PROBE HARD: Is there any other way you can tell me what a commercial is?)

LOW AWARENESS: NO CONCEPT OF ADVERTISING

01. Descriptions—specific commercials: "They show kids playing with dune buggies and the dune buggies go around the track."
02. Descriptions and generalized concrete properties of commercials: They're short, interrupt show, funny.
03. Affect answers: focus on one's own affective experience—I like/don't like them, they make me laugh.
97. Child doesn't understand the question. Child lacks ability to differentiate between programs and commercials.

MEDIUM AWARENESS: CONCEPT OF ADVERTISING WITHOUT UNDERSTANDING

04. Advertises—no further response: it's an ad.

05. Informs, shows people product: shows you things so you know what to buy.

06. Praises product: they tell you their product is best.

07. Idea of selling—generalized or hazy: they sell stuff.

08. Idea of selling—specific to product or category of products: they sell toys.

HIGH AWARENESS: CONCEPT OF INTENT, SPONSORSHIP AND/OR TECHNIQUE

09. Idea of affecting audience behavior—they want you to buy products—no idea of profit motive.

10. Idea that commercials are intended to affect audience behavior with some idea of profit motive: they want you to buy their products so they can make money.

11. Sponsors show: they pay for the show.

12. Idea of technique used to persuade audience to buy product— they make people look nice and liking their product so you'll want to buy it.

13. Combination of two or more of the above.

2. Why are commercials shown on television? (PROBE: Is there any other reason they're shown on TV?)

LOW AWARENESS

1. No understanding that there is a purpose: to show that commercial because they're important—n.f.s. not further specified, nonsense answer, DK.

2. Focus on one's own experience watching commercial: so you could watch them; because I can't sit that long to go to the bathroom. Viewer's experience.

3. Perceived needs of TV actors: because when something happens on TV they just put commercials on so actors can get dressed.

MEDIUM AWARENESS

4. Very specific recognition of information, focus on one type of commercial only, i.e., they show where kids can buy toys.

5. Some recognition of information or general teaching function: to

show people what's good and bad; to advertise things; people can ask for something they've seen advertised; to help you.

6. Some recognition of selling motive: to sell things; get you to buy stuff and make you believe theirs is the best.

HIGH AWARENESS

7. Recognition of selling motive which includes taking role of others.
    a) Subsumes information as part of selling process: they want people to know product and its qualities so they'll buy it.
    b) Idea of technique: talk you into buying things.
    c) Reasons behind selling motives: to get you to buy stuff so they can make money.
8. Sponsorship: to help pay for the show; to make money for TV station; to sponsor TV program.

2a. What do commercials try to do? (PROBE: Anything else they try to do?)

---

1. No understanding that there is a purpose: to show that commercial because they're important—n.f.s., DK, nonsense answers.
2. Focus on one's own viewer experience watching commercial: so you could watch them; because I can't sit that long to go to the bathroom.
3. Perceived needs to TV actors: because when something happens on TV they just put commercials on so actors can get dressed.
4. Some recognition of information; very specific type based on one thing: they show where kids can buy toys.
5. Some recognition of information or teaching general function: to show the people what's good and bad; to advertise things; people can ask for something they've seen advertised; to help you.
6. Some recognition of selling motive: to sell things; get you to buy stuff and make you believe theirs is the best.
7. Recognition of selling motive which includes taking role of others.
    a) Subsumes information as part of selling process; they want people to know product and its qualities so they'll buy it.

    b) Idea of technique: talk you into buying things.

    c) Reasons behind selling motives: to get you to buy stuff so they can make money.

  8. Sponsorship: to help pay for the show; to make money for TV station; to sponsor TV program.

3.   What is your favorite TV commercial—the one you like the most?

3a. Tell me what happens in this commercial. (PROBE: Anything else?)

---

  1. Recall unidimensional (descriptive): a boy's eating cereal.

  2. Recall unidimensional (message): they want you to buy Crest toothpaste.

  3. Recall multi-dimensional and *random:* there's a girl playing with a doll. The doll cries and it's green and purple. The doll has lots of clothes.

  4. Recall multi-dimensional and *coherent:* a woman says she has to paint her wall. Then a boy comes through the wall and says "use Wonder Wally." She uses it and says "now I don't have to paint my walls."

  5. Recall multi-dimensional, *coherent* with selling message: like the one where a boy is walking in the zoo. He has two lions with him and he has two candy bars. They're called Kit Kat. He says they are so light you can eat two and they want you to buy them.

3b. Why do you like it? (PROBE: What do you like about it? What's in it that you like?) (Three responses)

TYPE OF AFFECT

  01. Funny
  02. Scary
  03. Stupid, absurd
  07. Like it
  08. Don't like it
  18. Other affect

ELEMENT IN COMMERCIAL UPON WHICH AFFECT IS BASED

21. Entertainment
22. Information
23. Aesthetics
24. Product
25. Significant other (parents, kids, celebrities, animals, organization)
38. Other element
97. Irrelevant response (if only response)
99. NA
00. Inap.

4. When you watch TV you see both programs and commercials. What is the difference between a TV program and a TV commercial? (Anything else?)

---

1. Lack of ability to focus on dimensions which differentiate objects *(coincidental reasoning)*:
   a) Mention only one object—focus on experience rather than perception: cartoons make me happy; I like TV programs.
   b) Sentence with no differentiating elements: after program is over commercial comes on; they go under tunnels (car-truck); they love each other (mother-father); when I'm tired from school I come home.
2. *Perceptual:* refers to physical attributes of objects distinguished. Solely perceptual responses (coincidental reasoning): program is longer; schools bigger than homes; my mother has long hair.
3. *Transitional:* child refers to activities which object performs. Child does not grasp essential functional qualities of objects discriminated: At home you can sleep, at school you can't sleep; a car can go faster because a truck is heavier than a car.
4. *Conceptual:* focus on fuctional difference; statement must be complete rather than inferred (causal, logical reasoning): commercials show things to sell and a program is a long show with nothing to sell. It's a story; a truck carries things, a car is for riding; a school is to get your education, a home is to live in.
9. NA

4a. Let's see if you can tell me about differences between other things:

---

(1) SCHOOL-HOUSE

1. Lack of ability to focus on dimensions which differentiate objects *(coincidental reasoning):*
   a) Mention only one object—focus on experience rather than perception: cartoons make me happy; I like TV programs.
   b) Sentence with no differentiating elements: after program is over commercial comes on; they go under tunnels (car-truck); they love each other (mother-father); when I'm tired from school I come home.
2. *Perceptual:* refers to physical attributes of objects distinguished. Solely perceptual responses (coincidental reasoning): program is longer; schools bigger than homes; my mother has long hair.
3. *Transitional:* child refers to activities which object performs. Child does not grasp essential functional qualities of objects discriminated; at home you can sleep; at school you can't sleep; a car can go faster because a truck is heavier than a car.
4. *Conceptual:* focus on functional difference; statement must be complete rather than inferred (causal, logical reasoning): commercials show things to sell and a program is a long show with nothing to sell. It's a story; a truck carries things, a car is for riding; a school is to get your education, a home is to live in.
9. NA

(2) CAR-TRUCK

1. Lack of ability to focus on dimensions which differentiate objects *(coincidental reasoning):*
   a) Mention only one object—focus on experience rather than perception: cartoons make me happy; I like TV programs.
   b) Sentence with no differentiating elements: after program is over commercial comes on; they go under tunnels (car-truck); they love each other (mother-father); when I'm tired from school I come home.
2. *Perceptual:* refers to physical attributes of objects distinguished. Solely perceptual response (coincidental reasoning): program is longer; schools bigger than homes; my mother has long hair.

3. *Transitional:* child refers to activities which object performs. Child does not grasp essential functional qualities of objects discriminated; at home you can sleep, at school you can't sleep, a car can go faster because a truck is heavier than a car.

4. *Conceptual:* focus on functional difference; statement must be complete rather than inferred (causal, logical reasoning): commercials show things to sell and a program is a long show with nothing to sell. It's a story; a truck carries things, a car is for riding; a school is to get your education, a home is to live in.

(3) FATHER-MOTHER

1. Lack of ability to focus on dimensions which differentiate objects *(coincidental reasoning):*
   a) Mention only one object—focus on experience rather than perception: cartoons make me happy; I like TV programs.
   b) Sentence with no differentiating elements: after program is over commercial comes on; they go under tunnels (car-truck); they love each other (mother-father); when I'm tired from school I come home.

2. *Perceptual:* refers to physical attributes of objects distinguished. Solely perceptual responses (coincidental reasoning): program is longer; schools bigger than homes; my mother has long hair.

3. *Transitional:* child refers to activities which object performs. Child does not grasp essential functional qualities of objects discriminated: at home you can sleep, at school you can't sleep; a car can go faster because a truck is heavier than a car.

4. *Conceptual:* focus on functional difference; a statement must be complete rather than inferred (causal, logical reasoning): commercials show things to sell and a program is a long show with nothing to sell. It's a story; a truck carries things, a car is for riding; a school is to get your education, a home is to live in.

9. NA

5. Let's talk about TV again. Do you think TV commercials always tell the truth?

___

1. Yes (Code 0 in cols. 30-32)
2. Sometimes, no (Code 0 in cols. 28-29)

9. NA (Code 0 in cols. 28-32)

6.   How do you know they tell the truth?

---

1. Confused—no understanding of purpose and therefore, no basis for judgment: they just talk about things; we listen; they're lying because people can't fly; don't look right.
2. Authority-based responses: grownups tell the truth; mother tells me they lie; they're on TV; Sesame Street always tells the truth.
3. Concrete-specific experience—empirically based responses: you try to find it and it's not there; they say if you try Cheerios you'll get a big muscle and you don't get a big muscle all the time; see it at the market and it's the same as in the commercial.
4. Understanding of advertising techniques directed toward specific commercial: they make their product (specified) sound better than it is; in the commercial for aspirin, they're just being corny.
5. Generalized distrust—rejects function of persuading people to buy—nonauthority based generalized trust responses: they have interesting stories on so you watch and think their product is good; they're acting; they do tricks; exaggerate; they tell the truth because they want you to buy their products and if they don't tell the truth they wouldn't buy them, think it's a good company, etc.
6. Understanding of mixture of truth and untruth due to general psychological and/or social factors relevant to advertising.
9. NS
0. Inap.—commercials don't tell truth, coded 2 or 9 in col. 27.

6a.   Why do you think commercials tell the truth? (What do you think is the reason commercials tell the truth?)

---

1. No or egocentric concept of motivations of advertisers: cuz they don't lie; cuz if they don't they'd be lying and they'd stop TV—they'd get kicked out; they just want to fool you to see if you're smart.
2. Notion of desire to motivate (i.e., affect audience behavior) without specified ideas of profit motive: they want you to go

and get it; they know stuff doesn't really do it so they make stuff up to make people buy product.

3. Understanding or profit motives of advertisers: they want the money; for the $—they want you to buy stuff no matter what; company wants $ so they can keep going.

4. Understanding of selling motive plus societal constraints on advertising.

9. NA

0. Inap.—commercials don't tell truth, coded 2 or 9 in col. 27.

7. How often do they lie—most of the time, some of the time or just once in a while?

---

1. Most of the time
2. Some of the time
3. Just once in a while
9. NA
0. Inap.—always tell truth, coded 1 or 9 in col. 27.

7a. How do you know when they lie?

---

1. Confused—no understanding of purpose and therefore, no basis for judgment: they just talk about things; we listen; they're lying because people can't fly; don't look right.

2. Authority-based responses: grownups tell the truth; mother tells me they lie; they're on TV; Sesame Street always tells the truth.

3. Concrete-specific experience—empirically based responses: you go to find it and it's not there; they say if you try Cheerios you'll get a big muscle and you don't get a big muscle all the time; see it at the market and it's the same as in the commercial.

4. Understanding of advertising techniques directed toward specific commercial: they make their product (specified) sound better than it is; in the commercial for aspirin, they're just being corny.

5. Generalized distrust—rejects function of persuading people to buy—nonauthority based generalized trust responses: they have interesting stories on so you watch and think their product is good; they're acting; they do tricks, exaggerate; they tell the

truth because they want you to buy their products and if they don't tell the truth they wouldn't buy them, think it's a good company, etc.

6. Understanding of mixture of truth and untruth due to general psychological and/or social factors relevant to advertising.

9. NA

0. Inap.—commercials tell truth, coded 1 or 9 in col. 27.

7b. Why do you think they don't tell the truth? (What do you think is the reason commercials don't tell the truth?)

---

1. No or egocentric concept of motivations of advertisers: cuz they don't lie; cuz if they don't, they'd be lying and they'd stop TV—they'd get kicked out, they just want to fool you to see if you're smart.

2. Notion of desire to motivate (i.e., affect audience behavior) without specified idea of profit motive: they want you to go and get it; they know stuff doesn't really do it so they make stuff up; to make people buy product.

3. Understanding of profit motives of advertiser: they want the money; for the $—they want you to buy stuff no matter what; company wants $ so they can keep going.

4. Understanding of selling motive plus societal constraints on advertising.

9. NA

0. Inap.—commercials always tell truth, coded 1 or 9 in col. 27.

Appendix C ▓▓▓▓▓▓▓▓▓▓▓▓▓▓▓▓▓▓▓▓▓▓▓▓▓▓▓▓▓▓▓▓▓▓

REGRESSION ANALYSES:
SEPARATELY BY GRADE LEVEL

▓▓▓▓▓▓▓▓▓▓▓▓▓▓▓▓▓▓▓▓▓▓▓▓▓▓▓▓▓▓▓▓▓▓

AWARENESS OF THE PURPOSE OF TV COMMERCIALS

Kindergarten Mult R=.516 R^2=.266	*beta*
Frequency of negotiating purchase requests	.17
Frequency of *not* yielding to purchase requests	.23
Number of comments about commercials	.13
Degree of opposition to children's commercials	.19
Frequency of using price/appearance attributes in purchases	.15
Number of quality shopping goals	.16
Child power in making purchases	.12
Frequency of using contextual attributes in purchases	−.11
Frequency of exposure to television commercials	−.09
Family socio-economic status	.08
Budget accounting	−.12
Budget planning	.12
Number of different sources for money	.09

Third Grade   Mult R=.391 R^2=.153

Flexibility in responding to purchase requests	.21
Total child income	−.13
Degree of opposition to children's commercials	−.14
Frequency of taking child shopping	−.11
Frequency of using price/appearance attributes in purchases	.11
Frequency of refusal with explanation	−.09
Budget accounting	.11
Number of quality shopping goals	.13
Number of sources consulted in major purchases	.12
Frequency of exposure to television commercials	.10
Number of comments about commercials	−.08

Sixth Grade   Mult R=.230 R^2=.053

Number of different sources for money	−.12
Frequency of refusal with explanation	−.13
Number of bargain goals	−.08
Degree of opposition to children's commercials	.14
Family socio-economic status	.09
Flexibility in responding to purchase requests	−.08
Budget planning	.14
Budget accounting	−.12
Number of quality shopping goals	.14
Number of money goals	.13
Relative efficiency of information use in purchases	−.18
Frequency of using contextual attributes in purchases	.13

INFORMATION-PROCESSING SKILLS—HIGHER LEVEL

ASKING ABOUT PERFORMANCE ATTRIBUTES IN TV PURCHASE

Kindergarten   Mult R=.268 R^2=.072

	beta
Number of quality shopping goals	.16
Number of money goals	−.10
Frequency of *not* yielding to purchase requests	.12
Frequency of discussing consumption generally	.09
Frequency of taking child shopping	.08

Third Grade   Mult R=.354 R^2=.125

Frequency of exposure to television commercials	.23
Number of quality shopping goals	.15
Frequency of *not* yielding to purchase requests	−.12
Budget planning	−.13
Frequency of negotiating purchase requests	.11
Number of comments about commercials	−.13
Degree of opposition to children's commercials	.11
Number of sources consulted in major purchases	.11

Sixth Grade   Mult R=.304 R^2=.092

Frequency of refusal with explanation	−.21
Flexibility in responding to purchase requests	.09
Degree of opposition to children's commercials	−.12
Frequency of exposure to television commercials	.09
Relative efficiency of information use in purchases	.14
Number of bargain goals	.09
Frequency of *not* yielding to purchase requests	.08
Frequency of using price/appearance attributes in purchases	−.09

INFORMATION-PROCESSING SKILLS—HIGHER LEVEL

COMPARING BRANDS ON THE BASIS OF PERFORMANCE AND INGREDIENT CHARACTERISTICS

Kindergarten Mult R=.432 R^2=.186

	beta
Family socio-economic status	.16
Frequency of *not* yielding to child's purchase requests	.15
Number of money goals	.12
Number of quality shopping goals	.12
Frequency of using contextual attributes in purchases	−.23
Total information use in purchases	.20
Budget accounting	−.13
Number of different sources for money	.14
Budget planning	.09
Total child income	−.10
Frequency of exposure to television commercials	.08

Third Grade   Mult R=.433   R^2=.187

Frequency of using contextual attributes in purchases	.27
Number of money goals	.23
Frequency of taking child shopping	.15
Flexibility in responding to purchase requests	.11
Family socio-economic status	.12
Frequency of discussing consumption generally	.09
Number of quality shopping goals	−.09

Sixth Grade   Mult R=.091   R^2=.153

Number of comments about commercials	.16
Total information use in purchases	.10
Frequency of *not* yielding to purchase requests	.13
Budget planning	.13
Number of money goals	.18
Number of quality shopping goals	.16
Frequency of refusal with explanation	−.12
Number of different sources for money	.09
Child power in making purchases	−.09

INFORMATION-PROCESSING SKILLS—HIGHER LEVEL

AWARENESS OF MULTIPLE SOURCES FOR INFORMATION ABOUT NEW PRODUCTS

Kindergarten   Mult R=.366   R^2=.134   *beta*

Frequency of negotiating purchase requests	.17
Number of money goals	.11
Family socio-economic status	.10
Frequency of using price/appearance attributes in purchases	.12
Frequency of using contextual attributes in purchases	−.09
Degree of opposition to children's commercials	.12
Number of bargain goals	.09
Flexibility in responding to purchase requests	.09

Third Grade   Mult R=.323   R^2=.104

Frequency of refusal with explanation	.13
Family socio-economic status	.12

Relative efficiency in information use in purchases	.13
Frequency of using advertising attributes in purchases	−.10
Number of quality shopping goals	.09
Degree of opposition to children's commercials	.09
Frequency of *not* yielding to child's purchase requests	.09
Number of sources consulted in major purchases	.08

Sixth Grade Mult R=.372 R^2=.138

Frequency of using price/appearance attributes in purchases	.26
Number of sources consulted in major purchases	.10
Number of quality shopping goals	.06
Child power in making purchases	.12
Family socio-economic status	.09
Frequency of negotiating purchase requests	−.11
Frequency of *not* yielding to purchase requests	.08
Frequency of using contextual attributes in purchases	.09
Frequency of refusal with explanation	.08
Number of money goals	−.08

INFORMATION-PROCESSING SKILLS–HIGHER LEVEL

AWARENESS OF BRAND NAMES

Kindergarten Mult R=.366 R^2=.134   *beta*

Number of comments about commercials	.16
Frequency of using contextual attributes in purchases	.17
Family socio-economic status	.11
Frequency of taking child shopping	.12
Flexibility in responding to purchase requests	−.13
Frequency of negotiating purchase requests	.12
Frequency of using advertising attributes in purchases	−.03
Frequency of using price/appearance attributes in purchases	.14
Relative efficiency of information use in purchases	−.14
Frequency of exposure to television commercials	.08

Third Grade Mult R=.338 R^2=.114

Frequency of discussing consumption generally	.19
Number of comments about commercials	.13

Frequency of using contextual attributes in purchases	.09
Child power in making purchases	.08
Relative effectiveness of information use in purchases	.20
Frequency of using price/appearance attributes in purchases	−.15

Sixth Grade   Mult R=.441   R²=.195

Family socio-economic status	.25
Child power in making purchases	.20
Frequency of using contextual attributes in purchases	.14
Frequency of refusal with explanation	−.18
Frequency of taking child shopping	−.12
Relative effectiveness of information use in purchases	.14
Frequency of exposure to television commercials	.08

INFORMATION-PROCESSING SKILLS–LOW LEVEL

ASKING ABOUT PERCEPTUAL ATTRIBUTES IN TV PURCHASE

Kindergarten Mult R=.263   R²=.069   *beta*

Frequency of using price/appearance attributes in purchases	.23
Number of money goals	.13
Budget planning	.12
Frequency of using contextual attributes in purchases	.17
Total information use in purchases	−.20
Frequency of negotiating purchase requests	.08

Third Grade   Mult R=.307   R²=.094

Frequency of exposure to television commercials	−.22
Number of comments about commercials	.12
Number of quality shopping goals	−.12
Degree of opposition to children's commercials	−.08
Frequency of using contextual attributes in purchases	.12
Budget accounting	−.13
Budget planning	.09
Number of sources consulted in major purchases	−.09

Sixth Grade   Mult R=.336   R²=.113

Relative efficiency of information use in purchases	−.25
Degree of opposition to children's commercial	.17
Budget planning	−.10
Flexibility in responding to purchase requests	−.20
Frequency of refusal with explanation	.12
Frequency of using advertising attributes in purchases	.12
Frequency of using price/appearance attributes in purchases	.11

INFORMATION-PROCESSING SKILLS–LOW LEVEL

COMPARING BRANDS ON THE BASIS OF PERCEPTUAL CHARACTERISTICS

Kindergarten Mult R=.310   R²=.096   *beta*

Frequency of negotiating purchase requests	.11
Frequency of *not* yielding to purchase requests	.15
Relative efficiency of information use in purchases	.16
Frequency of using advertising attributes in purchases	−.14
Frequency of discussing consumption generally	.09
Frequency of exposure to television commercials	−.09
Frequency of taking child shopping	.08
Flexibility in responding to purchase requests	−.08

Third Grade   Mult R=.290   R²=.084

Frequency of discussing consumption generally	−.18
Number of money goals	.13
Number of different sources for money	.10
Frequency of using price/appearance attributes in purchases	−.11
Frequency of refusal with explanation	.10
Frequency of *not* yielding to purchase requests	.09

Sixth Grade   Mult R=.383   R²=.147

Relative effectiveness of information use in purchases	.30
Frequency of using contextual attributes in purchases	−.27
Frequency of refusal with explanation	−.16
Frequency of using advertising attributes in purchases	.13
Frequency of taking child shopping	.13
Frequency of negotiating purchase requests	.12

Number of different sources for money .... −.09
Frequency of *not* yielding to purchase requests .... −.08

INFORMATION-PROCESSING SKILLS–LOW LEVEL

AWARENESS OF IN-STORE SHOPPING FOR INFORMATION ABOUT NEW PRODUCTS

Kindergarten Mult R=.398 R²=.158 — beta

	beta
Frequency of negotiating purchase requests	.31
Frequency of refusal with explanation	.22
Number of comments about commercials	−.11
Frequency of using price/appearance attributes in purchases	.15
Total information use in purchase	−.13

Third Grade Mult R=.300 R²=.090

Flexibility in responding to purchase requests	.18
Number of sources consulted in major purchases	−.14
Frequency of using price/appearance attributes in purchases	.19
Frequency of exposure to television commercials	−.10
Relative effectiveness of information use in purchases	−.13
Number of quality shopping goals	.09
Child power in making purchases	.07

Sixth Grade Mult R=.281 R²=.097

Frequency of using advertising attributes in purchases	−.19
Frequency of using contextual attributes in purchases	−.19
Relative efficiency of information use in purchases	.15
Number of bargain goals	−.10
Number of comments about commercials	.10
Flexibility in responding to purchase requests	−.08

MONEY USE SKILLS–SAVINGS

PRESCRIPTIVE NORMS–SAVINGS

Kindergarten Mult R=.339 R²=.115 — beta

	beta
Frequency of *not* yielding to purchase requests	.16
Number of money goals	−.17
Child power in making purchases	.15
Frequency of exposure to television commercials	−.11
Number of different sources for money	.10

Frequency of taking child shopping .... −.10
Frequency of refusal with explanation .... .10
Number of quality shopping goals .... −.12
Frequency of negotiating purchase requests .... .08

Third Grade   Mult R=.340   R²=.116

Frequency of using contextual attributes in purchases .... −.22
Frequency of refusal with explanation .... .23
Number of sources consulted in major purchases .... .17
Number of money goals .... −.10
Frequency of taking child shopping .... −.10
Frequency of exposure to television commercials .... .11
Flexibility in responding to purchase requests .... −.12
Frequency of using advertising attributes in purchases .... .09
Degree of opposition to children's commercials .... .08

Sixth Grade   Mult R=.293   R²=.086

Family socio-economic status .... −.15
Flexibility in responding to purchase requests .... −.18
Relative efficiency of information use in purchases .... .13
Number of different sources for money .... .09
Number of comments about commercials .... −.09
Frequency of *not* yielding to purchase requests .... .09

MONEY USE SKILLS–SAVINGS

PROSCRIPTIVE NORMS–DON'T WASTE MONEY

Kindergarten Mult R=.229   R²=.052   *beta*

Child power in making purchases .... −.07
Number of sources consulted in major purchases .... −.15
Budget accounting .... −.09
Relative efficiency of information use in purchases .... .13
Frequency of using advertising attributes in purchases .... −.10
Frequency of *not* yielding to purchase requests .... .08

Third Grade   Mult R=.352   R²=.124

Total information use in purchases .... .17
Frequency of negotiating purchase requests .... .14

Number of comments about commercials	−.13
Number of money goals	.09
Number of different sources for money	−.10
Frequency of discussing consumption generally	.10
Child power in making purchases	.09
Frequency of taking child shopping	−.08

Sixth Grade   Mult R=.350   R^2=.123

Number of money goals	−.16
Frequency of using contextual attributes in purchases	.14
Total child income	.10
Family socio-economic status	−.15
Frequency of negotiating purchase requests	.17
Number of sources consulted in major purchases	−.10
Frequency of exposure to television commercials	−.08
Frequency of *not* yielding to purchase requests	.09
Number of bargain goals	.08

MONEY USE SKILLS–SAVINGS

PROSCRIPTIVE NORMS–DON'T BUY SPECIFIC PRODUCTS

Kindergarten Mult R=.336   R^2=.113   *beta*

Number of quality shopping goals	.15
Number of different sources for money	.18
Frequency of discussing consumption generally	.10
Flexibility in responding to purchase requests	.13
Frequency of *not* yielding to purchase requests	−.12
Frequency of exposure to television commercials	.10
Family socio-economic status	.09

Third Grade   Mult R=.209   R^2=.044

Frequency of negotiating purchase requests	−.12
Child power in making purchases	−.10
Flexibility in responding to purchase requests	−.07

Sixth Grade   Mult R=.384   R^2=.148

Frequency of *not* yielding to purchase requests	.21

Frequency of using price/appearance attributes in purchases	.10
Frequency of using contextual attributes in purchases	−.18
Relative efficiency of information use in purchases	.18
Flexibility in responding to purchase requests	−.12
Family socio-economic status	.10
Number of money goals	.09
Number of comments about commercials	.09

MONEY USE SKILLS–SAVINGS

NUMBER OF TYPES OF PRESCRIPTIVE MONEY NORMS

Kindergarten Mult R=.341   R^2=.116   *beta*

Flexibility in responding to purchase requests	.14
Frequency of taking child shopping	−.07
Frequency of using price/appearance attributes in purchases	−.11
Number of bargain goals	.13
Frequency of using contextual attributes in purchases	−12
Number of comments about commercials	.10
Frequency of discussing consumption generally	−.10
Child power in making purchases	.13
Frequency of *not* yielding to purchase requests	.08
Total child income	−.14
Number of different sources for money	.11
Budget planning	.08

Third Grade   Mult R=.374   R^2=.140

Family socio-economic status	.20
Budget planning	−.15
Frequency of discussing consumption generally	.10
Frequency of using advertising attributes in purchases	.13
Degree of opposition to children's commercials	.11
Flexibility in responding to child's purchase requests	−.19
Frequency of refusal with explanation	.16
Frequency of taking child shopping	−.10
Frequency of exposure to television commercials	.10
Frequency of negotiating purchase requests	.10

Sixth Grade   Mult R=.314   R^2=.099

Degree of opposition to children's commercials	.12
Relative efficiency of information use in purchases	.15
Family socio-economic status	−.09
Frequency of using contextual attributes in purchases	−.09
Total child income	.09
Flexibility in responding to purchase requests	−.10
Frequency of using price/appearance attributes in purchases	.11
Number of comments about commercials	−.09
Frequency of discussing consumption generally	.08

MONEY USE SKILLS–SAVINGS

NUMBER OF TYPES OF PROSCRIPTIVE MONEY NORMS

Kindergarten   Mult R=.318   R^2=.101   *beta*

Flexibility in responding to purchase requests	.16
Frequency of discussing consumption generally	.16
Budget accounting	−.12
Number of sources consulted in major purchases	−.15
Number of quality shopping goals	.10
Number of different sources for money	.08

Third Grade   Mult R=.288   R^2=.083

Number of money goals	.17
Relative effectiveness of information use in purchases	.10
Frequency of exposure to television commercials	−.07

Sixth Grade   Mult R=.297   R^2=.088

Total child income	.13
Frequency of negotiating purchase requests	.11
Frequency of *not* yielding to purchase requests	.10
Frequency of exposure to television commercials	−.11
Family socio-economic status	−.09
Number of money goals	−.09
Relative efficiency of information use in purchases	.09
Budget planning	.08

MONEY USE SKILLS–SAVINGS

MONEY BEHAVIOR–SAVINGS

Kindergarten Mult R=.275 R^2=.075   *beta*

Frequency of *not* yielding to purchase requests	.16
Frequency of discussing consumption generally	.14
Number of sources consulted in major purchases	−.10
Number of comments about commercials	.13
Frequency of refusal with explanation	−.08
Budget accounting	.08

Third Grade   Mult R=.283 R^2=.080

Frequency of *not* yielding to purchase requests	−.12
Frequency of using contextual attributes in purchases	.12
Number of bargain goals	−.10
Number of comments about commercials	−.09
Flexibility in responding to purchase requests	−.10
Relative effectiveness of information use in purchases	.11
Budget planning	−.08

Sixth Grade   Mult R=.407 R^2=.165

Relative effectiveness of information use in purchases	.19
Frequency of taking child shopping	.18
Number of different sources for money	.17
Flexibility in responding to purchase requests	−.16
Degree of opposition to children's commercials	−.13
Frequency of *not* yielding to purchase requests	.12
Budget accounting	−.09
Family socio-economic status	.08
Frequency of using contextual attributes in purchases	.09

MONEY USE SKILLS–SAVINGS

REGULARITY OF SAVING PART OF CHILD'S INCOME

Kindergarten Mult R=.306 R^2=.094   *beta*

Frequency of using contextual attributes in purchases	.16

Frequency of negotiating purchase requests	.18
Flexibility in responding to purchase requests	-.14
Number of different sources for money	.11
Frequency of exposure to television commercials	.10

Third Grade   Mult R=.376 R^2=.142

Frequency of taking child shopping	.18
Frequency of discussing consumption generally	.10
Frequency of using advertising attributes in purchases	-.22
Relative efficiency of information use in purchases	.17
Number of different sources for money	-.11
Frequency of *not* yielding to child's purchase requests	-.10

Sixth Grade   Mult R=.316 R^2=.100

Number of different sources for money	.10
Degree of opposition to children's commercials	.12
Family socio-economic status	-.14
Frequency of exposure to television commercials	-.09
Number of comments about commercials	.12
Number of quality shopping goals	-.17
Number of bargain goals	-.13
Number of money goals	-.12
Frequency of using advertising attributes in purchases	.08
Frequency of negotiating purchase requests	.08

MONEY USE SKILLS—SAVINGS

NUMBER OF DIFFERENT USES OF CHILD'S INCOME

Kindergarten Mult R=.333 R^2=.111	*beta*
Number of different sources for money	.20
Frequency of negotiating purchase requests	.10
Frequency of using contextual attributes in purchases	-.16
Number of bargain goals	.11
Budget planning	.08
Flexibility in responding to purchase requests	.08
Frequency of taking child shopping	.08
Frequency of exposure to television commercials	-.08
Number of sources consulted in major purchases	.08

Third Grade   Mult R=.409   R^2=.167

Number of money goals	.17
Child power in making purchases	.18
Budget planning	-.16
Frequency of using contextual attributes in purchases	.12
Frequency of using price/appearance attributes in purchases	-.32
Relative effectiveness of information use in purchases	.24
Frequency of exposure to television commercials	-.12

Sixth Grade   Mult R=.375   R^2=.441

Total information use in purchases	.13
Number of different sources for money	.20
Frequency of taking child shopping	.13
Total child income	-.10
Child power in making purchases	-.09
Family socio-economic status	.10
Degree of opposition to children's commercials	-.13
Frequency of using contextual attributes in purchases	.09
Budget planning	-.07

NONSKILL BEHAVIORS–SPENDING AND ASKING FOR PRODUCTS

PRESCRIPTIVE NORMS–SPEND

Kindergarten Mult R=.314   R^2=.098

	beta
Flexibility in responding to purchase requests	.20
Frequency of refusal with explanation low	.14
Number of comments about commercials	.15
Number of sources consulted in major purchases	-.15
Budget planning	.14
Frequency of using contextual attributes in purchases	.10
Frequency of negotiating purchase requests low	.11
Budget accounting	-.09
Degree of opposition to children's commercials	-.08

Third Grade   Mult R=.278   R^2=.077

Budget planning	-.13

Number of money goals	.13
Frequency of using contextual attributes in purchases	.11
Number of sources consulted in major purchases	−.12
Frequency of refusal with explanation low	.12
Frequency of using price/appearance attributes in purchases	.90

Sixth Grade   Mult R=.349 R^2=.122

Degree of opposition to children's commercials	.17
Budget planning	−.13
Frequency of discussing consumption generally	.16
Frequency of using price/appearance attributes in purchases	.13
Number of sources consulted in major purchases	−.13
Frequency of taking child shopping	−.10
Frequency of using advertising attributes in purchases	.08
Frequency of exposure to television commercials	−.08
Total child income	.08

NONSKILL BEHAVIORS–SPENDING AND ASKING FOR PRODUCTS

MONEY BEHAVIOR–SPENDING

Kindergarten Mult R=.337 R^2=.113   *beta*

Number of different sources for money	.19
Frequency of yielding to purchase requests	.18
Frequency of refusal with explanation low	.14
Flexibility in responding to purchase requests	.14
Budget accounting	−.11
Family socio-economic status	−.08

Third Grade   Mult R=.257 R^2=.066

Number of different sources for money	.11
Number of comments about commercials	.13
Number of sources consulted in major purchases	−.13
Degree of opposition to children's commercials	.11
Budget planning	−.09
Budget accounting	.08

Sixth Grade   Mult R=.352 R^2=.124

Frequency of yielding to purchase requests	.24
Budget planning	−.16
Budget accounting	.10
Frequency of taking child shopping	−.10
Frequency of using contextual attributes in purchases	.14
Frequency of discussing consumption generally	.08
Child power in making purchases	.07
Frequency of using price/appearance attributes in purchases	.17
Relative effectiveness of information use in purchase	−.16

NONSKILL BEHAVIORS–SPENDING AND ASKING FOR PRODUCTS

REGULARITY OF SPENDING PART OF CHILD'S INCOME

Kindergarten   Mult R=.353   R^2=.245   *beta*

Number of different sources for money	.16
Frequency of yielding to purchase requests	.18
Frequency of negotiating purchase requests low	−.17
Flexibility in responding to purchase requests	−.11
Number of comments about commercials	.09
Frequency of using advertising attributes in purchases	.09
Child power in making purchases	.09

Third Grade   Mult R=.319   R^2=.102

Number of different sources for money	−.20
Family socio-economic status	−.13
Number of quality shopping goals	.14
Frequency of refusal with explanation low	.14
Total child income	.10
Number of comments about commercials	.09
Frequency of using advertising attributes in purchases	.11
Total information use in purchases	−.10

Sixth Grade   Mult R=.378   R^2=.143

Number of different sources for money	−.24
Total child income	.17
Frequency of negotiating purchase requests low	.13
Child power in making purchases	.10

Frequency of using contextual attributes in purchases	.16
Relative effectiveness of information use in purchases	−.11
Number of bargain goals	.11
Number of quality shopping goals	.09
Number of sources consulted in major purchases	−.09

NONSKILL BEHAVIORS–SPENDING AND ASKING FOR PRODUCTS

ASKING FOR FOOD PRODUCTS

Kindergarten Mult R=.327 R^2=.107   *beta*

Child power in making purchases	.18
Number of comments about commercials	.12
Total information use in purchases	−.18
Frequency of using contextual attributes in purchases	.11

Third Grade   Mult R=.401 R^2=.161

Number of comments about commercials	.24
Frequency of refusal with explanation low	.13
Degree of opposition to children's commercials	−.16
Frequency of discussing consumption generally	.13
Frequency of negotiating purchase requests low	.13
Child power in making purchases	.13
Frequency of yielding to purchase requests	.10
Frequency of taking child shopping	−.09
Number of bargain goals	.08

Sixth Grade   Mult R=.375 R^2=.140

Frequency of negotiating purchase requests low	.16
Child power in making purchases	.12
Number of comments about commercials	.13
Budget planning	−.12
Number of different sources for money	.11
Frequency of discussing consumption generally	.09
Frequency of refusal with explanation low	.09
Total child income	−.09
Frequency of using price/appearance attributes in purchases	.24

Relative effectiveness of information use in purchases   −.19
Frequency of yielding to purchase requests   .10

NONSKILL BEHAVIORS–SPENDING AND ASKING FOR PRODUCTS

ASKING FOR ADULT PRODUCTS

Kindergarten   Mult R=.405   R^2=.164   *beta*

Child power in making purchases	.21
Frequency of refusal with explanation low	.16
Frequency of taking child shopping	.13
Frequency of using price/appearance attributes in purchases	−.04
Frequency of using contextual attributes in purchases	.20
Number of comments about commercials	.11
Relative effectiveness of information use in purchases	−.19

Third Grade   Mult R=.444   R^2=.197

Number of different sources for money	.19
Family socio-economic status	−.17
Frequency of using advertising attributes in purchases	.25
Number of sources consulted in major purchases	.16
Relative efficiency of information use in purchases	−.24
Frequency of discussing consumption generally	.16
Frequency of refusal with explanation low	.18
Frequency of negotiating purchase requests low	.15
Number of quality shopping goals	.13
Number of bargain goals	.11
Frequency of using price/appearance attributes in purchases	.13
Number of comments about commercials	.10
Budget accounting	.08

Sixth Grade   Mult R=.161   R^2=.026

Frequency of negotiating purchase requests low	.18
Number of bargain goals	.15
Frequency of taking child shopping	.08
Frequency of exposure to television commercials	−.11
Frequency of discussing consumption generally	.10
Child power in making purchases	.09

Budget planning	−.09
Frequency of using advertising attributes in purchases	.08

NONSKILL BEHAVIORS–SPENDING AND ASKING FOR PRODUCTS

ASKING FOR CHILD-RELATED PRODUCTS

Kindergarten Mult R=.497 R^2=.247   *beta*

Frequency of using price/appearance attributes in purchases	−.18
Frequency of exposure to television commercials	.25
Family socio-economic status	−.12
Frequency of refusal with explanation low	.15
Frequency of negotiating purchase requests low	.09
Budget planning	−.09

Third Grade   Mult R=.289   R^2=.084

Number of different sources for money	.15
Frequency of negotiating purchase requests low	.08
Number of comments about commercials	.14
Number of bargain goals	−.08
Family socio-economic status	−.09
Relative effectiveness of information use in purchases	.17
Frequency of using contextual attributes in purchases	−.11
Flexibility in responding to purchase requests	−.09
Frequency of exposure to television commercials	.07

Sixth Grade   Mult R=.373   R^2=.139

Frequency of using advertising attributes in purchases	.16
Total child income	.10
Budget planning	−.11
Child power in making purchases	.11
Frequency of exposure to television commercials	−.11
Family socio-economic status	−.09
Number of comments about commercials	.14
Frequency of using contextual attributes in purchases	−.10
Number of sources consulted in major purchases	.10
Number of quality shopping goals	−.10
Frequency of yielding to purchase requests	.08

Degree of opposition to children's commercials	.08
Frequency of discussing consumption generally	.08

NONSKILL BEHAVIORS—SPENDING AND ASKING FOR PRODUCTS

ASKING FOR BRANDS

Kindergarten Mult R=.336 R^2=.113   *beta*

Frequency of taking child shopping	.20
Frequency of negotiating purchase requests low	−.18
Frequency of exposure to television commercials	.11
Flexibility in responding to purchase requests	−.13
Frequency of refusal with explanation low	−.10
Number of comments about commercials	−.09
Number of quality shopping goals	.11
Relative effectiveness of information use in purchases	−.11
Number of bargain goals	.07

Third Grade   Mult R=.353 R^2=.125

Number of money goals	.27
Number of comments about commercials	.12
Family socio-economic status	.11
Flexibility in responding to purchase requests	.10
Degree of opposition to children's commercials	−.15

Sixth Grade   Mult R=.332 R^2=.110

Frequency of using advertising attributes in purchases	.25
Number of comments about commercials	.21
Frequency of yielding to purchase requests	.09

NONSKILL BEHAVIORS—SPENDING AND ASKING FOR PRODUCTS

STRENGTH OF BRAND PREFERENCE

Kindergarten Mult R=.396 R^2=.157   *beta*

Total information use in purchases	−.27

Degree of opposition to children's commercials	−.17
Total child income	−.18
Frequency of refusal with explanation low	.13
Number of sources consulted in major purchases	−.12
Number of different sources for money	.10
Frequency of yielding to purchase requests	.14
Number of quality shopping goals	−08
Frequency of using advertising attributes in purchases	.10
Frequency of taking child shopping	−.09
Flexibility in responding to purchase requests	.08
Number of bargain goals	.08

Third Grade   Mult R=.367 R^2=.135

Family socio-economic status	−.19
Frequency of exposure to television commercials	−.13
Degree of opposition to children's commercials	.15
Frequency of refusal with explanation low	.05
Relative efficiency of information use in purchases	−.25
Total information use in purchases	.23
Frequency of yielding to purchase requests	−.12
Flexibility in responding to purchase requests	−.11
Number of quality shopping goals	−.09
Frequency of taking child shopping	.08

Sixth Grade   Mult R=.283 R^2=.080

Flexibility in responding to purchase requests	.16
Frequency of yielding to purchase requests	.16
Number of different sources for money	−.12
Frequency of discussing consumption generally	.10
Number of bargain goals	.08
Relative efficiency of information use in purchases	.13
Frequency of exposure to television commercials	−.09
Frequency of refusal with explanation low	.10
Frequency of using advertising attributes in purchases	−.10

INDEXES

SUBJECT INDEX

Advertising 19, 20, 25-27, 28, 51, 55, 56, 74, 75, 140, 141, 177, 183
  cognitive filtering of 167-173
  regulation of 17, 165, 166
  role of research on 166-167
  (see also Television commericals
Attention processes 23, 25, 53-55, 140-141
Attitudes toward commercials
  children's 18, 64-66
  mothers' 129-130
Awareness
  of brands 67-68, 160, 161, 178
  of commercials 59-66, 159, 167, 171-173, 177, 178
  of sources of product information 56-58, 159

Brands
  awareness of 67, 68, 160, 161, 178
  comparison of 20, 71, 72, 178, 160,
  recall of from commercials 55, 178
  requests 72-73
  strength 70, 71, 178
Budget planning and accounting 126-127, 142-143

Central processing 20, 21, 26-28, 29, 178
  measures of 34, 35
  of TV commercials 59-66
  of product information 70-76
  (see also Information processing)
Centration 45, 46
Child opportunities for consumption 37, 88-91, 107, 135, 136, 153, 154, 179-181
Cognitive filter 64-66, 166-168, 170-183, 185
Cognitive development 23-25, 39-40, 43-48, 175-176, 189-192
  and cognitive structures 23-24, 44-45
  and information processing 45, 175, 189-192
  as independent variable 28-29
  as predictor variable 155
  developmental growth 24, 44, 46, 48, 58

environmental effects on 26-28, 46-48, 95-97, 101
  functional approaches to 47, 103-105, 191-192
  family impact on 156-161
  impact on consumer skill development 156-162
  learning and 47-48
  stages of 23, 38, 39, 44-45
Consumer behavior
  models of 21
  measures of 34-38
  children's 20-21, 81, 84-91, 135-136
  parents' 106-110, 113, 117-127, 146, 147, 152-155, 179, 181
Consumer goals 37, 108, 110, 114-117, 143, 146-147, 152-155, 181
  and teaching methods 116-117, 179
Consumer education 13, 179
  implications of research for 187-188
Consumer skills 48-50, 81-82, 91-92, 145-147
  correlations with grade level 36, 37
  development of 156-161
  family impact on 97, 98, 109-110, 146, 147, 151-153, 155, 181
  higher and lower level information processing 76-79, 181
Consumer socialization 11, 18, 19, 25, 59, 95-97, 175, 176, 179, 181, 190
  as information processing 19-23, 175, 189-192
  current research approaches to 25, 96, 97
  environmental influences on 26-28, 95, 140-144
  family influence on 97, 98, 106-110, 143-144, 181
  situational approach to 25-27, 96-97, 100
  research model 28-29
Consumerism 11, 17, 165, 186

Developmental stages (see Cognitive development)

Environmental influence (see Cognitive development, Consumer socialization)

Family context
37, 38, 40, 101-110, 116, 179, 180
as predictor variable 148-149
conceptualization of 113-115
influence on cognitive development 156-161
influence on consumer socialization 18-20, 26-27, 96-97, 106-110, 143-146, 151-155
past approaches to measurement of 98-103
patterns of influence 141-143
(see also Mother and Parent-child interaction)

Income
children's 84-85, 137
sources of children's 137-140
Information gathering strategies 58, 107
Information processing 11, 23, 26, 29, 175, 181
definition 20, 25
measures of 34-38
model 18-22, 25, 28-29
mother's 121-125
of TV commercials 52-66
of product information 66-76
outcomes of 81
past research on 25
situational approach to 25
skills 36-37, 48-59, 76-79, 146, 147, 157-161
Information selection 20, 177, 178
children's from TV commercials 55, 56
children's about products 67-70
Information sources
children's 51, 55-58, 158-159
mothers' 117-120
Information use 122-126
Initial processing 20, 25-29, 177, 178
measures 34-38
of TV commercials 52-59
of product information 67-70
past research on 25
(see also Information processing)
Interview (see Survey)

Learning
and development 46-48, 106
approaches to socialization 96-97, 99, 100
theories 19, 27, 109

Marketing 17, 168
implications of research for 176, 188, 189
Media influence (see Cognitive development, Information processing, TV commercials)
Modeling (see Family context, Mother)
Money use
behavior 84-88, 147, 178
mothers' goals regarding 114-115
norms 82-84, 178
skills 48-50, 91, 147-148
Mother
attitudes toward commercials 129-130
consumer behavior 106-110, 113, 117-127, 146, 147, 152-155, 179, 181
consumer goals 37, 108, 110, 114-117, 143, 146-147, 152-155, 181
consumer teaching methods 116-117, 179
interaction with child 107, 108, 113, 114, 127-129, 143, 188
interview schedule 37-38
yielding to purchase requests 131-135
(see also Family context and Parent-child interaction)
Multiattribute models 21, 66, 67

Nonskilled consumer behavior 81, 91-92, 109, 110, 145-147, 153-155

Object-attribute matrix 66, 67

Parent-child interaction 36, 106, 107, 108, 113, 114, 143, 179, 180, 181
parent initiated 127-130
child initiated 130-135
impact on child's consumer behavior 153-155, 171-172
Perceptual boundedness 38-40, 45, 53-55, 157-161
Premium advertising 25-26, 55, 56, 74-75

Policy decisions 11, 13, 23
  implications of research for 176, 182-187
Product attributes
  children's use 69, 70-76, 170, 171
  mothers' use 121-126
  information processing of 20, 66-76
Product purchase requests 49-50, 74-75, 88-91, 168, 170, 178
  yielding to 131-135

Savings behavior (see Money use)
Situational approach
  to information processing research 25-27
  to studying environmental influences on socialization 96, 97, 100-105

Survey
  sampling procedures 32-33
  interview procedures 33
  interview schedules 34-38

Television commercials 18, 51, 56-58
  attention to 53-55
  attitudes toward 64-66, 129-130
  awareness of 59-66
  exposure to 51, 140-141
  perceived truthfulness of 60-63
  related to consumer skill learning 171-173, 177
  separation from program 177, 178

Yielding 131-135, 143, 154

Association of National Advertisers (ANA) 166, 185, 193
Action for Children's Television (ACT) 166, 193
Adler, R. et al. 166, 193
Atkin, C.K. 25, 66, 74, 193

Baldwin, A.L. 28, 58, 190, 193
Barcus, E.F. 18, 193
Bauer, R. 13, 193
Bettman, J.R. 21, 193
Belk, R. W. 111n, 193
Bucklin, L.P. 117, 193
Burgess, E.W. 101, 193

Carman, J.M. 118, 193
Caron, A. 25, 51, 97, 193
Case, R. 47, 103, 104, 156, 191, 192n, 193
Chaffee, S. 100, 102, 121, 193
Child, I.L. 111n, 197
Children's Review Unit, National Council of Better Business Bureaus 166, 184
Council of Children, Media and Merchandising 166
Cox, D.F. 121, 194
Crandall, J.J. et al. 28, 104, 105, 194

Dervin, B. 120, 194

Ettema, J. 25, 53, 54, 196

Faber, R. 51, 194
Farnham-Diggory, S. 190, 194
Federal Communications Commission (FCC) 166
Federal Trade Commission (FTC) 166, 167, 183, 184
Fishbein, M. 66, 194
Flavell, J.H. 24, 194

Gans, H. 120, 194
Gerlach, G.C. 13, 184, 194
Ginsburg, H. 46, 194
Greenberg, B. 120, 193

Hemple, D.J. 121, 194
Hoffman, L. 27, 194
Hollingshead, A.B. 118, 194

Howard, J.A. 167, 194
Hughes, G.D. 30n, 121, 190, 194
Hulbert, J. 167, 194

Inhelder, B. 47, 194

Jacoby, J. 21, 194
Jain, S.C. 118, 196

Kagan, J. 28, 101, 104, 195
Katz, E. 118, 195
Kohlberg, L. 27, 44, 45, 106, 195

Lazarsfeld, P.F. 118, 195
Leifer, A.D. et al. 55, 195
Lesser, G.S. 185, 195
Lippitt, R. 27, 194
Locke, J. 101, 193
Lyle, J. 51, 195

Magruder, L. 82, 88, 195
Marshall, H.R. 82, 88, 195
McGuire, W.J. 190, 195
McLeod, J.M. 100, 102, 121, 194
McNeal, J.R. 19, 30n, 81, 195
Miller, D.R. 101, 195
Moss, H. 28, 101, 104, 195

National Association of Broadcasters (NAB) 166, 184, 185
Nie, N.H. et al. 148, 195

Opper, S. 46, 194

Pascual-Leone, J. 47, 103, 104, 156, 191, 192n, 195
Piaget, J. 23, 24, 43-48, 82, 95, 116, 194, 195
Pillemer, D.B. 192n, 195

Ray, M.L. 21, 30n, 121, 190, 195
Reilly, G. 25, 74, 195
Rich, S. 118, 196
Robertson, T.S. 25, 52, 66, 196
Rosenberg, M.J. 66, 196
Rossiter, J.R. 25, 52, 66, 196
Rubin, R.S. 25, 55, 77, 196

Schramm, W. 119, 196
Schuessler, K. 49, 82, 88, 196
Sears, R.R. et al. 100, 196
Shimp, T.A. et al. 26, 196
Simon, H.A. 53, 190, 196
Smith, J. 47, 195
Strauss, A. 49, 82, 88, 196
Swanson, G.E. 101, 195

Tichenor, P.J. et al. 119, 196

Wackman, D.B. 25, 52-54, 59, 88, 92n,
    100, 102, 196
Wade, S.E. 119, 196
Ward, S. 21, 25, 30n, 51-54, 59, 88, 92n,
    97, 190, 193, 196
Wartella, E. 25, 53, 54, 196
Wells, W.D. 19, 196
Williams, W.C. 101, 197
Wohlwill, J.F. 45, 197
Wright, P.L. 21, 197

Zigler, E. 111n, 197

ABOUT THE AUTHORS

SCOTT WARD is Associate Professor of Business Administration at Harvard University, and Senior Research Associate at the Marketing Science Institute, a non-profit research organization affiliated with the Business School. He received his B.S., M.S. and Ph.D. degrees from the University of Wisconsin. His current research interests are in understanding consumer behavior processes in family units, focusing on how parents and offspring interact and influence purchase decisions, and in understanding how major purchases—such as insurance and health care—occur in families throughout the life cycle.

DANIEL B. WACKMAN is an Associate Professor and Director of the Communication Research Division, School of Journalism and Mass Communication, University of Minnesota. His research focuses on the role of communication—both interpersonal and mass communication—in childhood and adult socialization. He has recently co-authored the book ALIVE AND AWARE: IMPROVING COMMUNICATION IN RELATIONSHIPS. Currently, he is examining the impact of television and family models on children's learning of modes of conflict resolution.

ELLEN WARTELLA is an Assistant Professor in the Department of Communication, Ohio State University. Her research focuses on the application of cognitive development theory to children's perception and comprehension of television programming and advertising.

The three authors are continuing their studies of children's consumer development with a recent grant from the National Science Foundation.